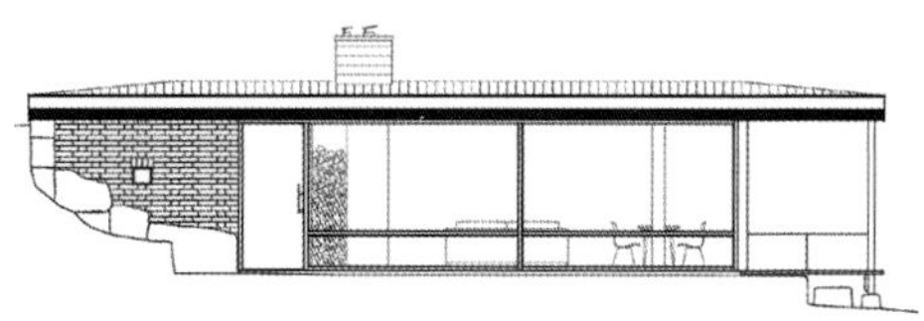

Editorial project:
2020 © **booq** publishing, S.L.
c/ Domènech, 7-9, 2º 1ª
08012 Barcelona, Spain
T: +34 93 268 80 88
www.booqpublishing.com

ISBN 978-84-9936-712-5 [EN]
ISBN 978-84-9936-705-7 [DE]

© Editions du Layeur
Dépôt Légal : 2020
ISBN : 978-2-915126-66-2
Espagne, juin 2020

© 2020 Instituto Monsa de ediciones, S.L.
c/ Gravina, 43
08930 Sant Adrià de Besós, Barcelona, Spain
T: +34 93 381 00 50
www.monsa.com
monsa@monsa.com
ISBN 978-84-17557-23-2

Editorial coordinator:
Claudia Martínez Alonso

Art director:
Mireia Casanovas Soley

Editor and layout:
David Andreu Bach

Translation:
© **booq** publishing, S.L.

Printing in Spain

**ARKÍS ARCHITECTS**
HOLMEN AQUATICS CENTER
© Tove Lauluten

**WÅHLIN ARKITEKTER**
VILLA BJÖRKNÄS

© Ola Österling

Until the late nineteenth century, Scandinavian Architecture was based on vernacular wooden, stone, and brick structures constructed by those without formal architectural training. Although unheralded, they offered practical solutions to problems specific to the north, including maximizing natural light and heat during the dark, cold winter days.
Nordic Architecture is nowadays functional, attractive in a minimalist way, and in balance with nature. At the same time, architects play a role in the emergence of the region's social welfare model, which requires quality in housing and public buildings.
With more than 400 illustrations and floor plans, this book provides a visual introduction of the most relevant architects in the region, showing how Scandinavian architects use their own resources and traditions to generate ideas that currently influence other international firms.

Bis ins späte neunzehnte Jahrhundert stützte sich die skandinavische Architektur auf Holz-, Stein- und Ziegelbauten, die im Volksmund von Menschen ohne formale Architekturausbildung errichtet wurden. Obwohl sie nicht angekündigt waren, boten sie praktische Lösungen für spezifische Probleme des Nordens, einschließlich der Maximierung von natürlichem Licht und Wärme während der dunklen, kalten Wintertage.
Die nordische Architektur ist heute funktional, auf minimalistische Weise attraktiv und im Gleichgewicht mit der Natur. Gleichzeitig spielen Architekten eine Rolle bei der Entstehung des sozialen Wohlfahrtsmodells der Region, das Qualität im Wohnungsbau und bei öffentlichen Gebäuden erfordert.
Mit mehr als 400 Abbildungen und Grundrissen bietet dieses Buch eine visuelle Einführung in die wichtigsten Architekten der Region und zeigt, wie skandinavische Architekten ihre eigenen Ressourcen und Traditionen nutzen, um Ideen zu entwickeln, die derzeit andere internationale Firmen beeinflussen.

Jusqu'à la fin du XIXe siècle, l'architecture scandinave était basée sur des structures vernaculaires en bois, en pierre et en brique construites par des personnes sans formation architecturale formelle. Bien qu'elles n'aient pas été annoncées, elles offraient des solutions pratiques aux problèmes spécifiques au Nord, notamment l'optimisation de la lumière et de la chaleur naturelles pendant les jours sombres et froids de l'hiver.
L'architecture nordique est aujourd'hui fonctionnelle, attrayante de manière minimaliste et en équilibre avec la nature. En même temps, les architectes jouent un rôle dans l'émergence du modèle de bien-être social de la région, qui exige la qualité des logements et des bâtiments publics.
Avec plus de 400 illustrations et plans, ce livre fournit une introduction visuelle des architectes les plus importants de la région, montrant comment les architectes scandinaves utilisent leurs propres ressources et traditions pour générer des idées qui influencent actuellement d'autres cabinets internationaux.

Hasta finales del siglo XIX, la arquitectura escandinava se basaba en estructuras vernáculas de madera, piedra y ladrillo construidas por personas sin formación arquitectónica formal. Aunque no se anunciaban, ofrecían soluciones prácticas a los problemas específicos del norte, incluyendo la maximización de la luz natural y el calor durante los oscuros y fríos días de invierno.
La arquitectura nórdica es hoy en día funcional, atractiva de forma minimalista y en equilibrio con la naturaleza. Al mismo tiempo, los arquitectos desempeñan un papel en el surgimiento del modelo de bienestar social de la región, que exige calidad en la vivienda y en los edificios públicos.
Con más de 400 ilustraciones y planos, este libro ofrece una introducción visual de los arquitectos más relevantes de la región, mostrando cómo los arquitectos escandinavos utilizan sus propios recursos y tradiciones para generar ideas que actualmente influyen en otras firmas internacionales.

Our aim at AIX is to create architecture that makes a difference and creates a better society. We design high-quality contemporary architecture, taking careful account of existing buildings. Our aim is to form spatial experiences where function and beauty intermingle, reinforcing one another: spaces that evoke feelings, change with the times and provide the best setting for people to live and to interact.

With our wide variety of expertise our team can work together to find the best solution for every individual project. We operate city planning and residential properties, cultural environment and restoration, commercial, public and educational premises, theater technology, interior and lighting design. Wood constructions is one of our special areas of expertise.

Unser Ziel bei AIX ist es, eine Architektur zu schaffen, die einen Unterschied macht und eine bessere Gemeinschaft schafft. Wir entwerfen qualitativ hochwertige zeitgenössische Architektur unter Berücksichtigung bestehender Gebäude. Unser Ziel ist es, Raumerlebnisse zu schaffen, in denen sich Funktion und Schönheit vermischen und sich gegenseitig verstärken: Räume, die Gefühle hervorrufen, sich mit der Zeit verändern und den Menschen den besten Rahmen zum Leben und zur Interaktion bieten.

Mit unserer vielseitigen Erfahrung können unsere Teammitglieder zusammenarbeiten, um die beste Lösung für jedes einzelne Projekt zu finden. Wir sind in den Bereichen Stadtplanung und Wohnimmobilien, kulturelles Umfeld und Gastronomie, gewerbliche, öffentliche und Bildungseinrichtungen, Theatertechnik, Innenarchitektur und Beleuchtung tätig. Der Holzbau ist eines unserer Spezialgebiete.

# AIX ARCHITECTER

Notre objectif, chez AIX, est de créer une architecture qui fait la différence et crée une société meilleure. Nous concevons une architecture contemporaine de haute qualité, en tenant le plus grand compte des constructions d'origine. Nous visons à former des expériences spatiales là où fonctionnalité et beauté se rejoignent, se renforçant l'une l'autre : des espaces qui évoquent des sentiments, changent avec le temps et offrent le meilleur cadre de vie et d'interaction pour leurs occupants.

Avec notre large variété de compétences, notre équipe peut collaborer pour trouver la meilleure solution pour chaque projet individuel. Nous intervenons dans la planification urbaine et la propriété résidentielle, l'environnement culturel et la restauration, les locaux commerciaux, publics et éducatifs, la technologie théâtrale, le design d'intérieur et la conception d'éclairage. La construction en bois est l'une de nos spécialités.

Nuestro objetivo en AIX es crear una arquitectura que marque la diferencia y cree una mejor comunidad. Diseñamos arquitectura contemporánea de alta calidad, teniendo muy en cuenta los edificios existentes. Nuestro objetivo es formar experiencias espaciales en las que la función y la belleza se entremezclen, reforzándose mutuamente: espacios que evocan sentimientos, cambian con los tiempos y proporcionan el mejor escenario para que las personas vivan e interactúen.

Con nuestra variada experiencia, los miembros de nuestro equipo pueden trabajar juntos para encontrar la mejor solución para cada proyecto individual. Operamos en urbanismo y propiedades residenciales, entorno cultural y restauración, locales comerciales, públicos y educativos, tecnología teatral, diseño de interiores e iluminación. La construcción en madera es una de nuestras especialidades.

KATA FARM

DRESSYRHALLEN

## KATA FARM

Varnhem, Sweden
Photos: © Antonius van Arkel

When archaeologists excavated a hill near Varnhem monastery church, they found the ruins of one of Sweden's oldest churches. A private yard church from the Viking era, ruled by a woman named Kata. The church crypt is perhaps the oldest preserved room in Sweden. Our task was to protect its foundations and graves while making its history accessible to all visitors. The shelter consists of a simple triangular roof structure.
As the visitor enters the space, its unearthed underside unfolds. The wooden architecture is meant to bring warmth into the space while the detailing is visible and tactile to all senses. There are two windows in the room. One small vertical slot in the eastern gable overlooking both chancel and crypt of the original church. The other window makes visible connection to the Varnhem church at distance.

Als Archäologen einen Hügel in der Nähe der Klosterkirche von Varnhem ausgruben, entdeckten sie die Überreste einer der ältesten Kirchen Schwedens. Eine Privatkirche aus der Wikingerzeit, die von einer Frau namens Kata regiert wird. Unsere Aufgabe bestand darin, ihre Fundamente und Gräber zu schützen und gleichzeitig ihre Geschichte allen Besuchern zugänglich zu machen. Der Unterstand besteht aus einer einfachen dreieckigen Dachkonstruktion.
Wenn der Besucher den Raum betritt, entfaltet sich seine ausgegrabene Unterseite. Die Holzarchitektur soll Wärme in den Raum bringen, während die Details für alle Sinne sichtbar und fühlbar sind. Ein kleiner vertikaler Schlitz im östlichen Giebel überblickt das Presbyterium und die Krypta der ursprünglichen Kirche, und ein Fenster ermöglicht eine visuelle Verbindung mit der Kirche.

Lorsque des archéologues ont excavé une colline près du monastère de Varnhem, ils ont trouvé les ruines d'une des plus anciennes églises de Suède. Un enclos paroissial privé de l'époque viking, dirigé par une femme nommée Kata. La crypte de cette église est peut-être la plus ancienne salle conservée de Suède. Notre tâche était de protéger ses fondations et ses tombes tout en rendant son histoire accessible à tous les visiteurs. L'abri consiste en une structure de toit triangulaire simple.
À mesure que le visiteur pénètre dans l'espace, la partie inférieure mise au jour se révèle. L'architecture en bois sert à apporter de la chaleur à l'espace et les détails de construction sont visibles et font appel à tous les sens. Cette pièce est percée de deux fenêtres. L'une, fente verticale pratiquée sur le pignon, donne à la fois sur le choeur et la crypte de l'église d'origine. L'autre rend visible le lien avec l'église de Varnem au loin.

Cuando los arqueólogos excavaron una colina cerca de la iglesia del monasterio de Varnhem, descubrieron restos de una de las iglesias más antiguas de Suecia. Una iglesia privada de la época vikinga, gobernada por una mujer llamada Kata. Nuestra tarea consistía en proteger sus cimientos y sus tumbas al tiempo que poníamos su historia al alcance de todos los visitantes. El refugio consiste en una sencilla estructura de tejado triangular.
A medida que el visitante entra en el espacio, su parte inferior desenterrada se despliega. La arquitectura de madera está pensada para aportar calidez al espacio mientras que los detalles son visibles y táctiles para todos los sentidos. Una pequeña ranura vertical en el frontón oriental tiene vistas al presbiterio y a la cripta de la iglesia original y una ventana hace posible la conexión visual con la iglesia.

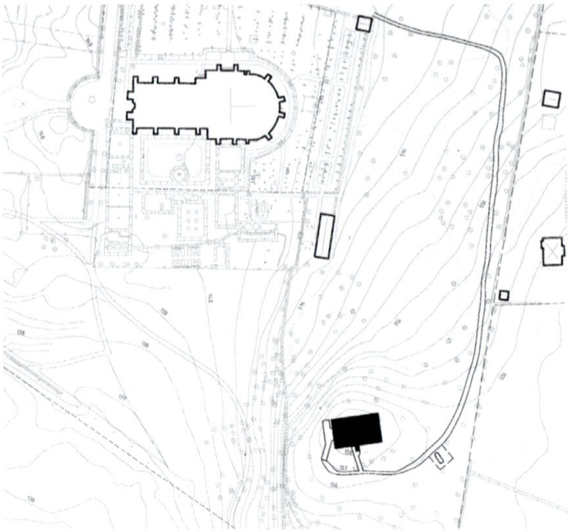

Site plan

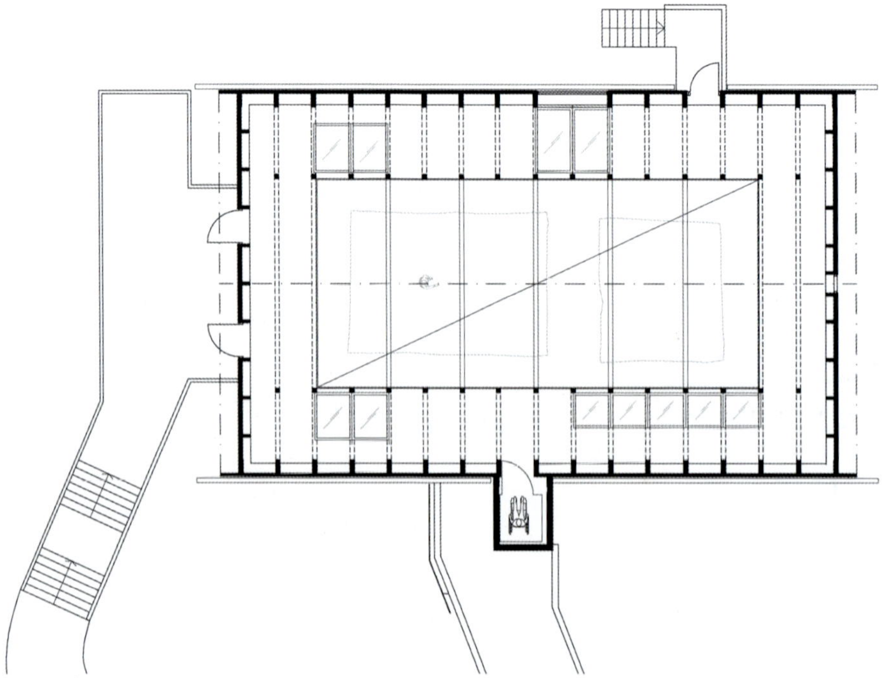

Floor plan

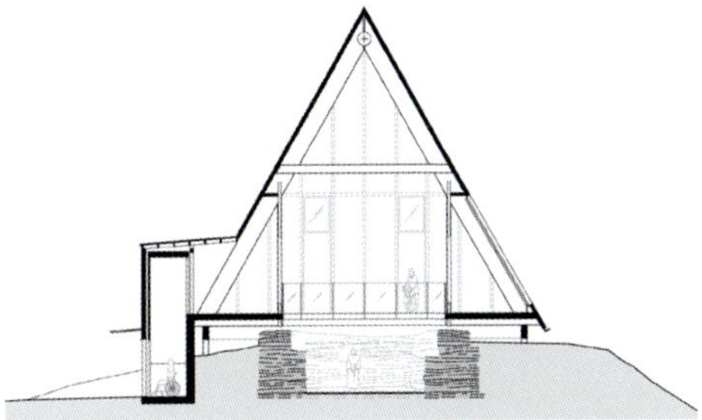

Section

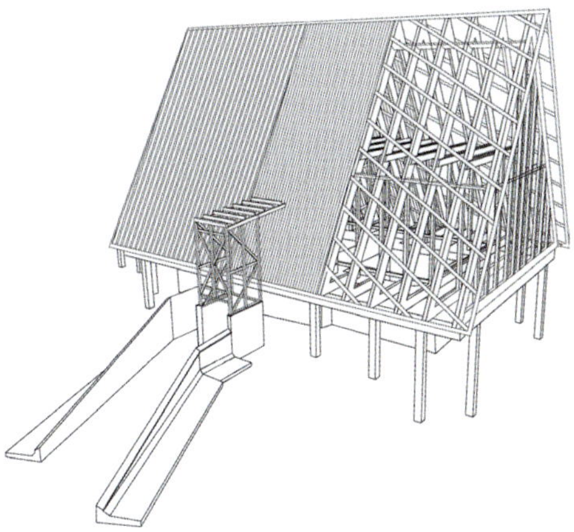

Construction perspective

## DRESSYRHALLEN

Rosersberg, Sweden
Photos: © Peder Lindbom

The Swedish Police Force needed a new training facility. A simple, rational structure—in a sensitive culturalhistorical environment. While being cost effective, the demand on building expression was high, one that needed to offer high caliber architecture most suitable for Rosersberg Palace.
The solution: making the best out of a modern yet noble material: cross laminated timber slabs. The 1.2 x 11 m elements were used as would an upside-down clinker boat. The capacity to absorb the load of the 5.8 m. span without secondary trusses was met by overlapping these slabs creating exceptional shear strength. In this way full-length slabs needed only one truss support. In the end the form indeed stood out amongst the older structures while the architecture lives up to the same principles: rationality, robustness and a functional beauty.

Die schwedische Polizei brauchte ein neues Ausbildungszentrum. Eine einfache und rationale Struktur - in einem kulturell und historisch sensiblen Umfeld. Das Projekt war zwar rentabel, musste aber dem architektonischen Charakter von Schloss Rosersberg entsprechen.
Die Lösung: die Nutzung eines modernen und zugleich edlen Materials: Holzböden. Wie bei der Konstruktion eines gelaschten Rumpfes wurden Elemente von 1,2 x 11 m verwendet. Die Tragfähigkeit der 5,8 m Spannweite ohne sekundäre Fachwerkträger wurde durch die Überlappung dieser Geschosse und damit die Verstärkung der Konstruktion erreicht. Auf diese Weise benötigten die durchgehenden Decken nur eine einzige Fachwerkstütze. Letztendlich stach die Form unter den älteren Strukturen hervor, während die Architektur den gleichen Prinzipien folgt: Rationalität, Robustheit und funktionelle Schönheit.

La police suédoise avait besoin de nouveaux locaux d'entraînement. Une structure simple, rationnelle – dans un environnement culturel et historique sensible. Tout en étant économiquement rentable, l'exigence de caractère pour le bâtiment était élevée, demandant une architecture du niveau de celle du Palais de Rosersberg.
La solution : tirer le meilleur parti d'un matériau moderne et noble : des lames de bois stratifié-croisé. Les éléments de 1,2 x 11 m ont été utilisés comme pour une embarcation à clin renversée. La capacité d'absorption de la charge des 5.8 m de portée sans avoir recours à des fermes secondaires a été obtenue par le chevauchement de ces lames, créant une résistance en cisaillement exceptionnelle. Ainsi les lames de bois n'ont nécessité qu'un seul soutien supplémentaire. Finalement cette forme s'est démarquée parmi des structures plus anciennes tandis que son architecture respecte les mêmes principes : la rationalité, la robustesse et une beauté fonctionnelle.

La Policía sueca necesitaba un nuevo centro de formación. Una estructura simple y racional –en un entorno cultural-histórico sensible. El proyecto, aunque rentable, tenía que estar a la altura del carácter arquitectónico del palacio de Rosersberg.
La solución: sacar el máximo provecho de un material moderno y a la vez noble: los suelos de madera. Se utilizaron elementos de 1,2 x 11 m como en la realización de un casco trincado. La capacidad de absorber la carga del vano de 5,8 m sin cerchas secundarias se consiguió solapando estos suelos reforzando así la estructura. De esta manera, los suelos continuos solo necesitaban un solo soporte de cerchas. Al final, la forma destacó entre las estructuras más antiguas, mientras que la arquitectura sigue los mismos principios: racionalidad, robustez y belleza funcional.

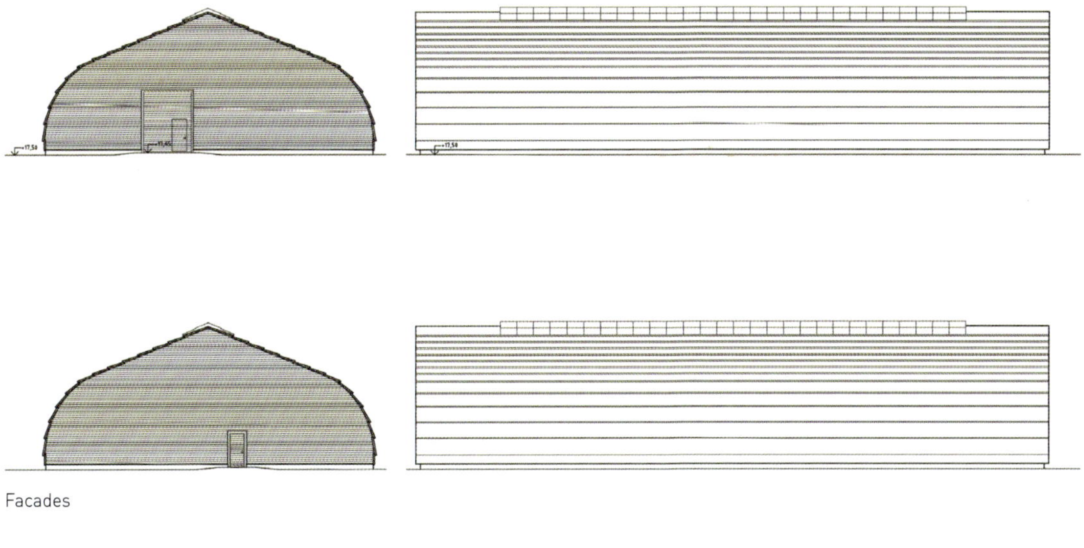

Facades

ARKÍS Architects is a progressive design partnership practicing architecture, design, planning and green design consultancy. ARKÍS was founded in 1997, but from the firm's founding ARKÍS architects have executed projects at various scales and levels of complexity, both in Iceland and internationally, for institutional, private, and civic clients.
ARKÍS architects are driven by the pursuit of quality and the belief that the built environment has the inherent potential to improve the quality of our lives. Moreover, ARKÍS architects are committed to sustainable design practices.
ARKÍS architects are the recipient of numerous awards and honors. Significant works include Holmen Aquatics Center, Holmsheidi Prison, the Icelandic Institute of Natural History, and Snaefellsstofa Visitor Center. The office of ARKÍS architects is located in Reykjavik, Iceland.

ARKIS Architects ist ein Designverband, der Architektur, Design, Planung und ökologische Designberatung betreibt. Das Atelier wurde 1997 gegründet, hat aber seit seiner Gründung sowohl in Island als auch international Projekte unterschiedlichen Umfangs und unterschiedlicher Komplexität für institutionelle, private und öffentliche Auftraggeber durchgeführt.
Die Architekten von ARKIS werden von dem Streben nach Qualität und der Überzeugung angetrieben, dass die gebaute Umwelt das inhärente Potenzial hat, unsere Lebensqualität zu verbessern. Darüber hinaus haben sie sich zu nachhaltigen Gestaltungspraktiken verpflichtet.
ARKIS Architekten haben zahlreiche Auszeichnungen und Ehrungen erhalten. Zu ihren bedeutendsten Werken gehören das Holmen Aquatic Centre, das Holmsheidi-Gefängnis, das Isländische Institut für Naturgeschichte und das Besucherzentrum Snaefellsstofa. Das Architekturbüro ARKIS Architects hat seinen Sitz in Reykjavik, Island.

© Hreinn Magnússon

# ARKÍS ARCHITECTS

ARKÍS Architects est une association de design qui pratique l'architecture, le design, la planification et le conseil en design écologique. Le studio a été fondé en 1997, mais depuis sa création, il a réalisé des projets à différentes échelles et à différents niveaux de complexité, tant en Islande qu'à l'étranger, pour des clients institutionnels, privés et publics.
Les architectes d'ARKIS sont animés par la recherche de la qualité et la conviction que l'environnement bâti a le potentiel inhérent d'améliorer la qualité de notre vie. En outre, ils s'engagent à adopter des pratiques de conception durable.
Les architectes d'ARKIS ont reçu de nombreux prix et distinctions. Parmi leurs œuvres les plus importantes, on peut citer le centre aquatique de Holmen, la prison de Holmsheidi, l'Institut islandais d'histoire naturelle et le centre de visiteurs Snaefellsstofa. Le bureau ARKIS Architects est situé à Reykjavik, en Islande.

ARKÍS Architects es una asociación de diseño que practica la arquitectura, el diseño, la planificación y la consultoría de diseño ecológico. El estudio se fundó en 1997, pero desde su origen ha ejecutado proyectos en varias escalas y niveles de complejidad, tanto en Islandia como internacionalmente, para clientes institucionales, privados y públicos.
Los arquitectos de ARKÍS están impulsados por la búsqueda de la calidad y la creencia de que el entorno construido tiene el potencial inherente de mejorar la calidad de nuestras vidas. Además, están comprometidos con las prácticas de diseño sostenible.
ARKÍS Architects han recibido numerosos premios y honores. Entre sus obras más significativas se incluyen el Centro Acuático de Holmen, la Prisión de Holmsheidi, el Instituto Islandés de Historia Natural y el Centro de Visitantes de Snaefellsstofa. El despacho de ARKIS Architects se encuentra en Reykjavik, Islandia.

HOLMEN AQUATICS CENTER

ÁSTJÖRN PARISH HALL

VILLA PANORAMA

FJAÐRÁRGLJÚFUR VIEWING PLATFORM

## HOLMEN AQUATICS CENTER

Asker, Norway
Photos: © Lasse Leonhardsen, Tove Lauluten

Holmen Aquatics Center is located at the edge of a forest's edge coinciding with a foot of a slope. The building is a continuation of the landscape embracing Asker's Holmskæret beach.
The building is designed and constructed according to the Passive House standard. That impacts the building's insulative qualities, but more importantly it impacts the recycling of the thermal energy found both in the building's operations and in the immediate surroundings. A total of 15 geothermal wells surround the building, 650 m² of solar panels are located on its surfaces and heat is recycled from parking lots and from waste water.
Holmen Aquatics Center was selected as on of 50 model projects for Future Built in Norway. Holmen Aquatics Center received the Norwegian Building of the Year Award in 2017 (Byggeindustriens pris).

Das Holmen's Water Centre liegt am Rande eines Waldes, der mit einem Fuß eines Hügels zusammenfällt. Das Gebäude ist eine Fortsetzung der Landschaft, die den Strand von Asker's Holmskæret umfasst.
Das Gebäude ist nach dem „Passivhaus"-Standard geplant und gebaut. Dies wirkt sich auf die Dämmeigenschaften des Gebäudes aus, vor allem aber auf die Wiederverwertung von Wärmeenergie, die sowohl beim Betrieb des Gebäudes als auch in der unmittelbaren Umgebung anfällt. Insgesamt 15 geothermische Brunnen für die Wiederverwertung von Abwasser umgeben das Gebäude. 650 m² Sonnenkollektoren befinden sich auf den Oberflächen des Gebäudes, die die Wärme von den Parkplätzen zurückgewinnen.
Holmen's Water Centre wurde als eines von 50 Modellprojekten für die Zukunft des Bauens in Norwegen ausgewählt und erhielt die Auszeichnung „Norwegisches Bauen" des Jahres 2017 (Byggeindustriens pris).

Le Centre de l'eau de Holmen est situé à la lisière d'une forêt, coïncidant avec un pied de colline. Le bâtiment s'inscrit dans le prolongement du paysage qui englobe la plage d'Asker's Holmskæret.
Le bâtiment est conçu et construit conformément à la norme « Maison passive ». Cela affecte les qualités isolantes du bâtiment, mais surtout le recyclage de l'énergie thermique présente dans le fonctionnement du bâtiment et dans son environnement immédiat. Un total de 15 puits géothermiques, pour le recyclage des eaux usées, entourent le bâtiment. 650 m² de panneaux solaires sont situés sur les surfaces du bâtiment, recyclant la chaleur des aires de stationnement.
Le Centre de l'eau de Holmen a été sélectionné comme l'un des 50 projets modèles pour l'avenir de la construction en Norvège, recevant le prix du « Bâtiment norvégien » de l'année en 2017 (Byggeindustriens pris).

El Centro Acuático de Holmen está situado en el borde de un bosque, coincidiendo con un pie de ladera. El edificio es una continuación del paisaje que abarca la playa Holmskæret de Asker.
El edificio está diseñado y construido de acuerdo con el estándar de «Casa Pasiva». Esto afecta a las cualidades aislantes del edificio, pero lo más importante es que afecta al reciclaje de la energía térmica que se encuentra tanto en las operaciones del edificio como en el entorno inmediato. Un total de 15 pozos geotérmicos, para el reciclaje de las aguas residuales, rodean el edificio. 650 m² de paneles solares están ubicados en las superficies del edificio, reciclando el calor de las zonas de aparcamiento.
El Centro Acuático de Holmen fue seleccionado como uno de los 50 proyectos modelo para el futuro de la construcción de Noruega, recibiendo el premio al «Edificio Noruego» del año en 2017 (Byggeindustriens pris).

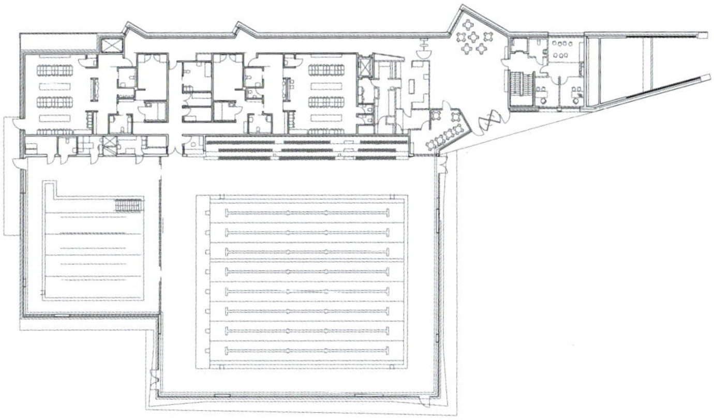

Floor plan

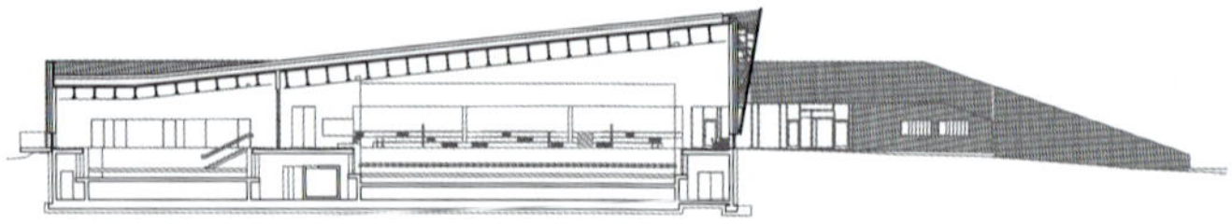

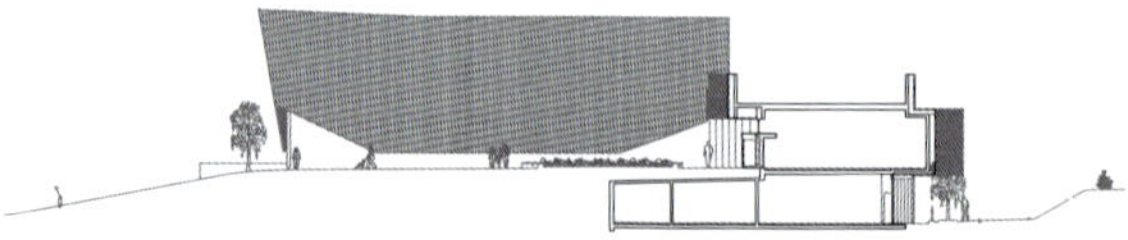

Sections

dame

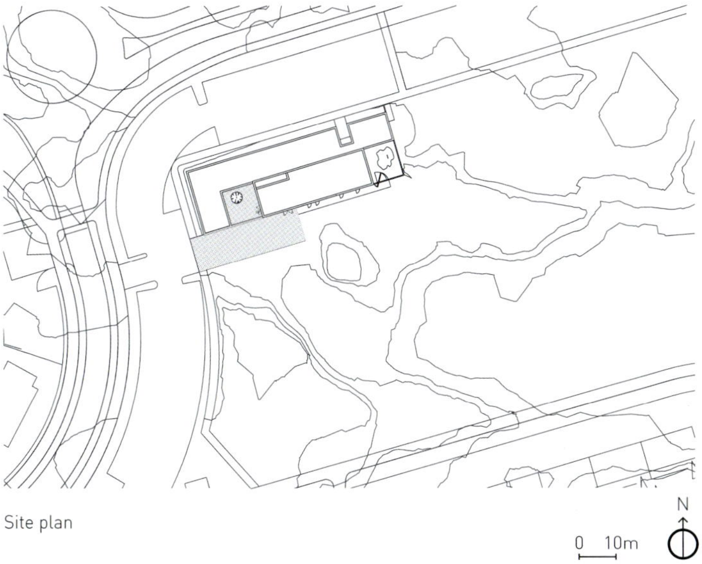


Site plan

## ÁSTJÖRN PARISH HALL

Hafnarfjörður, Iceland
Photos: © Thorgils G. Gunnthorsson

Being the first phase of the Ástjörn church, the parish hall holds the unique status of taking on all of the functions of the parish, church services included. The anticipated second phase is a church to the south of the main hall.
The Parish hall is modest, warm and accessible. It provides a warm embrace for those who enter to seek protective shelter, peace and inner strength within. The design approach of the parish hall is to enhance the church's role as a servant.
The building is tucked comfortably into the lava field and together, building and landscape, create a sheltered and pleasant external environment. Building and landscape blend together through the way the building's color- and material palette are derived from the surrounding lava.

Als erste Phase des Baus der Kirche von Ástjörn hat das Gemeindehaus den einzigartigen Status, alle Funktionen der Gemeinde, einschließlich der kircheneigenen Gottesdienste, zu übernehmen. Als zweite Phase ist eine Kapelle südlich der Haupthalle geplant.
Das Gemeindehaus ist bescheiden, warm und zugänglich. Sie umarmt diejenigen, die auf der Suche nach Zuflucht, Frieden und innerer Stärke zu uns kommen. Der Schwerpunkt des Entwurfs liegt darauf, die Rolle der Kirche als Dienerin der Gläubigen zu stärken.
Das Gebäude ist behaglich in ein Lavafeld eingebettet, und gemeinsam schaffen sie eine geschützte und angenehme äußere Umgebung durch eine Palette von Farben und Materialien, die zur umgebenden Lavalandschaft passen.

En tant que première phase de la construction de l'église d'Ástjörn, la salle paroissiale a le statut unique de reprendre toutes les fonctions de la paroisse, y compris les services propres à l'église. La deuxième phase prévue est une chapelle au sud de la salle principale.
La salle paroissiale est modeste, chaleureuse et accessible. Il offre une étreinte chaleureuse à ceux qui y entrent en quête de refuge, de paix et de force intérieure. L'objectif de ce projet est de renforcer le rôle de l'église en tant que servante des fidèles.
Le bâtiment est confortablement niché dans un champ de lave et, ensemble, ils créent un environnement extérieur protégé et agréable grâce à une palette de couleurs et de matériaux qui s'harmonisent avec le paysage de lave environnant.

Constituyendo la primera fase de la construcción de la iglesia de Ástjörn, el salón parroquial tiene el estatus único de asumir todas las funciones de la parroquia, incluyendo los servicios propios de la iglesia. La segunda fase prevista es una capilla al sur del salón principal.
El salón parroquial es modesto, cálido y accesible. Proporciona un cálido abrazo a aquellos que entran en busca de refugio, paz y fuerza interior. El enfoque del diseño consiste en mejorar el papel de la iglesia como sirviente de los fieles.
El edificio está cómodamente arropado en un campo de lava y juntos, crean un ambiente externo protegido y agradable a través de una paleta de colores y materiales que concuerdan con el paisaje de lava circundante.

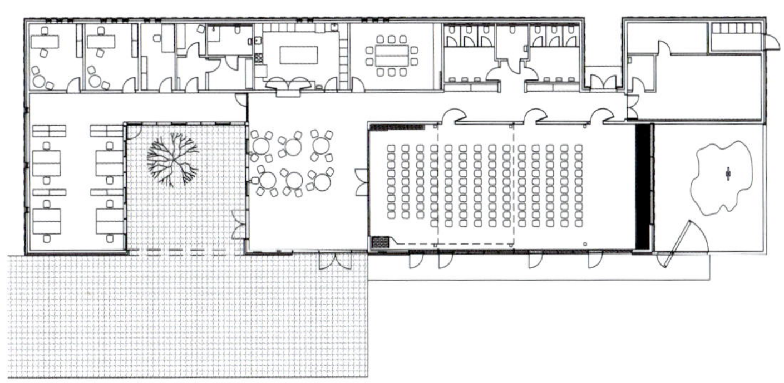

Floor plan

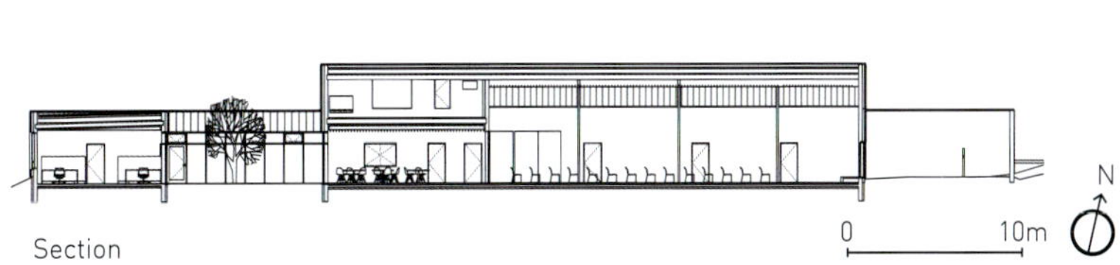


Section

## VILLA PANORAMA

Akureyri, Iceland
Photos: © Alex Fradkin

The site is located in a beautiful birch forest across the water from Akureyri. In this location, it was possible to utilize spectacular views towards the town of Akureyri and see the entire fjord Eyjafjordur from north to south. With this magnificent location in mind the concept developed to having a massive and secluded lower level that carries the weight of an elevated glass house floating above. One might refer to the upper level as a tribute to Mies van der Rohe's Farnsworth house where the boundary between inside and outside are visually blurred and the entire horizon can be experienced from the house's living room.

Das Land liegt in einem schönen Birkenwald auf der anderen Seite einer Wasserzone in der Nähe der Stadt Akureyri. Auf diese Weise wurden die spektakulären Aussichten auf Akureyri und den Eyjafjordur-Fjord genutzt. Bei dieser herrlichen Lage wurde das Konzept auf der Grundlage einer isolierten unteren Ebene entwickelt, die das Gewicht eines erhöhten, schwebenden Glashauses tragen sollte. Man könnte das Obergeschoss als eine Hommage an Mies van der Rohes Farnsworth-Haus bezeichnen, in dem die Grenzen zwischen Innen und Außen visuell verschwimmen und der Horizont vom Wohnzimmer des Hauses aus erfahrbar ist.

Le terrain est situé dans une belle forêt de bouleaux de l'autre côté d'une zone d'eau près de la ville d'Akureyri. De cette façon, les vues spectaculaires d'Akureyri et du fjord de l'Eyjafjordur ont été mises à profit. Avec ce magnifique emplacement, le concept a été développé sur la base de la réalisation d'un niveau inférieur isolé qui supporterait le poids d'une maison de verre surélevée et flottante. On pourrait qualifier le niveau supérieur d'hommage à la maison Farnsworth de Mies van der Rohe, où les frontières entre l'intérieur et l'extérieur sont visuellement floues et où l'horizon peut être expérimenté depuis le salon de la maison.

El terreno está situado en un hermoso bosque de abedules al otro lado de una zona de agua cercana a la población de Akureyri. De esta forma se aprovecharon las espectaculares vistas de Akureyri y del fiordo Eyjafjordur. Con esta magnífica ubicación, el concepto se desarrolló en base a conseguir un nivel inferior aislado que soportara el peso de una casa de cristal elevada y flotante. Uno podría referirse al nivel superior como un tributo a la casa Farnsworth de Mies van der Rohe, donde los límites entre el interior y el exterior son visualmente borrosos y el horizonte puede ser experimentado desde la sala de estar de la casa.

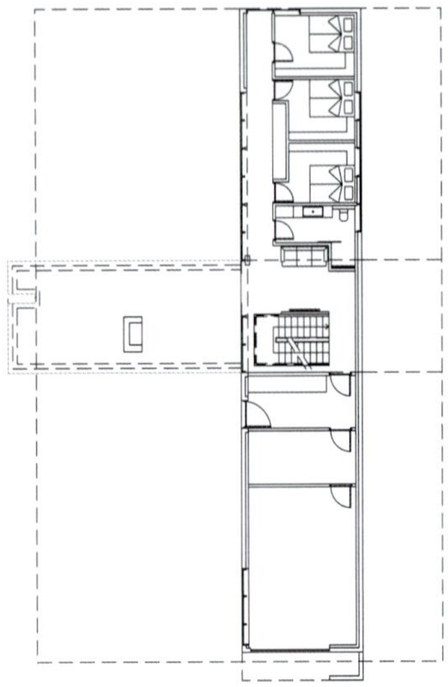

Ground floor plan

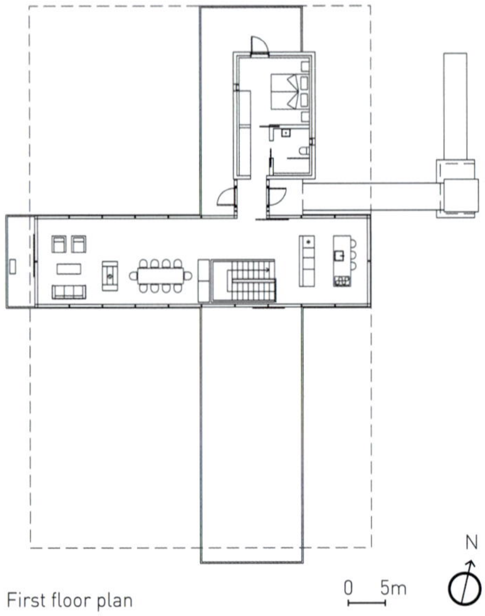


First floor plan

## FJAÐRÁRGLJÚFUR VIEWING PLATFORM

Skaftárhreppur, Vestur Skaftafellssýsla, Iceland
Photos: © Karl Vilhjálmsson

Fjadrargljufur viewing platform is located at the top of the canyon where the views are most spectacular. The platform is constructed of weathering steel, with an open grille floor and transparent railing so that visitors can enjoy looking through and down to the canyon. Handrails are also of weathering steel with delicate rust-free steel wires. The platform is designed for deconstruction and removal so that minimal impact will be left on site after the structure's lifecycle.

Die Beobachtungsplattform Fjadrargljufur befindet sich auf der Spitze einer Schlucht und bietet spektakuläre Aussichten. Es ist aus witterungsbeständigem Stahl gebaut, mit einem offenen Gitterboden und einem transparenten Geländer, so dass die Besucher die Aussicht genießen können. Die Handläufe sind ebenfalls aus Stahl gefertigt und mit feinen Edelstahlseilen versehen. Die Plattform ist so konzipiert, dass sie nach Ablauf ihres Lebenszyklus so rückgebaut und entfernt werden kann, dass sie nur minimale Auswirkungen auf den Boden hinterlässt.

La plate-forme d'observation Fjadrargljufur est située au sommet d'un canyon, avec une vue spectaculaire. Il est construit en acier résistant aux intempéries, avec un plancher en grille ouverte et une rampe transparente pour que les visiteurs puissent profiter des vues. Les mains courantes sont également en acier, terminées par de délicats câbles en acier inoxydable. La plate-forme est conçue pour être déconstruite et retirée de manière à laisser un impact minimal sur le sol une fois son cycle de vie terminé.

La plataforma de observación Fjadrargljufur está situada en la cima de un cañón, con vistas espectaculares. Está construida con acero resistente a la intemperie, con un suelo de rejilla abierta y una barandilla transparente para que los visitantes puedan disfrutar de las vistas. Los pasamanos también son de acero, acabados con delicados cables de acero inoxidable. La plataforma está diseñada para ser deconstruida y retirada de manera que se deje un impacto mínimo en el terreno una vez acabado su ciclo de vida.

Buster, borned 1967, was educated at Beckmans School of Design in Stockholm, where he now teaches architecture and interior design.
He has broad experience of design in many different fields, from graphic design, industrial design, furniture design, exhibitions, offices, shops, restaurants and commissions for private clients such as kitchens, bathrooms, holiday homes and villas.
He has been active since 1997 and has extensive experience in construction engineering and and how to implement advanced projects together with a well-established network of contractors. As a client, you can trust that Buster is dedicated and meticulous and performs all tasks with utmost dedication.

Buster, geboren 1967, wurde an der Beckmans School of Design in Stockholm ausgebildet, wo er heute Architektur und Innendesign lehrt.
Er verfügt über umfassende Erfahrung mit Design in vielen verschiedenen Bereichen, von Grafikdesign, Industriedesign, Möbeldesign, Ausstellungen, Büros, Geschäften, Restaurants und Aufträgen für private Auftraggeber wie Küchen, Bäder, Ferienhäuser und Villen.
Er ist seit 1997 tätig und verfügt über umfassende Erfahrung im Bauingenieurwesen und in der Umsetzung fortgeschrittener Projekte zusammen mit einem gut etablierten Netzwerk von Auftragnehmern. Als Kunde können Sie darauf vertrauen, dass Buster engagiert und akribisch ist und alle Aufgaben mit größter Hingabe ausführt.

# DELIN ARKITEKTKONTOR

Buster, né en 1967, a fait ses études à l'école de design Beckmans à Stockholm, où il enseigne aujourd'hui l'architecture et le design d'intérieur.
Il a une grande expérience du design dans de nombreux domaines, du graphisme au design industriel, en passant par la conception de meubles, les expositions, les bureaux, les magasins, les restaurants et les commandes pour des clients privés comme les cuisines, les salles de bains, les maisons de vacances et les villas.
Il est actif depuis 1997 et possède une vaste expérience de l'ingénierie de la construction et de la mise en œuvre de projets avancés en collaboration avec un réseau d'entrepreneurs bien établi. En tant que client, vous pouvez être sûr que Buster est dévoué et méticuleux et qu'il accomplit toutes les tâches avec le plus grand dévouement.

Buster, nacido en 1967, se educó en la Escuela de Diseño de Beckmans en Estocolmo, donde ahora enseña arquitectura y diseño de interiores.
Tiene una amplia experiencia en diseño en muchos campos diferentes, desde diseño gráfico, diseño industrial, diseño de muebles, exposiciones, oficinas, tiendas, restaurantes y encargos para clientes privados como cocinas, baños, casas de vacaciones y villas.
Ha estado activo desde 1997 y tiene una amplia experiencia en la ingeniería de construcción y en cómo implementar proyectos avanzados junto con una red bien establecida de contratistas. Como cliente, puede confiar en que Buster es dedicado y meticuloso y realiza todas las tareas con la máxima dedicación.

## LUNDNÄS HOUSE

Hälsingland, Sweden
Photos: © Johan Sellén

The Lundnäs House is built in the granite foundation from a turn of the century ceramic stove factory. The architect designed and built the house as a case study with design and construction evolving simultaneously using experimental ideas, such as a floor that is heated by hot air from the fireplace and passive solar heating. The secluded location and scenery made it desirable to have glass walls around the living area while the bedrooms and bathroom are located in the back of the house between walls built of granite and bricks recovered from the site. The house is an example of how thoughtful construction, using locally produced materials, and taking into account the nature and history of the region can combine contemporary aesthetics and philosophy with functional requirements, low construction costs, and a small ecological footprint.

Das Lundnäs-Haus ist im Granitfundament einer Keramikofenfabrik aus der Jahrhundertwende erbaut. Der Architekt entwarf und baute das Haus als Fallstudie, wobei sich Entwurf und Konstruktion gleichzeitig mit experimentellen Ideen weiterentwickelten, wie beispielsweise ein Fußboden, der durch heiße Luft aus dem Kamin und passive Solarheizung beheizt wird. Aufgrund der abgeschiedenen Lage und Landschaft war es wünschenswert, den Wohnbereich mit Glaswänden zu umgeben, während sich die Schlafzimmer und das Badezimmer im hinteren Teil des Hauses zwischen Wänden aus Granit und Ziegelsteinen befinden, die vor der Baustelle verborgen wurden. Das Haus ist ein Beispiel dafür, wie durchdachtes Bauen unter Verwendung lokal produzierter Materialien und unter Berücksichtigung der Natur und Geschichte der Region zeitgenössische Ästhetik und Philosophie mit funktionalen Anforderungen, niedrigen Baukosten und einem kleinen ökologischen Fußabdruck verbinden kann.

La maison Lundnäs est construite dans les fondations en granit d'une usine de poêles en céramique du tournant du siècle. L'architecte a conçu et construit la maison comme une étude de cas ; la conception et la construction évoluant simultanément grâce à des idées expérimentales, comme un plancher chauffé par l'air chaud de la cheminée et le chauffage solaire passif. L'emplacement et le paysage isolés ont rendu souhaitable la présence de murs en verre autour de la zone de séjour, tandis que les chambres et la salle de bain sont situées à l'arrière de la maison entre des murs construits en granit et en briques récupérées sur le site. La maison est un exemple de la manière dont une construction réfléchie, utilisant des matériaux produits localement et tenant compte de la nature et de l'histoire de la région, peut combiner l'esthétique et la philosophie contemporaines avec des exigences fonctionnelles, de faibles coûts de construction et une faible empreinte écologique.

La casa Lundnäs está construida en los cimientos de granito de una fábrica de estufas de cerámica de principios de siglo. El arquitecto diseñó y construyó la casa como un caso de estudio, donde el diseño y la construcción evolucionan simultáneamente usando ideas experimentales, como un suelo que se calienta con el aire caliente de la chimenea y la calefacción solar pasiva. La ubicación aislada y el paisaje hicieron que fuera deseable tener paredes de vidrio alrededor de la zona de estar, mientras que los dormitorios y el baño se encuentran en la parte trasera de la casa entre paredes construidas de granito y ladrillos recuperados del lugar. La casa es un ejemplo de cómo una construcción cuidadosa, utilizando materiales producidos localmente y teniendo en cuenta la naturaleza y la historia de la región, puede combinar la estética y la filosofía contemporáneas con requisitos funcionales, bajos costos de construcción y una pequeña huella ecológica.

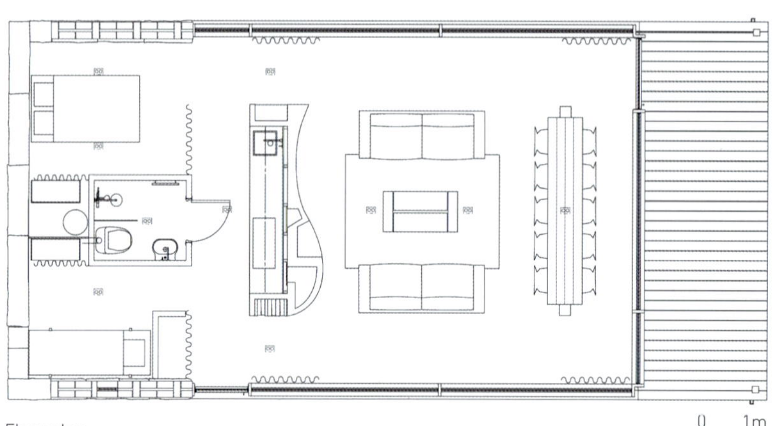


Floor plan

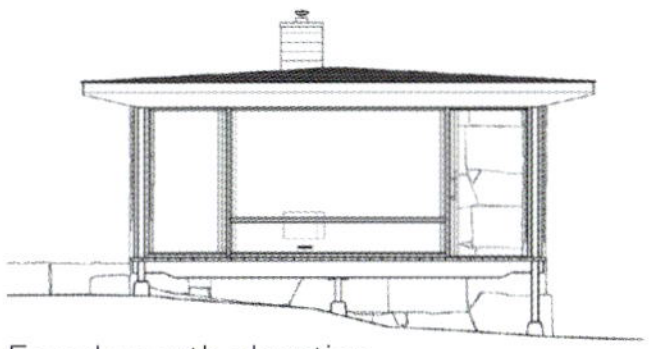

Facade south elevation

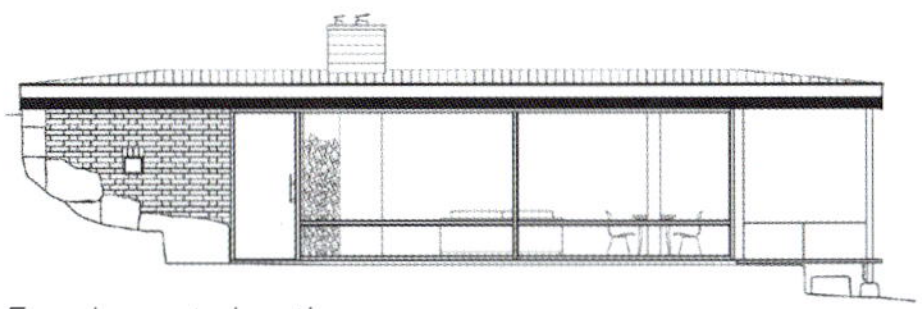

Facade west elevation

The office started as a studio collective in 1985 and was officially founded in 1993 by the three partners Nils Johan Mannsåker, Odd Sørhus and Petter Bergerud. Fortunen Arkitektur has today 17 employees located in an industrial building in the harbour, by the water, in Bergen, Norway. The office is organized as three departments: building, landscape and design. This ensures a high level of professional breadth in all our work tasks; project planning and planning at all levels, both in large and small construction projects, outdoor work, urban spaces, overall planning, interior design, exhibitions and object design.
Since the start-up, Fortunen Arkitektur have placed great emphasis on participation in architectural competitions and have so far won 24 entries.

Das Büro begann 1985 als Atelierkollektiv und wurde 1993 offiziell von den drei Partnern Nils Johan Mannsåker, Odd Sørhus und Petter Bergerud gegründet. Fortunen Arkitektur hat heute 17 Mitarbeiter in einem Industriegebäude in Bergen, Norwegen, im Hafen direkt am Wasser. Das Büro ist in drei Abteilungen organisiert: Gebäude, Landschaft und Design. Dies gewährleistet eine hohe fachliche Breite bei allen Arbeitsaufgaben; Projektplanung und Planung auf allen Ebenen, sowohl bei großen als auch bei kleinen Bauvorhaben, Außenarbeiten, städtischen Räumen, Gesamtplanung, Innenarchitektur, Ausstellungen und Objektgestaltung.
Seit der Gründung legt Fortunen Arkitektur großen Wert auf die Teilnahme an Architekturwettbewerben und hat bisher mit 24 Einreichungen gewonnen.

# FORTUNEN ARKITEKTUR

Le bureau a commencé comme un collectif de studios en 1985 et a été officiellement fondé en 1993 par les trois partenaires Nils Johan Mannsåker, Odd Sørhus et Petter Bergerud. Fortunen Arkitektur compte aujourd'hui 17 employés dans un bâtiment industriel situé dans le port, au bord de l'eau, à Bergen, en Norvège. Le bureau est organisé en trois départements : bâtiment, paysage et design. Cela garantit un haut niveau de professionnalisme dans toutes nos tâches de travail ; de la planification à l'élaboration de projets à tous les niveaux, tant pour les grands que pour les petits projets de construction, le travail en extérieur, les espaces urbains, la planification globale, la décoration intérieure, les expositions et la conception d'objets.
Depuis son lancement, Fortunen Arkitektur a accordé une grande importance à la participation à des concours d'architecture et a remporté

La oficina comenzó como un estudio colectivo en 1985 y fue fundada oficialmente en 1993 por los tres socios Nils Johan Mannsåker, Odd Sørhus y Petter Bergerud. Fortunen Arkitektur tiene hoy 17 empleados ubicados en un edificio industrial en el puerto, junto al agua, en Bergen, Noruega. La oficina está organizada en tres departamentos: construcción, paisaje y diseño. Esto asegura un alto nivel de amplitud profesional en todas nuestras tareas de trabajo; planificación a todos los niveles, tanto en proyectos de construcción grandes como pequeños, trabajo al aire libre, espacios urbanos, planificación general, diseño de interiores, exposiciones y diseño de objetos.
Desde su inicio, Fortunen Arkitektur ha puesto gran énfasis en la participación en concursos de arquitectura y hasta el momento ha ganado 24 de ellos.

▼ BRYGGENS MUSEUM´S PERMANENT EXHIBITION (2017-2019)

▼ HESTAD CHAPEL REST AREA

▼ LOGEN THEATER

## BRYGGENS MUSEUM

Bergen, Norway
Photos: © Dag Randen

The aim of the exhibition is to convey life in the Middle Ages in Bergen, Norway. New communication was established between the entrance area and main plan with shop, cafe and service rooms that are opened up to get light from all directions. The exhibition area is a "black box" where artificial lighting and environment can be controlled and a dramatic atmosphere can be created.
The exhibition is based on the actual drawings in soil layers made by archaeologists at the excavation in 1955, which is best explanatory of what was found and later exhibited. An abstracted world of the Middle Ages was created where visitors meet objects from that era. Another inspiration came from Nordic Runes, which were taken by the technique of painting in a material or as a graphic element.

Ziel der Ausstellung ist es, das Leben im Mittelalter in Bergen, Norwegen, zu vermitteln. Es wurde eine neue Kommunikation zwischen dem Eingangsbereich und dem Hauptplan mit Laden, Café und Serviceräumen geschaffen, die geöffnet sind, um Licht aus allen Richtungen zu erhalten. Der Ausstellungsbereich ist eine „Black Box", in der künstliche Beleuchtung und Umgebung gesteuert werden können und eine dramatische Atmosphäre geschaffen werden kann.
Die Ausstellung basiert auf den tatsächlichen Zeichnungen in Bodenschichten, die von Archäologen bei der Ausgrabung 1955 angefertigt wurden und die am besten erklären, was gefunden und später ausgestellt wurde. Es wurde eine abstrahierte Welt des Mittelalters geschaffen, in der die Besucher auf Objekte aus dieser Epoche treffen. Eine weitere Inspiration kam von den nordischen Runen, die von der Technik der Malerei in einem Material oder als grafisches Element aufgenommen wurden.

L'objectif de l'exposition est de faire connaître la vie au Moyen Âge à Bergen, en Norvège. Une nouvelle communication a été établie entre la zone d'entrée et le plan principal avec des boutiques, des cafés et des salles de service qui sont ouverts pour recevoir la lumière de toutes les directions. La zone d'exposition est une «boîte noire» où l'éclairage artificiel et l'environnement peuvent être contrôlés et où une atmosphère dramatique peut être créée.
L'exposition est basée sur les dessins réels dans les couches du sol réalisés par les archéologues lors des fouilles de 1955, ce qui est la meilleure manière d'expliquer ce qui a été trouvé et exposé par la suite. Un monde abstrait du Moyen Âge a été créé, où les visiteurs rencontrent des objets de cette époque. Une autre inspiration est venue des runes nordiques, qui ont été prises par la technique de la peinture dans un matériau ou comme élément graphique.

El objetivo de la exposición es transmitir la vida en la Edad Media en Bergen, Noruega. Se ha establecido una nueva comunicación entre la zona de entrada y el plano principal con la tienda, el café y las salas de servicio que se abren para recibir luz desde todas las direcciones. El área de exposición es una «caja negra» donde la iluminación artificial y el ambiente pueden ser controlados, creando una atmósfera dramática.
La exposición se basa en los dibujos reales en capas de suelo realizados por los arqueólogos en la excavación de 1955. Se creó un mundo abstracto de la Edad Media donde los visitantes se encuentran con objetos de esa época. Otra inspiración provino de las Runas Nórdicas, que fueron tomadas por medio de la técnica de la pintura en un material o como elemento gráfico.

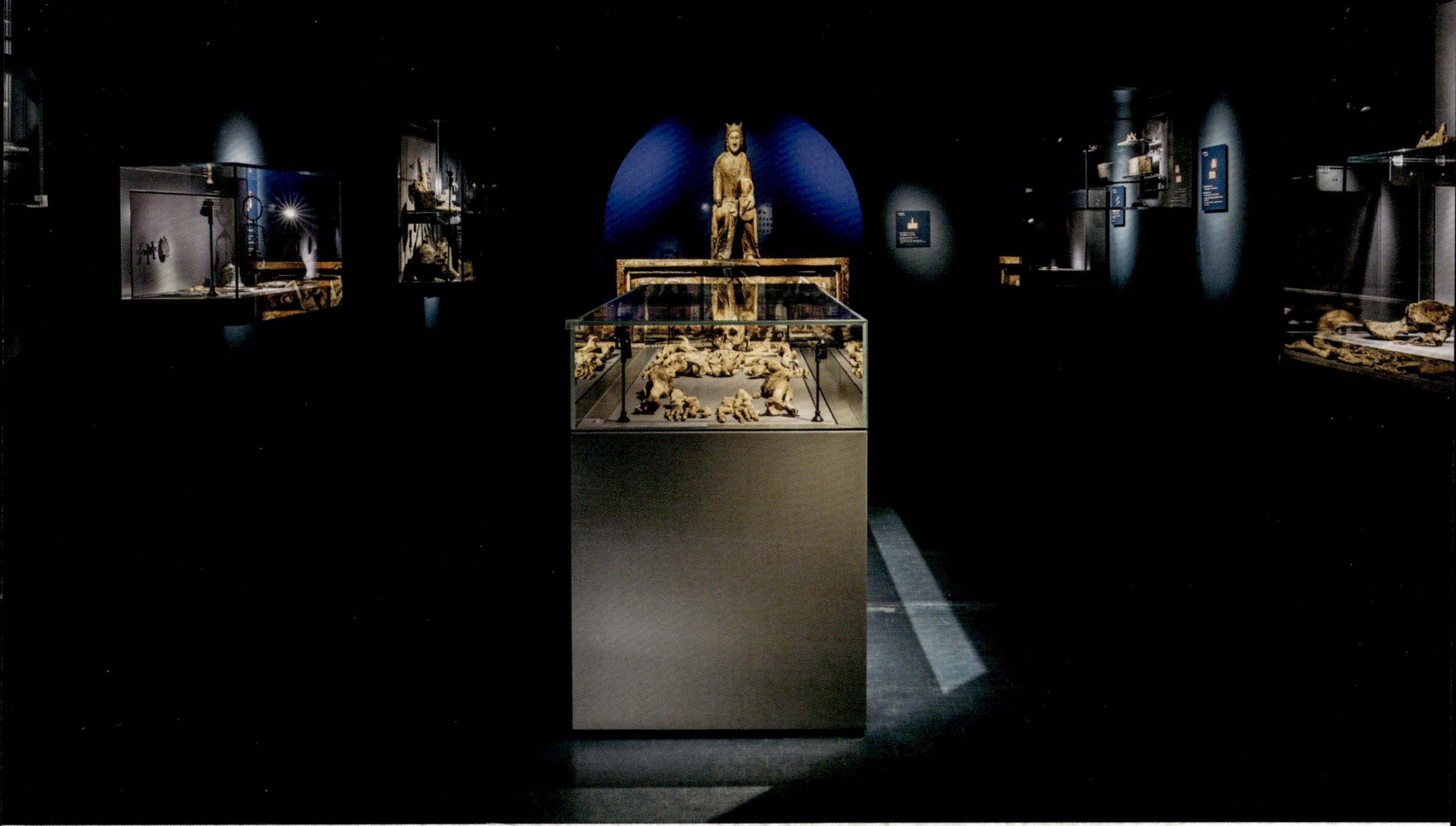

## HESTAD CHAPEL

Gaular, Norway
Photos: © Fortunen Arkitektur

The Hestad chapel area is a beautiful and popular stopping point, with sets of resting places and service buildings planned in collaboration with the Norwegian National Scenic Routes and Gaular Municipality, in western Norway. The Chapel building was constructed in 1805 with parts of an older church dated back from the 12th century.
The rest area, service building and assistance point are located besides the existing chapel by the water. The rest area is joined by groups of tall cylinders which form a great circle. It is an important premise of the project that the entire area is flooded two times a year, and parts of the structures are then under water. A walk along the water's south edge returns through a low stone portal and back into the church backyard.

Das Gebiet der Hestad-Kapelle ist ein schöner und beliebter Erholungsort mit einer Reihe von Rastplätzen und Dienstgebäuden, die in Zusammenarbeit mit den norwegischen Nationalen Landschaftspfaden und der Gemeinde Gaular in Westnorwegen geplant wurden. Das Kapellengebäude wurde 1805 mit Teilen einer älteren Kirche aus dem 12. Jahrhundert errichtet.
Der Erholungsbereich, das Dienstgebäude und der Hilfspunkt befinden sich neben der bestehenden Kapelle am Wasser. Der Erholungsbereich ist durch Gruppen von hohen Zylindern verbunden, die einen großen Kreis bilden. Es ist eine wichtige Prämisse des Projekts, dass der gesamte Bereich zweimal im Jahr geflutet wird und Teile der Strukturen dann unter Wasser stehen. Ein Spaziergang entlang der Südkante des Wassers führt durch ein niedriges Steinportal zurück in den Hinterhof der Kirche.

Le quartier de la chapelle de Hestad est un point d'arrêt magnifique et populaire, avec des ensembles de lieux de repos et de bâtiments de service planifiés en collaboration avec les Routes Scénographiques Nationales Norvégiennes et la Municipalité Gaular, dans l'ouest de la Norvège. Le bâtiment de la chapelle a été construit en 1805 avec des parties d'une église plus ancienne datant du 12ème siècle.
L'aire de repos, le bâtiment de service et le point d'assistance sont situés à côté de la chapelle existante au bord de l'eau. L'aire de repos est reliée par des groupes de hauts cylindres qui forment un grand cercle. Un des principes importants du projet est que toute la zone est inondée deux fois par an et que des parties des structures sont alors sous l'eau. Une promenade le long du bord sud de l'eau revient par un portail de pierre bas et ramène dans le jardin de l'église.

La zona de la capilla Hestad es un hermoso y popular punto de parada con conjuntos de lugares de descanso y edificios de servicios planificados en colaboración con las Rutas Escénicas Nacionales de Noruega y el Municipio Gaular, en el oeste del país. El edificio de la capilla se construyó en 1805 con partes de una iglesia más antigua que data del siglo XII.
El área de descanso, el edificio de servicios y el punto de asistencia están situados al lado de la capilla existente junto al agua. El área de descanso está unida por grupos de altos cilindros que forman un gran círculo. Es una premisa importante del proyecto que toda el área se inunde dos veces al año, quedando entonces bajo agua, partes de las estructuras. Un paseo por el borde sur del agua regresa a través de un portal bajo de piedra y vuelve al patio trasero de la iglesia.

## LOGEN THEATER

Bergen, Norway
Photos: © Richard Seymour, Fortunen Arkitektur

The project consists of an extension and renovation of a neoclassical theater building in Bergen, Norway in collaboration with 3RW architects. The undulating movement of the front curtain is used as unifying element in the rehabilitation of the service area in the theater, and to the planned façade´s extension. The bar is built up by sections of CNC-cut elements plastered to a solid shape. The lightning consists of traditional stage lights with a golden abstraction. The façade has a steel mesh screen on the outside of the glacing that captures the Nordic light while flowing seamlessly into the historical surroundings. The movement and colours repeat themselves in furniture and columns inside the new and old building, which gives am integrated impression.

Das Projekt besteht aus einer Erweiterung und Renovierung eines neoklassizistischen Theatergebäudes in Bergen, Norwegen, in Zusammenarbeit mit 3RW Architekten. Die wellenförmige Bewegung des Frontvorhangs wird als verbindendes Element bei der Sanierung des Sitzbereichs im Theater und bei der geplanten Fassadenverlängerung eingesetzt. Die Stange wird aus Abschnitten von CNC-geschnittenen Elementen aufgebaut, die zu einer massiven Form verputzt werden. Die Beleuchtung besteht aus traditionellen Bühnenleuchten mit einer goldenen Abstraktion. Die Fassade hat an der Außenseite der Verglasung ein Stahlgittergewebe, das das nordische Licht einfängt und sich nahtlos in die historische Umgebung einfügt. Die Bewegung und die Farben wiederholen sich in Möbeln und Säulen im Inneren des neuen und alten Gebäudes, wodurch ein integrierter Eindruck entsteht.

Le projet consiste en une extension et une rénovation d'un bâtiment de théâtre néoclassique à Bergen, en Norvège, en collaboration avec les architectes du 3RW. Le mouvement ondulant du rideau avant est utilisé comme élément unificateur dans la réhabilitation de l'aire de service du théâtre et dans l'extension prévue de la façade. La barre est constituée de sections d'éléments découpés par CNC et plâtrés pour obtenir une forme solide. L'éclairage est constitué de lumières de scène traditionnelles avec une abstraction dorée. La façade est dotée d'un écran en maille d'acier à l'extérieur du vitrage qui capte la lumière nordique tout en s'intégrant parfaitement à l'environnement historique. Le mouvement et les couleurs se répètent dans les meubles et les colonnes à l'intérieur du nouveau et de l'ancien bâtiment, ce qui donne une impression d'intégration.

El proyecto consiste en la ampliación y renovación de un teatro neoclásico en Bergen, Noruega, en colaboración con los arquitectos de 3RW. El movimiento ondulante de la cortina frontal se utiliza como elemento unificador en la rehabilitación del área de servicio del teatro, y en la ampliación prevista de la fachada. La barra está formada por secciones de elementos cortados con CNC enyesados a una forma sólida. La iluminación consiste en luces de escenario tradicionales con una abstracción dorada. La fachada tiene una pantalla de malla de acero en el exterior que captura la luz nórdica mientras fluye sin problemas hacia el entorno histórico. El movimiento y los colores se repiten en los muebles y las columnas del interior del nuevo y del viejo edificio, ayudando a conseguir una impresión de conjunto.

Gudmundur Jonsson Arkitektkontor was established in 1987 in Oslo. Ever since they have won 37 different prizes in Norwegian, Icelandic and Nordic competitions, some of them 1st and 2nd prizes.
The essence of «reading the site» has been of utmost importance and the emphasis of the dialog between nature and the house. Construction and materiality is supposed to clarify the concept, and the heritage of functionalism is often an inspiration in the projects.
Definition of volumes are often made more distinctive by the cantilevered roofs and balconies, simultaneously defining the spaces and giving excitement and dialog between the building and the landscape. An extensive use of glass is strengthening the constructive challenges.
In the interior the purpose is to make surfaces appear as a softening unity, integrating closets, cabinets and technical installations to obtain maximum harmony and tranquility, enforced by the colour-palette.

Das Gudmundur Jonsson Arkitektkontor wurde 1987 in Oslo gegründet. Seitdem hat es 37 verschiedene Preise in norwegischen, isländischen und weiteren nordischen Wettbewerben gewonnen, darunter erste und zweite Preise.
Die Essenz des „Lesens des Ortes" war von größter Bedeutung, sowie die Betonung des Dialogs zwischen Natur und Haus. Konstruktion und Materialität sollen das Konzept verdeutlichen, und das Erbe des Funktionalismus ist oft eine Inspiration in den Projekten.
Die Definition der Volumina wird oft durch die auskragenden Dächer und Balkone verstärkt, die gleichzeitig die Räume definieren und für Spannung und Dialog zwischen dem Gebäude und der Landschaft sorgen. Ein umfangreicher Einsatz von Glas verstärkt die konstruktiven Herausforderungen.
Im Inneren sollen die Oberflächen als eine weichmachende Einheit erscheinen, indem Schränke, Vitrinen und technische Installationen integriert werden, um ein Maximum an Harmonie und Ruhe zu erreichen, die durch die Farbpalette verstärkt wird.

# GUDMUNDUR JONSSON ARKITEKTKONTOR

Gudmundur Jonsson Arkitektkontor a été créé en 1987 à Oslo. Depuis, ils ont remporté 37 prix différents dans des concours norvégiens, islandais et nordiques, dont certains 1er et 2e prix.
L'essence de la «lecture du site» a été de la plus haute importance et l'accent a été mis sur le dialogue entre la nature et la maison. La construction et la matérialité sont censées clarifier le concept et l'héritage du fonctionnalisme est souvent une source d'inspiration dans les projets.
Les toits et les balcons en porte-à-faux permettent de définir des volumes de manière plus distinctive. Ils définissent simultanément les espaces et donnent de l'animation et du dialogue entre le bâtiment et le paysage. L'utilisation intensive du verre renforce les défis de construction.
À l'intérieur, l'objectif est de faire apparaître les surfaces comme une unité adoucissante, en intégrant les placards, les armoires et les installations techniques pour obtenir une harmonie et une tranquillité maximales, renforcées par la palette de couleurs.

Gudmundur Jonsson Arkitektkontor se estableció en 1987 en Oslo. Desde entonces han ganado 37 premios en competiciones noruegas, islandesas y nórdicas, algunos de ellos el primer y segundo premio.
La lectura e interpretación del lugar es de suma importancia en sus proyectos, así como el énfasis del diálogo entre la naturaleza y la casa. Se supone que la construcción y la materialidad aclaran el concepto, y por ello, la herencia del funcionalismo se convierte a menudo en su fuente de inspiración
La definición de los volúmenes se distingue por los tejados en voladizo y los balcones, delimitando simultáneamente los espacios y dando emoción y diálogo entre
edificio y paisaje. El uso extensivo del vidrio refuerza estos desafíos.
En el interior, el propósito es hacer que las superficies aparezcan en suave unidad, integrando armarios e instalaciones técnicas para obtener la máxima armonía y tranquilidad, reforzadas por una elegante paleta de colores.

CASA G

CASA MYHRER HAUGE

## CASA G

Fljotshlid, Iceland
Photos: © Bragi Thor Josefsson

The concept of Casa G is based on reading and feedback to the landscape it exists on. The characteristic landscape situation and view differences distinctively in each direction. Towards south the view to the sea and islands, towards north the characteristic triangular mountain, towards east the glacier and towards west the river and canyon.
Those elements are the creator of the project, the transitions between the landscape views giving the entrance from the north and the curved plan giving a vitalized focus towards the seaside in south. When turning back the north view towards the mountain is as well enhanced with the widening view due to the fan-shape of the tilting wooden wall, being a mediator between the northern and southern landscape characteristic.

Das Konzept von Casa G basiert auf der Lektüre und dem Feedback der Landschaft, in der es existiert. Die charakteristische Lage und die Aussicht unterscheiden sich in jeder Richtung deutlich. Nach Süden der Blick auf das Meer und die Inseln, nach Norden der charakteristische dreieckige Berg, nach Osten der Gletscher und nach Westen der Fluss und die Schlucht.
Diese Elemente bilden die Grundlage des Projekts: Übergänge zwischen den Landschaftsansichten vom Eingang und dem gekrümmten Grundriss, die einen belebten Fokus auf die Meerseite im Süden geben. Auch der Blick zurück zum Berg wird durch die Fächerform der kippbaren Holzwand, die als Vermittler zwischen der nördlichen und südlichen Landschaft wirkt, mit der sich der Blick weitet, verstärkt.

Le concept de la Casa G est basé sur la lecture et la rétroaction du paysage sur lequel elle se trouve, sur son emplacement caractéristique et sur les différences de points de vue dans chaque direction. Vers le sud, la vue sur la mer et les îles, vers le nord la montagne triangulaire caractéristique, vers l'est le glacier et vers l'ouest la rivière et le canyon.
Ces éléments sont à la base du projet : des transitions entre les vues du paysage depuis l'entrée et le plan courbe donnant une orientation vitalisée vers le bord de mer au sud. Le retour vers la montagne est également mis en valeur par l'élargissement de la vue grâce à la forme en éventail du mur en bois basculant qui sert de médiateur entre le paysage du nord et celui du sud.

El concepto de la Casa G se basa en la lectura y la retroalimentación del paisaje en el que existe. La característica ubicación y las vistas difieren en cada dirección: hacia el sur, la vista al mar y las islas; al norte, la montaña triangular; hacia el este, el glaciar y hacia el oeste el río y el cañón. Esos elementos son la base del proyecto: transiciones entre las vistas del paisaje desde la entrada y el plano curvo que permiten un enfoque hacia la costa. El giro hacia la montaña se realza con la ampliación de las vistas debido a la forma de abanico de la pared de madera inclinada que funciona como mediador entre el paisaje del norte y el del sur.

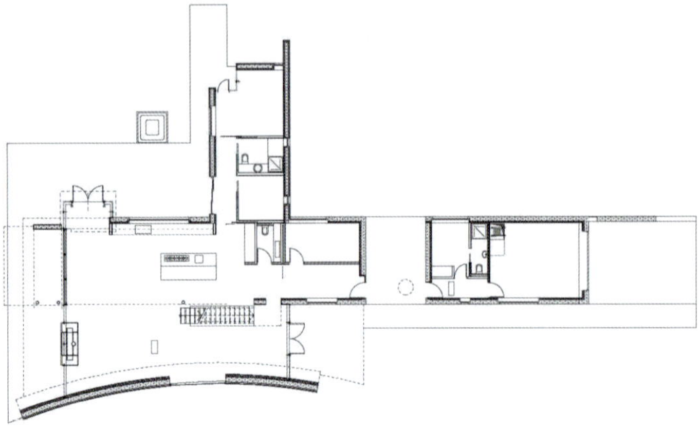

Ground floor plan

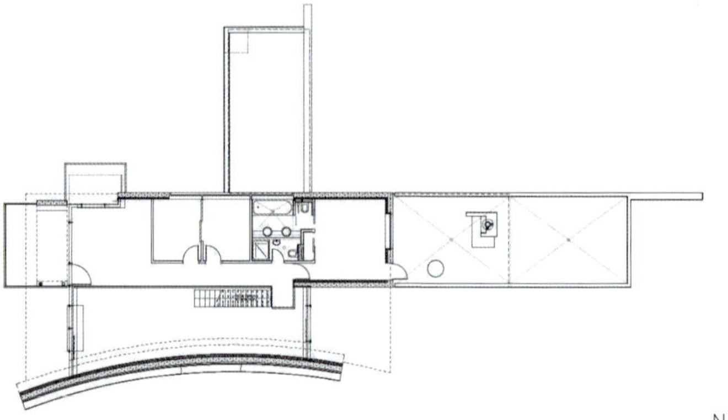

First floor plan

## CASA MYHRER HAUGE

Oslo, Norway
Photos: © Jiri Havran

The concept of Casa Myhrer Hauge is a synthesis of bringing difficult landscape and regulation factors together. The factors being a river down the valley on the s-vest side of the site, with prohibitions to build closer than 100 meters, and the partly closed river/stream, that I found important to open up, make use of, preserve the nature, and bring the stream into the project as an important feature.
Due to those issues, and the wish to enhance the importance between the stream and the project, the garage and the house are connected with a bridge floating over the landscape, not touching it, but bringing it into importance and meditative experience when entering the house. The nature will be brought back as natural as possible, as it was initially in this Maridalen forest, just enhancing the nature with simple means, with the treatment of the Stream.

Das Konzept der Casa Myhrer Hauge ist eine Synthese aus der Zusammenführung von schwierigem Gelände und Vorschriften. Ein talabwärts verlaufender Fluss auf der Südseite des Geländes, mit Bauverboten näher als 100 Meter, und der teilweise geschlossene Flusslauf, den der Architekt für wichtig erachtete, unter Wahrung der Natur zu erschließen und den Bach in das Projekt einzubringen, waren die wichtigsten Merkmale.
Aus diesen Gründen und aus dem Wunsch heraus, die Bedeutung zwischen dem Bach und dem Projekt zu erhöhen, sind die Garage und das Haus mit einer schwimmenden Brücke verbunden, die das Betreten des Gebäudes in eine meditative Erfahrung verwandelt. Die Natur wird so natürlich wie möglich zurückgebracht, so wie sie in diesem Maridalen-Wald ursprünglich war.

Le concept de la Casa Myhrer Hauge est une synthèse entre un paysage difficile et des réglementations. Parmi les éléments les plus importants on trouve une rivière descendant la vallée sur le côté sud du site, avec des interdictions de construire à moins de 100 m et le cours d'eau partiellement fermé, que l'architecte a jugé important d'ouvrir tout en préservant la nature et d'intégrer le cours d'eau dans le projet.
En raison de ces problèmes et du souhait d'accroître l'importance entre le ruisseau et le projet, le garage et la maison sont reliés par un pont flottant, ce qui permet de vivre une expérience méditative en entrant dans le bâtiment. La nature sera ramenée aussi naturelle que possible, comme elle l'était initialement dans cette forêt de Maridalen.

La Casa Myhrer Hauge es el resultado de unir un entorno complicado y las regulaciones legales: la presencia de un río en el lado sur del terreno, las prohibiciones de construir a menos de 100 m., y un arroyo que el arquitecto consideró importante ampliar preservando la naturaleza.
Debido a esas cuestiones y al deseo de resaltar la importancia del arroyo en el proyecto, el garaje y la casa se conectaron por medio de un puente flotante, convirtiendo la intervención en una experiencia meditativa durante la entrada al edificio. La naturaleza se recupera de la manera más natural posible, tal como ya sucedió originalmente en este bosque de Maridalen.

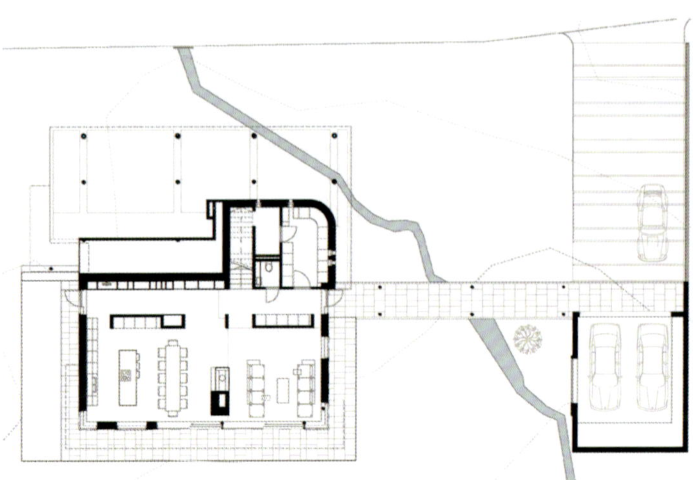

Ground floor plan

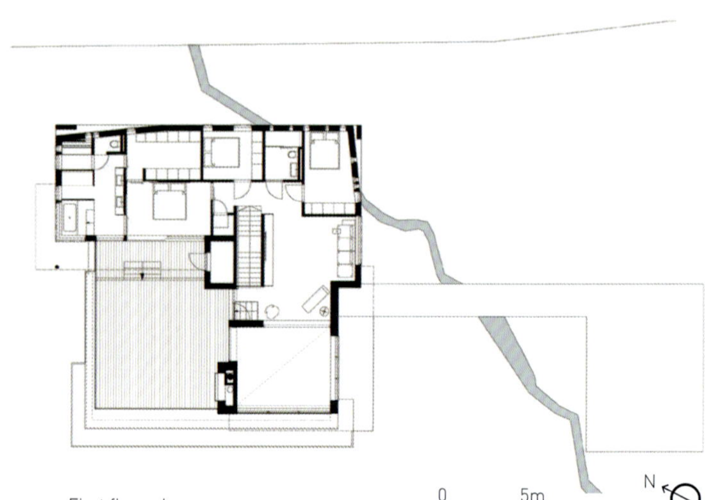


First floor plan

Sections

Jan Henrik Jansen is a Danish/German architect based in Copenhagen, Denmark. He holds degrees from Leibniz Universität, Hannover and Aarhus School of Architecture and has taught at the University of applied science in Lübeck, Germany and DIS in Copenhagen.
Between 2002 and 2016 Jansen designed and single-handedly built three distinctive, award winning summer houses, "Langelinie", "Black+Bright" and "Birkedal", on the Danish island of Møn. These three houses served as a laboratory where Jansen experimented with design, details and materials and led to the launch of his practice, Jan Henrik Jansen arkitekter, in 2012. Jansen now works internationally, designing quietly radical, materially-rich and geometrically precise houses that are highly sensitive to the diverse landscapes that they occupy.

Jan Henrik Jansen ist ein dänisch-deutscher Architekt mit Sitz in Kopenhagen, Dänemark. Er hat Abschlüsse der Leibniz-Universität, Hannover und der Aarhus School of Architecture und lehrte an der Fachhochschule Lübeck, Deutschland, und der DIS in Kopenhagen.
Zwischen 2002 und 2016 entwarf und baute Jansen eigenhändig drei unverwechselbare, preisgekrönte Sommerhäuser, „Langelinie", „Black+Bright" und „Birkedal", auf der dänischen Insel Møn. Diese drei Häuser dienten als Laboratorium, in dem Jansen mit Design, Details und Materialien experimentierte, und führten zur Gründung seines Büros Jan Henrik Jansen arkitekter im Jahr 2012. Heute arbeitet Jansen international und entwirft leise, radikale, materialreiche und geometrisch präzise Häuser, die sehr sensibel auf die vielfältigen Landschaften reagieren, die sie besetzen.

# JAN HENRIK JANSEN ARKITEKTER

Jan Henrik Jansen est un architecte danois-allemand basé à Copenhague, au Danemark. Il est diplômé de l'université Leibniz, de Hanovre et de l'école d'architecture d'Aarhus. Il a enseigné à l'université des sciences appliquées de Lübeck, en Allemagne et à la DIS de Copenhague.
Entre 2002 et 2016, Jansen a conçu et construit à lui seul trois maisons d'été distinctes et primées : « Langelinie », « Black+Bright » et « Birkedal », sur l'île danoise de Møn. Ces trois maisons ont servi de laboratoire où Jansen a expérimenté le design, les détails et les matériaux et ont conduit au lancement de sa pratique, Jan Henrik Jansen arkitekter, en 2012. Jansen travaille maintenant à l'échelle internationale, concevant des maisons discrètement radicales, riches en matériaux et géométriquement précises, très sensibles aux divers paysages qu'elles occupent.

Jan Henrik Jansen es un arquitecto danés/alemán con sede en Copenhague, Dinamarca. Tiene títulos de la Leibniz Universität, Hannover y la Escuela de Arquitectura de Aarhus y ha enseñado en la Universidad de Ciencias Aplicadas de Lübeck, Alemania y en la DIS de Copenhague.
Entre 2002 y 2016, Jansen diseñó y construyó por su cuenta tres casas de verano distintivas y premiadas, «Langelinie», «Black+Bright» y «Birkedal», en la isla danesa de Møn. Estas tres casas sirvieron como un laboratorio donde Jansen experimentó con el diseño, los detalles y los materiales y condujo al lanzamiento de su estudio, Jan Henrik Jansen arkitekter, en 2012. Jansen trabaja ahora internacionalmente, diseñando casas silenciosamente radicales, ricas en materiales y geométricamente precisas que son altamente sensibles a los diversos paisajes que ocupan.

BIRKEDAL

LANDHUS I MIDTJYLLAND

VILLA KORUP

## BIRKEDAL

Møn, Denmark
Photos: © Jesper Ray, Lene K Fotografi

"Birkedal", or "Birch Dale" in English, was designed and built single handily by Jan Henrik Jansen with the goal to create a sustainable and peaceful family retreat on the bucolic Danish island of Møn. The house comprises nine interlinked cylindrical volumes constructed with intricate timber frames and clad with narrow spruce trunks which are a waste product of the forestry industry. Each of the cylinders encloses a single idiosyncratic room, finished with richly textured white surfaces; river pebble floors and painted board and batten wall cladding, which, like the walls of a gallery, provide a calm backdrop for the constantly changing textures and colours of the agricultural landscape visible through the punctured rectangular windows. The unique layout of the house demanded specially designed furniture, materials and details throughout.

Birkedal, oder auf Deutsch „Birkental", wurde von Jan Henrik Jansen eigenhändig entworfen und gebaut, mit dem Ziel, ein nachhaltiges und friedliches Familienrefugium auf der bukolischen dänischen Insel Møn zu schaffen. Das Haus besteht aus neun miteinander verbundenen zylindrischen Volumina, die mit komplizierten Holzrahmen gebaut und mit schmalen Fichtenstämmen verkleidet wurden, die ein Abfallprodukt der Forstwirtschaft sind. Jeder der Zylinder umschließt einen einzelnen, eigenwilligen Raum, der mit reich strukturierten, weißen Oberflächen versehen ist; Böden aus Flusskieselsteinen und Wandverkleidungen aus gestrichenen Brettern und Latten, die wie die Wände einer Galerie einen ruhigen Hintergrund für die ständig wechselnden Texturen und Farben der Agrarlandschaft bilden, die durch die durchbrochenen rechteckigen Fenster sichtbar sind. Der einzigartige Grundriss des Hauses erforderte durchgehend speziell entworfene Möbel, Materialien und Details.

« Birkedal », ou « Birch Dale » en anglais, a été conçu et construite à la main par Jan Henrik Jansen dans le but de créer une retraite familiale durable et paisible sur la bucolique île danoise de Møn. La maison se compose de neuf volumes cylindriques reliés entre eux, construits avec des charpentes en bois complexes et habillés d'étroites branches d'épicéa qui sont un déchet de l'industrie forestière. Chacun des cylindres renferme une pièce unique, avec des surfaces blanches richement texturées, des sols en galets de rivière et un revêtement mural en planches et lattes peintes. Cela offre, au même titre que les murs d'une galerie, une toile de fond calme aux textures et couleurs en constante évolution du paysage agricole, visible à travers les fenêtres rectangulaires percées. L'agencement unique de la maison exigeait des meubles, des matériaux et des détails spécialement conçus pour l'ensemble de la maison.

«Birkedal» fue diseñado y construido a mano por Jan Henrik Jansen con el objetivo de crear un refugio familiar sostenible y pacífico en la bucólica isla danesa de Møn. La casa comprende nueve volúmenes cilíndricos entrelazados, construidos con intrincados marcos de madera y revestidos con estrechas ramas de abeto que son un producto de desecho de la industria forestal. Cada uno de los cilindros encierra una única habitación acabada con superficies blancas de rica textura; suelos de guijarros de río y revestimientos de tablas y listones pintados, que, como las paredes de una galería, proporcionan un tranquilo telón de fondo para las texturas y colores constantemente cambiantes del paisaje agrícola visible a través de las ventanas rectangulares perforadas. La disposición única de la casa exigía muebles, materiales y detalles especialmente diseñados.

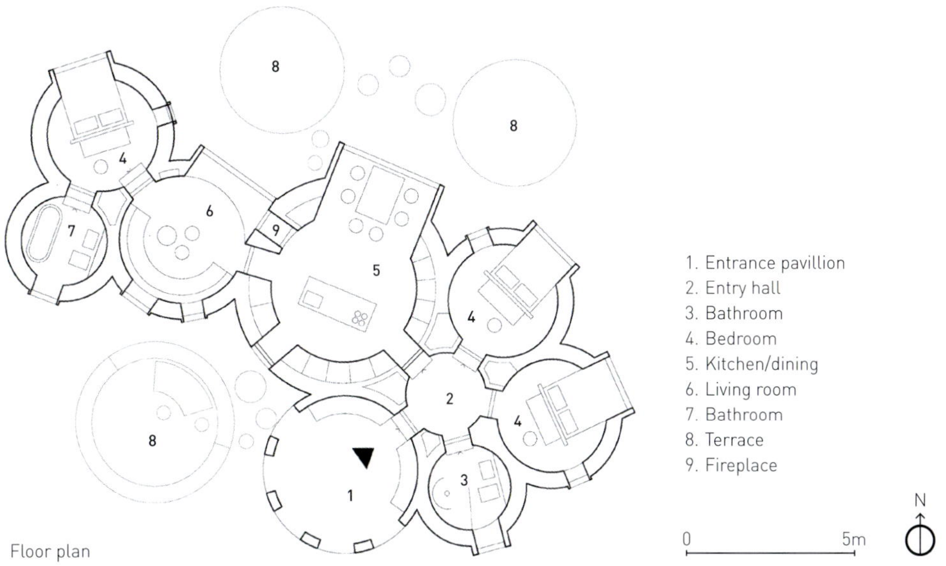


1. Entrance pavillion
2. Entry hall
3. Bathroom
4. Bedroom
5. Kitchen/dining
6. Living room
7. Bathroom
8. Terrace
9. Fireplace

Floor plan

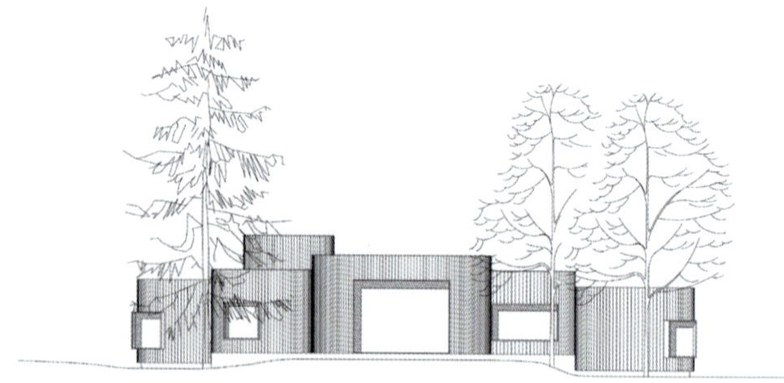

North elevation

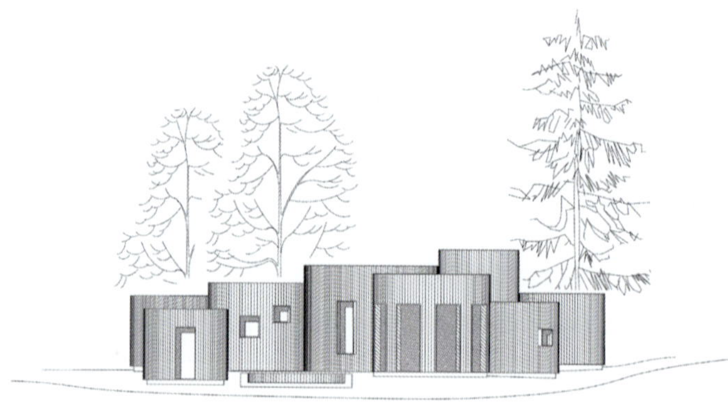

South elevation

## LANDHUS I MIDTJYLLAND

Søhøjlandet, Denmark
Photos: © Konrad Wojcik

"Landhus i Midtjylland" is a unique and highly sustainable timber house built in the densely forested and sparsely populated Danish region of 'søhøjlandet' The house offers a dramatic response to the site with a wing shaped section which opens up and invites views of the wildflower meadow and private lake deep into the house. Wide, angular openings are shielded to maximise the intake of sun and block prevailing winds while outdoor covered terraces adjoin the house ensuring that there is a sunny and protected space for all conditions. The house was one of the first private dwellings constructed in Denmark from cross laminated timber (CLT) which has in this case been exposed throughout the house and treated in a traditional Danish manner with soap and lye which protects the timber and gives it a soft, resilient finish.

Das „Landhus i Midtjylland" ist ein einzigartiges und sehr nachhaltiges Holzhaus, das in der dicht bewaldeten und dünn besiedelten dänischen Region Søhøjlandet gebaut wurde. Das Haus bietet eine dramatische Antwort auf den Ort mit einem flügelförmigen Schnitt, der sich öffnet und den Blick auf die Wildblumenwiese und den privaten See tief ins Haus hinein einlädt. Breite, eckige Öffnungen sind abgeschirmt, um den Sonneneinfall zu maximieren und die vorherrschenden Winde zu blockieren, während überdachte Außenterrassen an das Haus angrenzen, so dass für alle Bedingungen ein sonniger und geschützter Platz zur Verfügung steht. Das Haus war eines der ersten Wohnhäuser, die in Dänemark aus Brettsperrholz (CLT) gebaut wurden, das in diesem Fall im ganzen Haus exponiert und auf traditionelle dänische Weise mit Seife und Lauge behandelt wurde, was das Holz schützt und ihm eine weiche, robuste Oberfläche verleiht.

« Landhus i Midtjylland » est une maison en bois unique et hautement durable, construite dans la région danoise du « søhøjlandet », densément boisée et peu peuplée. La maison offre une réponse spectaculaire au site avec une section en forme d'aile qui s'ouvre et invite à des vues sur la prairie de fleurs sauvages et le lac privé au fond de la maison. De larges ouvertures angulaires sont protégées pour maximiser l'apport de soleil et bloquer les vents dominants, tandis que des terrasses extérieures couvertes jouxtent la maison, garantissant un espace ensoleillé et protégé, en toutes conditions. La maison a été l'une des premières habitations privées construites au Danemark à partir de bois lamellé croisé (CLT). Ce dernier a été, dans ce cas, exposé dans toute la maison et traité à la manière danoise traditionnelle avec du savon et de la lessive qui protègent le bois et lui donnent une finition douce et résistante.

«Landhus i Midtjylland» es una casa de madera única y altamente sostenible construida en la región danesa densamente forestada y poco poblada de «Søhøjlandet». La casa ofrece una respuesta dramática al lugar con una sección en forma de ala que se abre e invita a las vistas de la pradera de flores silvestres y al lago privado. Las amplias y angulosas aberturas están protegidas para maximizar la entrada del sol y bloquear el viento, mientras que las terrazas cubiertas exteriores colindan con la casa asegurando que haya un espacio soleado y protegido para todas las condiciones climáticas. La casa fue una de las primeras viviendas privadas construidas en Dinamarca con madera laminada en cruz (CLT) que en este caso ha sido expuesta en toda la casa y tratada de manera tradicional danesa con jabón y lejía que protege la madera y le da un acabado suave y resistente.

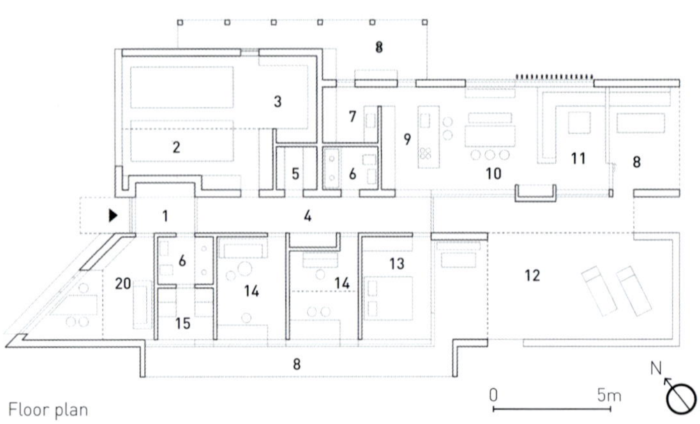


1. Entry hall
2. Garage
3. Bike store
4. Hall
5. Storeroom
6. Bathroom
7. Pantry
8. Covered terrace
9. Kitchen
10. Dining
11. Living room
12. Terrace
13. Master bedroom
14. Bedroom
15. Sauna
16. Office

Floor plan

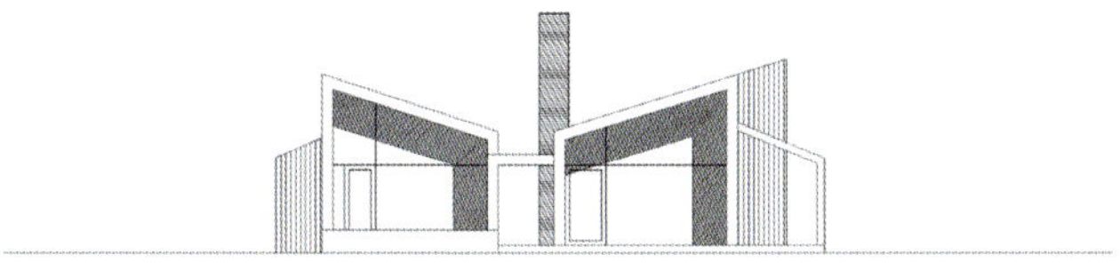

Southeast elevation

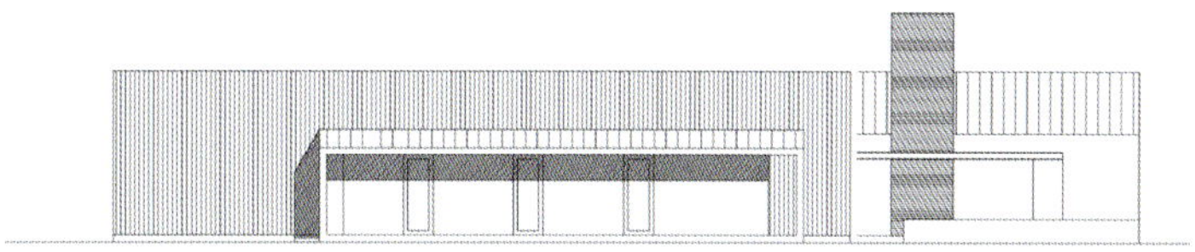

Southwest elevation

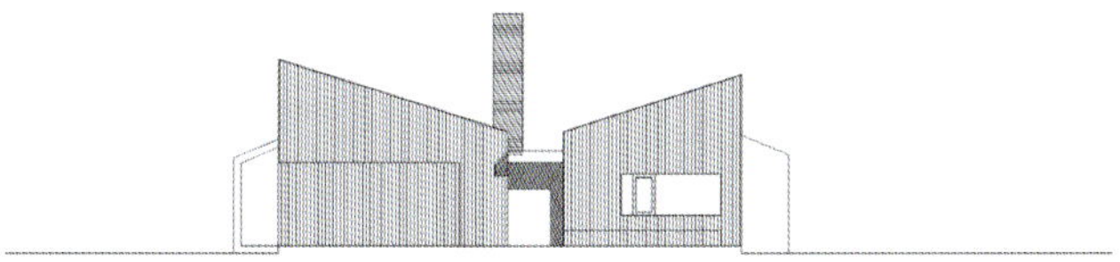

Northest elevation

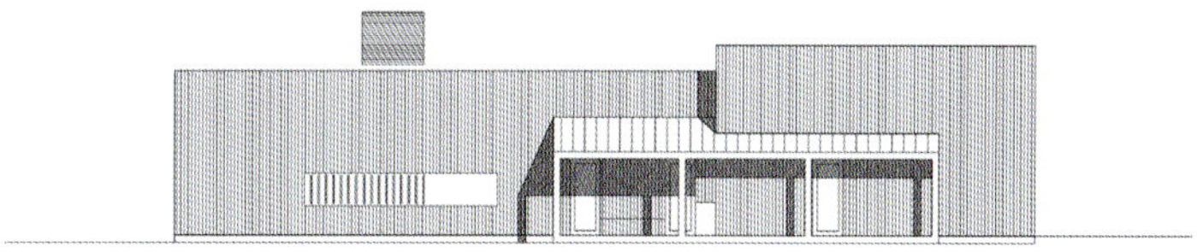

Northeast elevation

## VILLA KORUP

Fyn, Denmark
Photos: © Gabrielle Gualdi, Marshall Blecher

Villa Korup was designed for a young family of six on the Danish island of Fyn. The characteristic 'three legged' plan was developed in order to delineate the different aspects of the landscape, accentuating their qualities and creating three characteristic courtyard like spaces; a sunny south facing sloped area to the south, a protected kitchen garden to the east and an orchard cum playground to the west. Internally, the plan provides central communal spaces for the large family to gather as well as more private, secluded spaces at the ends of the wings. The house is constructed entirely from cross laminated timber (CLT) and clad with panels of weathering steel which change tone and respond to the sites conditions. Villa Korup was designed in collaboration with Australian architect Marshall Blecher.

Die Villa Korup wurde für eine junge sechsköpfige Familie auf der dänischen Insel Fünen entworfen. Der charakteristische „dreibeinige" Grundriss wurde entwickelt, um die verschiedenen Aspekte der Landschaft abzugrenzen, ihre Qualitäten hervorzuheben und drei charakteristische hofähnliche Räume zu schaffen: einen sonnigen, nach Süden ausgerichteten Hang, einen geschützten Nutzgarten im Osten und einen Obstgarten mit Spielplatz im Westen. Im Inneren sieht der Plan zentrale Gemeinschaftsräume vor, in denen sich die große Familie versammeln kann, sowie privatere, abgelegene Räume an den Enden der Flügel. Das Haus ist vollständig aus Brettsperrholz (CLT) gebaut und mit Paneelen aus verwitterndem Stahl verkleidet, die ihren Farbton ändern und auf die Bedingungen des Standortes reagieren. Die Villa Korup wurde in Zusammenarbeit mit dem australischen Architekten Marshall Blecher entworfen.

La Villa Korup a été conçue pour une jeune famille de six personnes sur l'île danoise de Fyn. Le plan caractéristique « à trois pattes » a été élaboré afin de délimiter les différents aspects du paysage, en accentuant leurs qualités et en créant trois espaces caractéristiques ressemblant à des cours. Il s'agit d'une zone en pente ensoleillée orientée au sud, d'un potager protégé à l'est et d'un verger et une aire de jeu à l'ouest. À l'intérieur, le plan prévoit des espaces communs centraux pour que la grande famille puisse se réunir, ainsi que des espaces plus privés et isolés aux extrémités des ailes. La maison est entièrement construite en bois lamellé-collé croisé (CLT) et revêtue de panneaux d'acier résistants aux intempéries qui changent de ton et réagissent aux conditions du site. La Villa Korup a été conçue en collaboration avec l'architecte australien Marshall Blecher.

Villa Korup fue diseñada para una joven familia de seis miembros en la isla danesa de Fyn. El característico plan de «tres patas» se desarrolló para delinear los diferentes aspectos del paisaje, acentuando sus cualidades y creando tres espacios característicos a modo de patio; una zona soleada orientada al sur con pendiente al sur, un jardín con cocina exterior protegido al este y un huerto con patio de recreo al oeste. Internamente, el plan prevé espacios comunitarios centrales para que se reúna la familia numerosa, así como espacios más privados y aislados en los extremos de las alas. La casa está construida enteramente de madera laminada en cruz (CLT) y revestida con paneles de acero resistente a la intemperie que cambian de tono y responden a las condiciones del lugar. Villa Korup fue diseñada en colaboración con el arquitecto australiano Marshall Blecher.

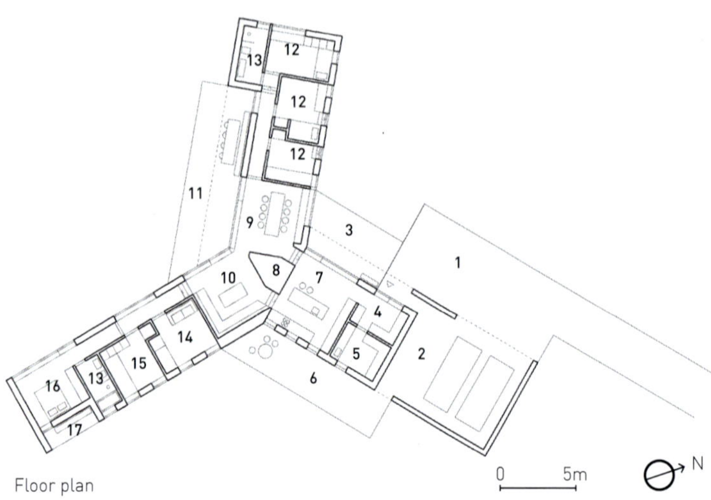


Floor plan

1. Driveway
2. Carpot
3. Western terrace
4. Entry
5. Laundry
6. Eastern terrace
7. Kitchen
8. Technical
9. Dining room
10. Living
11. Southern terrace
12. Bedroom
13. Bathroom
14. Guest
15. Office
16. Master bedroom
17. Private terrace

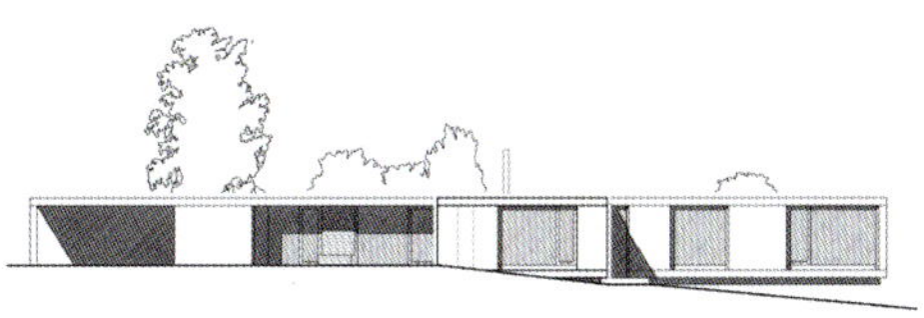

Northwest elevation

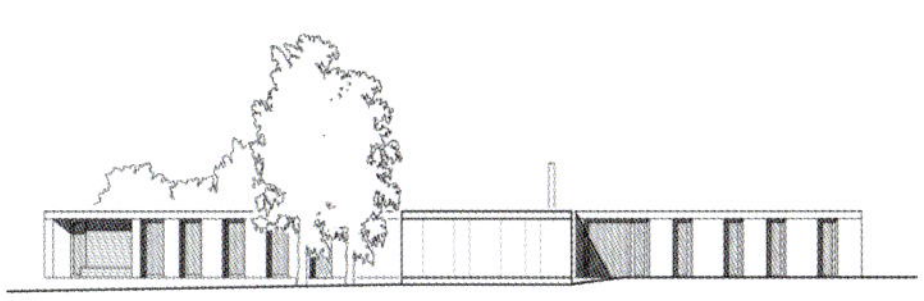

Northeast elevation

South elevation

Knut Hjeltnes was born in Drøbak, Norway in 1961, and was raised in Ås, a small university town south of Oslo. He studied at the Norwegian Institute of Technology in Trondheim from 1980 -1986. During the latter half of his studies and for one and a half years after graduating he worked for 4B Architects. Since 1988 he has had his on practice. He taught at the Oslo school of Architecture from 1988-2016, the last 12 years as professor. He has lectured in several countries, been awarded several prizes and his work is widely published.
The practice was established in Oslo as a one-man practice, slowly expanding to its current size of six employees. The office concentrate on houses, weekend homes and smaller public works. In a period over several years in the 1990s he cooperated with Haga and Grov Architects in Stavanger.

Knut Hjeltnes wurde 1961 in Drøbak, Norwegen, geboren und wuchs in Ås, einer kleinen Universitätsstadt südlich von Oslo, auf. Er studierte von 1980 bis 1986 am Norwegischen Institut für Technologie in Trondheim. Während der zweiten Hälfte seines Studiums und eineinhalb Jahre nach seinem Abschluss arbeitete er für 4B Architects. Seit 1988 hat er sein eigenes Büro. Von 1988 bis 2016 unterrichtete er an der Oslo School of Architecture, die letzten 12 Jahre als Professor. Er hat in mehreren Ländern Vorlesungen gehalten, wurde mit mehreren Preisen ausgezeichnet, und seine Arbeiten werden vielfach veröffentlicht.
Das Büro wurde in Oslo als Ein-Mann-Praxis gegründet, die sich langsam auf ihre derzeitige Größe von sechs Mitarbeitern ausweitete. Das Büro konzentriert sich auf Häuser, Wochenendhäuser und kleinere öffentliche Arbeiten. In den 1990er Jahren arbeitete er über mehrere Jahre hinweg mit Haga and Grov Architects in Stavanger zusammen.

# KNUT HJELTNES

Knut Hjeltnes est né à Drøbak, en Norvège, en 1961, et a grandi à Ås, une petite ville universitaire au sud d'Oslo. Il a étudié à l'Institut norvégien de technologie de Trondheim de 1980 à 1986. Pendant la seconde moitié de ses études et pendant un an et demi après l'obtention de son diplôme, il a travaillé pour 4B Architects. Depuis 1988, il a son propre cabinet. Il a enseigné à l'école d'architecture d'Oslo de 1988 à 2016, les 12 dernières années en tant que professeur. Il a donné des conférences dans plusieurs pays, a reçu plusieurs prix et ses travaux sont largement publiés.
Le cabinet a été créé à Oslo en tant que cabinet unipersonnel et s'est lentement développé pour atteindre sa taille actuelle de six employés. Le bureau se concentre sur les maisons, les résidences secondaires et les petits travaux publics. Dans les années 1990, il a coopéré pendant plusieurs années avec Haga and Grov Architects à Stavanger.

Knut Hjeltnes nació en Drøbak, Noruega, en 1961, y se crió en Ås, una pequeña ciudad universitaria al sur de Oslo. Estudió en el Instituto Noruego de Tecnología en Trondheim de 1980 a 1986. Durante la última mitad de sus estudios y durante un año y medio después de graduarse trabajó para 4B Architects. Desde 1988 ha tenido su propio estudio. Enseñó en la Escuela de Arquitectura de Oslo de 1988 a 2016, los últimos 12 años como profesor. Ha dado conferencias en varios países, ha recibido varios premios y su trabajo es ampliamente publicado.
El estudio se estableció en Oslo como un estudio de un solo hombre, expandiéndose lentamente hasta su tamaño actual de seis empleados. La oficina se concentra en el diseño de casas, casas de fin de semana y pequeñas obras públicas. En un período de varios años en la década de 1990 cooperó con Haga and Grov Architects en Stavanger.

## WEEKEND HOUSE STRAUME

Outside of Remøya, Norway
Photos: © Knut Hjeltnes

An old timber warehouse was washed away by a hurricane in 1992 leaving only the stone foundation intact. We were allowed to erect a new building, with the same volume, reusing the old foundations. It was decided to construct the complete 70 tons house on a nearby shipyard and lift it in place with an offshore crane. Seven steel frames establish the main construction, kept in place by the new concrete floor forming ground floor kitchen and living room. Four wooden volumes are mounted to these frames containing bathrooms, bedrooms and a media room. The attic is a large uninsulated storage space. Sheltered outdoor areas between the outer timber envelope and the proper insulated facade are used for outside work, dining, relaxation and all kinds of odd storage needed for fishing and other outdoor activities.

Ein altes Holzlager wurde 1992 von einem Hurrikan weggespült, wobei nur das steinerne Fundament intakt blieb. Wir durften ein neues Gebäude mit dem gleichen Volumen errichten, wobei die alten Fundamente wiederverwendet wurden. Wegen der schwierigen Baustelle wurde beschlossen, das komplette 70-Tonnen-Haus auf einer nahe gelegenen Werft zu errichten und mit einem Offshore-Kran an Ort und Stelle zu heben. Sieben Stahlrahmen bilden die Hauptkonstruktion, die durch den neuen Betonboden, der im Erdgeschoss Küche und Wohnzimmer bildet, an ihrem Platz gehalten wird. Auf diesen Rahmen sind vier Holzvolumina montiert, die Bäder, Schlafzimmer und einen Medienraum enthalten. Das Dachgeschoss ist ein großer, nicht isolierter Lagerraum. Geschützte Außenbereiche zwischen der äußeren Holzhülle und der entsprechend gedämmten Fassade werden für Arbeiten im Freien, Essen, Entspannung und alle Arten von unregelmäßigen Lagerräumen genutzt, die zum Angeln und für andere Aktivitäten im Freien benötigt werden.

Un ancien entrepôt de bois a été emporté par un ouragan en 1992, ne laissant que les fondations en pierre intactes. Nous avons été autorisés à construire un nouveau bâtiment, avec le même volume, en réutilisant les anciennes fondations. Il a été décidé de construire la maison complète de 70 tonnes sur un chantier naval voisin et de la soulever sur place avec une grue offshore. Sept charpentes en acier constituent la construction principale, maintenue en place par le nouveau sol en béton formant la cuisine et le salon du rez-de-chaussée. Quatre volumes en bois sont montés sur ces charpentes, contenant des salles de bain, des chambres et une salle de presse. Le grenier est un grand espace de rangement non isolée. Les espaces extérieurs abrités entre l'enveloppe extérieure en bois et la façade isolée appropriée sont utilisés pour le travail extérieur, les repas, la détente et toutes sortes de rangements bizarres nécessaires à la pêche et à d'autres activités de plein air.

Un viejo almacén de madera fue arrastrado por un huracán en 1992 dejando sólo los cimientos de piedra intactos. Se nos permitió erigir un nuevo edificio, con el mismo volumen, reutilizando los viejos cimientos. Se decidió construir la casa completa de 70 toneladas en un astillero cercano y levantarla en su lugar con una grúa *offshore*. Siete marcos de acero establecen la construcción principal, mantenida en su lugar por el nuevo suelo de hormigón que forma la cocina y la sala de estar de la planta baja. Cuatro volúmenes de madera están montados en estos marcos que contienen baños, dormitorios y una sala de ocio. El ático es un gran espacio de almacenamiento sin aislamiento. Las áreas exteriores protegidas entre la envoltura exterior de madera y la fachada aislada adecuada se utilizan para el trabajo exterior, la cena, la relajación y todo tipo de almacenamiento extraño necesario para la pesca y otras actividades al aire libre.

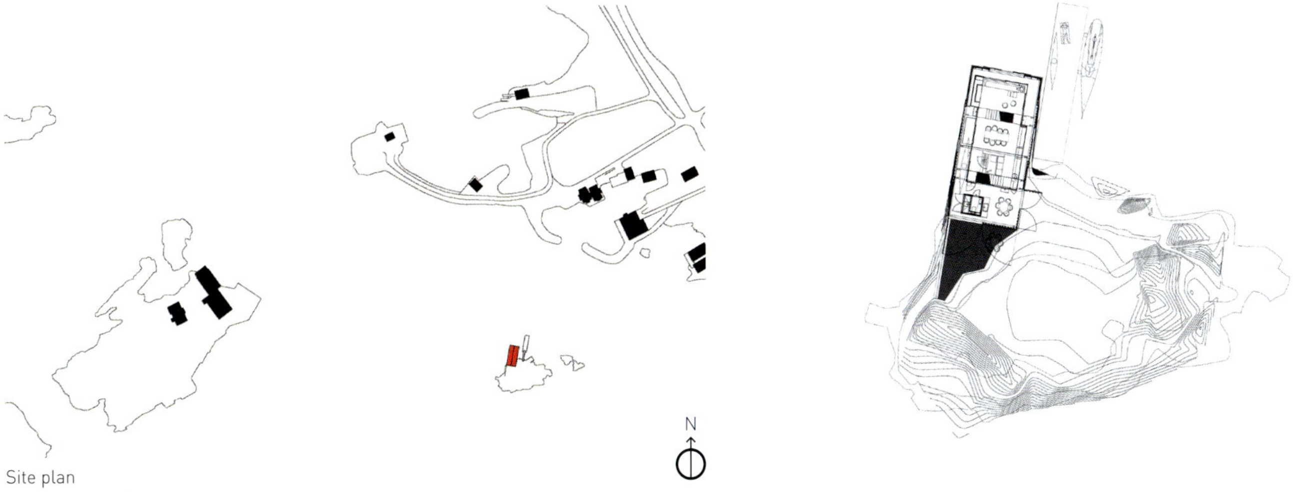


Site plan

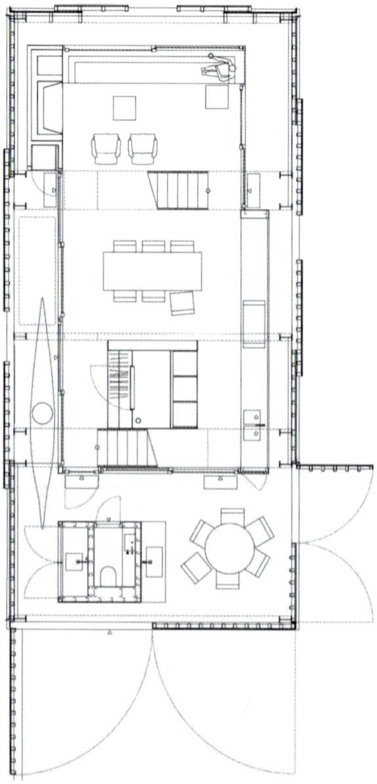
Ground floor plan

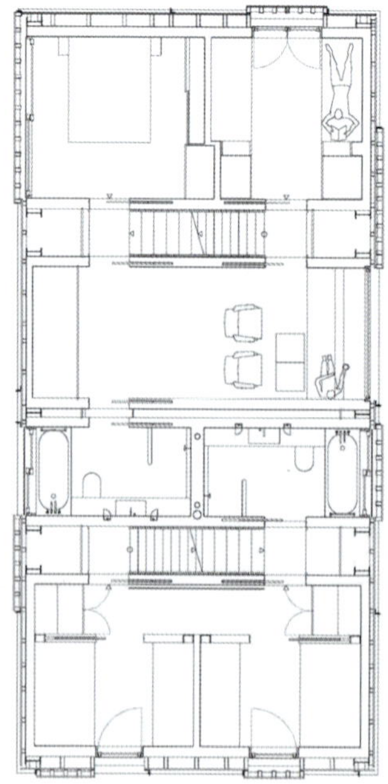
First floor plan

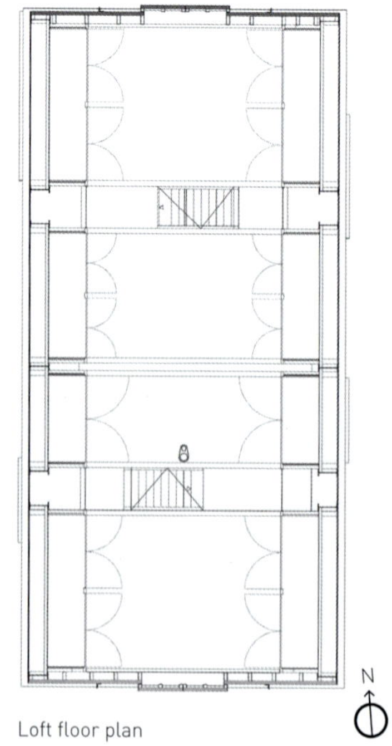

Loft floor plan

Lund Hagem is an architecture and urban design practice based in Oslo. The office was founded in 1990, and today it is managed by five partners; Svein Lund, Einar Hagem, Mette Røsbekk, Per Suul and Kristine Strøm-Gundersen. All projects are informed by a sensitive approach to the surrounding landscape and a dynamic dialogue between nature and the built environment. The work of Lund Hagem focuses on critical detailing and economic of means both poetically and practically.
Our designs reflect our belief in combining the latest advances in building technology with sustainable techniques and materiality drawn from local tradition. This provides us with key knowledge and experience in designing energy efficient Passive Houses and sustainable BREEAM certified buildings. We have in-office certification BREEAM Accredited Professional (BREEAM AP). Lund Hagem is a member of Norwegian Green Building Council.

Lund Hagem ist ein Architektur- und Stadtplanungsbüro mit Sitz in Oslo. Das Büro wurde 1990 gegründet und wird derzeit von fünf Partnern geführt: Svein Lund, Einar Hagem, Mette Røsbekk, Per Suul und Kristine Strøm-Gundersen. Alle Projekte basieren auf einem sensiblen Umgang mit der umgebenden Landschaft und einem dynamischen Dialog zwischen Natur und gebauter Umwelt. Lund Hagems Arbeit konzentriert sich auf die Bedeutung des Details und die Sparsamkeit der Mittel sowohl in poetischer als auch in praktischer Hinsicht.
Unsere Entwürfe spiegeln unsere Überzeugung wider, die neuesten Fortschritte in der Bautechnologie mit nachhaltigen Techniken und Materialien aus der lokalen Tradition zu kombinieren. Dadurch verfügen wir über das Schlüsselwissen und die Erfahrung bei der Planung energieeffizienter Passivhäuser und BREEAM-zertifizierter nachhaltiger Gebäude. Wir sind BREEAM Accredited Professional (BREEAM AP) zertifiziert. Lund Hagem ist Mitglied des norwegischen Green Building Council.

# LUND HAGEM ARKITEKTER

Lund Hagem est un cabinet d'architecture et d'urbanisme basé à Oslo. Ce bureau a été fondé en 1990, et il est aujourd'hui géré par cinq partenaires : Svein Lund, Einar Hagem, Mette Røsbekk, Per Suul et Kristine Strøm-Gundersen. Tous les projets sont nourris par un rapport sensible au paysage environnant et par un dialogue entre la nature et l'environnement bâti. Les travaux de Lund Hagem se concentrent sur les détails primordiaux d'exécution et sur l'économie de moyens au point de vue à la fois poétique et pratique. Nos designs reflètent notre foi dans l'alliance entre les derniers progrès de la technologie du bâtiment et les techniques durables et la matérialité tirées de la tradition locale.
Cela nous procure des connaissances et une expérience primordiales dans la conception de maisons passives et de constructions certifiées BREEAM à haute efficacité énergétique. Nous comptons parmi nous un professionnel accrédité BREEAM (BREEAM AP). Lund Hagem est membre du Conseil norvégien de l'habitat écologique (Norwegian Green Building Council).

Lund Hagem es un estudio de arquitectura y diseño urbano con sede en Oslo. La oficina fue fundada en 1990 y en la actualidad está dirigida por cinco socios: Svein Lund, Einar Hagem, Mette Røsbekk, Per Suul y Kristine Strøm-Gundersen. Todos los proyectos se basan en un enfoque sensible del paisaje circundante y en un diálogo dinámico entre la naturaleza y el entorno construido. El trabajo de Lund Hagem se centra en la importancia del detalle y economía de medios tanto poética como prácticamente.
Nuestros diseños reflejan nuestra creencia en la combinación de los últimos avances en tecnología de construcción con técnicas sostenibles y materiales extraídos de la tradición local. Esto nos proporciona el conocimiento y la experiencia claves en el diseño de casas pasivas energéticamente eficientes y edificios sostenibles con certificado BREEAM. En la oficina contamos con certificación BREEAM Accredited Professional (BREEAM AP). Lund Hagem es miembro del Consejo Noruego de Edificios Ecológicos.

▼ CABIN KVITFJELL

▼ LILLE ARØYA

## CABIN KVITFJELL

Kvitfjell, Norway
Photos: © Sam Hughes, Marc Goodwin

The site is located at one of the highest buildable plots within the Kvitfjell Ski Resort hosting. The two volumes are placed near the site boarders, thus creating a sheltered "courtyard" open to the evening sun. The main cabin and the annex are built on stilts, not to interfere with the ground. To emphasise the idea of the summer cabin in the mountain, the volumes are wrapped in thin, vertical louvers. Creating a light "veil-like" quality towards the courtyard as well as protecting the recessed glass behind. The plan is shaped to frame the remarkable views over the mountains. Ore-pine louvers treated with iron sulphate cover the exterior layer whereas painted Pine covers the inner exterior and interior facades. The outside floors and ceilings are untreated Pine, the inside is oiled Oak.

Die Hütte befindet sich auf einem der höchstgelegenen Baugrundstücke im Kvitfjell-Skigebiet. Die beiden Bände liegen nahe an den Grenzen des Geländes und bilden so einen geschützten „Hof", der zur Abendsonne hin offen ist. Die Hauptkabine und das Nebengebäude sind auf Stelzen gebaut, um den Boden nicht zu beeinträchtigen. Um die Idee einer Sommerhütte in den Bergen zu unterstreichen, sind die Volumen mit dünnen vertikalen Lamellen umhüllt, die zum Hof hin eine Art leichten „Schleier" bilden und das dahinter liegende Glas schützen. Der Grundriss ist so gestaltet, dass er die beeindruckende Aussicht über die Berge einrahmt. Mit Eisensulfat behandelte Kiefernfensterläden bedecken die äußere Schicht, während lackierte Kiefernfensterläden die Innen- und Außenfassaden bedecken. Die Außenböden und -decken bestehen aus unbehandelter Kiefer, das Innere aus geölter Eiche.

Ce site se trouve sur l'une des parcelles constructibles les plus élevées de la station de ski Kvitfjell. Ces deux volumes sont placés près des frontières du site, créant ainsi une « cour » abritée ouverte au soleil du soir. La cabane principale et l'annexe sont construites sur pilotis, pour éviter toute interférence avec le sol. Pour accentuer le concept de la cabane d'été dans la montagne, les volumes sont enveloppés dans de fines persiennes verticales, créant une qualité légèrement « voilée » du côté de la cour tout en protégeant le renfoncement vitré situé derrière. La forme du plan est conçue pour encadrer les vues remarquables au-dessus des montagnes. Les persiennes de pin durci traité au sulfate de fer recouvrent l'enveloppe extérieure tandis que des lames peintes enveloppent les façades internes à l'intérieur et à l'extérieur. Les sols et plafonds sont en pin non-traité, l'intérieur en chêne huilé.

La cabaña está situada en una de las parcelas edificables más altas de la estación de esquí de Kvitfjell. Los dos volúmenes están situados cerca de los límites del terreno, creando así un «patio» protegido abierto al sol de la tarde. La cabaña principal y el anexo están construidos sobre pilotes, para no interferir con el suelo. Para enfatizar la idea de cabaña de verano en la montaña, los volúmenes están envueltos en finas lamas verticales que crean una especie de «velo» ligero hacia el patio y protegen el cristal de detrás. El plano está diseñado para enmarcar las impresionantes vistas sobre las montañas. Las persianas de madera de pino tratada con sulfato de hierro cubren la capa exterior, mientras que las de pino pintado cubren las fachadas interiores y exteriores. Los suelos y techos exteriores son de pino sin tratar, el interior de roble aceitado.

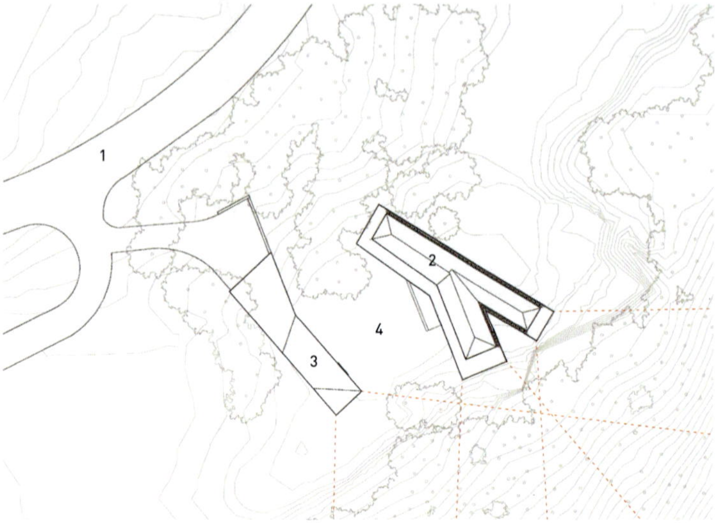


1. Road
2. Main cabin
3. Carport / annex
4. Courtyard

Site plan

Sections

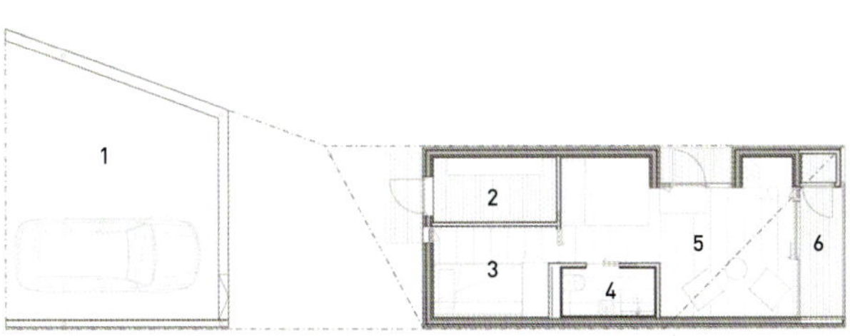

Annex plan

1. Carpot
2. Ski storage
3. Bedroom
4. Bathroom
5. Living room
6. Balcony

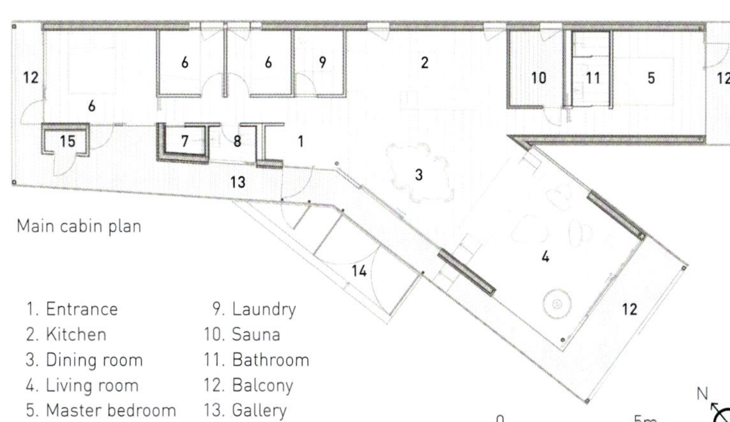

Main cabin plan

1. Entrance
2. Kitchen
3. Dining room
4. Living room
5. Master bedroom
6. Bedroom
7. Shower
8. WC
9. Laundry
10. Sauna
11. Bathroom
12. Balcony
13. Gallery
14. Terrace
15. Storage

## LILLE ARØYA

Larvik, Norway
Photos: © Alexander Westberg, Ivar Kvaal, Lund Hagem

The building creates a site on stilts that latches onto the island to unite the new with the old. Bedrooms and bathrooms are located in volumes placed on the threshold between the island and the new surface, whereas the roof spanning across the new deck creates a shelter for living.
The timber structure is visible forming the exterior and the interior. Glulam beams span from inside to outside and together with raw steel columns and a white concrete fireplace shape and colour the interior. Solid steel columns carry the "new site" for the house. The materials are kept to a minimum. Ore Pine is used outside and inside. Some of the exterior is stained black to tie in with the surroundings, the rest is left to patinate.

Das Gebäude ruht auf Pfählen, die auf die Insel genagelt werden, um das Neue mit dem Alten zu verbinden. Die Schlaf- und Badezimmer befinden sich in Volumina auf der Schwelle zwischen der Insel und der neuen Oberfläche, während das Dach, das den neuen Boden bedeckt, einen geschützten Wohnbereich schafft.
Die Holzkonstruktion ist sichtbar und bildet den Außen- und Innenbereich. Die Brettschichtholzbalken reichen von innen nach außen und geben zusammen mit den rohen Stahlsäulen und einem Kamin aus weißem Beton dem Innenraum Form und Farbe. Massive Stahlstützen tragen das „Neuland" für das Haus. Die Materialien werden auf ein Minimum beschränkt. Kiefer wird sowohl außen als auch innen verwendet. Ein Teil der Außenseite ist schwarz eingefärbt, um sich in die Umgebung einzufügen, der Rest wird belassen, um seine Patina zu erhalten.

Ce bâtiment crée un site sur pilotis qui s'accroche à l'île pour réunir l'ancien et le nouveau. Les chambres et salles-de-bain sont situées dans des volumes implantés sur le seuil entre l'île et la nouvelle surface, tandis que le toit qui s'étend sur la nouvelle terrasse crée un abri à vivre.
La structure en bois est visible, formant l'extérieur et l'intérieur. Les poutres en lamellé-collé filent de l'intérieur vers l'extérieur et, alliées à des colonnes d'acier brut et à un âtre en béton blanc, façonnent et colorent l'intérieur. Des colonnes d'acier massif soutiennent le « nouveau site » de la maison. Le nombre de matériaux est restreint. Le pin durci est utilisé pour l'extérieur comme l'intérieur. À l'extérieur il est parfois teint en noir pour se fondre dans son environnement, le reste étant destiné à être patiné par le temps.

El edificio descansa sobre pilotes que se clavan a la isla para unir lo nuevo con lo viejo. Los dormitorios y los baños están situados en volúmenes situados en el umbral entre la isla y la nueva superficie, mientras que el tejado que abarca la nueva planta crea una zona de estar protegida.
La estructura de madera es visible formando el exterior y el interior. Las vigas de madera laminada se extienden desde el interior hacia el exterior y junto con las columnas de acero en bruto y una chimenea de hormigón blanco dan forma y color al interior. Sólidas columnas de acero soportan el «nuevo terreno» para la casa. Los materiales se mantienen al mínimo. El pino se utiliza tanto en el exterior como en el interior. Parte del exterior está teñido de negro para encajar con el entorno, el resto se deja que adquiera su pátina.

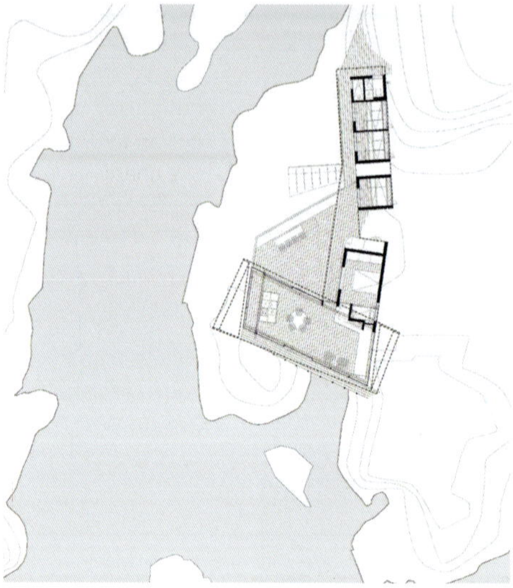

Site plan

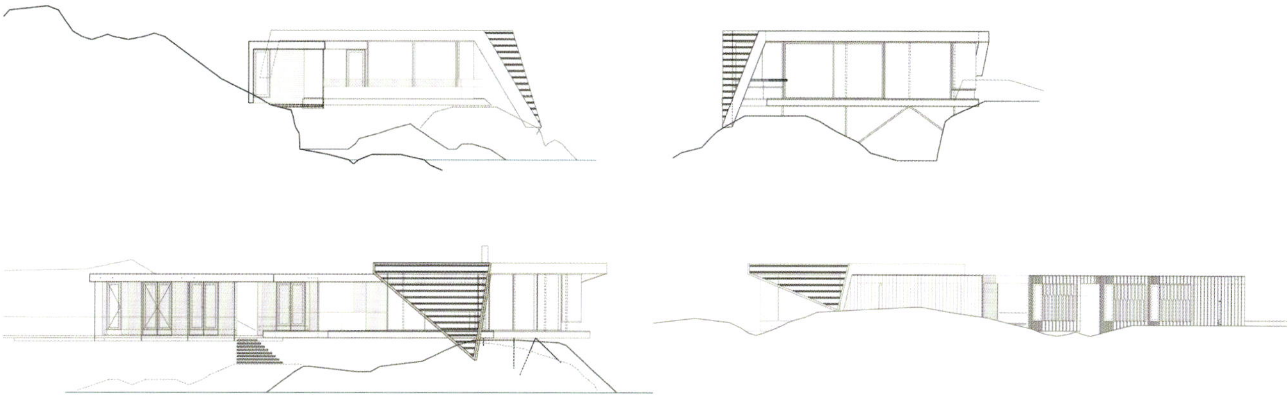

Sections

Marge Arkitekter was established in 2002 by Pye Aurell Ehrström, Katarina Grundsell, Louise Masreliez and Susanne Ramel. The firm rapidly became recognised as one of the young firms representing a contemporary development of architecture in Sweden and today has an extensive portfolio including private, commercial and public projects. Marge Arkitekter has received publicity in the national and international press and has exhibited in Sweden and around Europe. The firm currently has 36 employees.
Marge Arkitekter works in architecture on every scale, from town planning to interior fittings and product design. Common to the projects is a spatially exploratory architecture that is characterised by innovative organization and new applications for materials.

Marge Arkitekter wurde 2002 von Pye Aurell Ehrström, Katarina Grundsell, Louise Masreliez und Susanne Ramel gegründet. Das Büro wurde schnell als eines der jungen Büros anerkannt, die für eine zeitgenössische Entwicklung der Architektur in Schweden stehen, und verfügt heute über ein umfangreiches Portfolio, das private, gewerbliche und öffentliche Projekte umfasst. Marge Arkitekter wurde in der nationalen und internationalen Presse bekannt gemacht und hat in Schweden und in ganz Europa ausgestellt. Das Büro hat derzeit 36 Mitarbeiter.
Marge Arkitekter arbeitet in der Architektur in jeder Größenordnung, von der Stadtplanung bis zur Innenausstattung und zum Produktdesign. Gemeinsam ist den Projekten eine räumlich explorative Architektur, die sich durch innovative Organisation und neue Materialanwendungen auszeichnet.

# MARGE ARKITEKTER

Marge Arkitekter a été créée en 2002 par Pye Aurell Ehrström, Katarina Grundsell, Louise Masreliez et Susanne Ramel. Le cabinet a rapidement été reconnu comme l'un des jeunes cabinets représentant un développement contemporain de l'architecture en Suède et possède aujourd'hui un vaste portefeuille comprenant des projets privés, commerciaux et publics. Marge Arkitekter a fait l'objet d'une publicité dans la presse nationale et internationale et a exposé en Suède et dans toute l'Europe. La société compte actuellement 36 employés.
Marge Arkitekter travaille dans le domaine de l'architecture à toutes les échelles, de l'urbanisme à l'aménagement intérieur et à la conception de produits. Les projets ont en commun une architecture exploratoire dans l'espace qui se caractérise par une organisation innovante et de nouvelles applications des matériaux.

Marge Arkitekter fue fundada en 2002 por Pye Aurell Ehrström, Katarina Grundsell, Louise Masreliez y Susanne Ramel. La empresa se convirtió rápidamente en una de las jóvenes firmas que representan un desarrollo contemporáneo de la arquitectura en Suecia y hoy en día tiene una amplia cartera que incluye proyectos privados, comerciales y públicos. Marge Arkitekter ha recibido publicidad en la prensa nacional e internacional y ha expuesto en Suecia y en toda Europa. La empresa tiene actualmente 36 empleados.
Marge Arkitekter trabaja en la arquitectura a todas las escalas, desde el urbanismo hasta el equipamiento interior y el diseño de productos. Lo común en sus proyectos es una arquitectura de exploración espacial que se caracteriza por una organización innovadora y nuevas aplicaciones de materiales.

SERGELHUSET

VILLA HEDBERG

NATURUM TROLLSKOGEN

RÖHSSKA MUSEUM

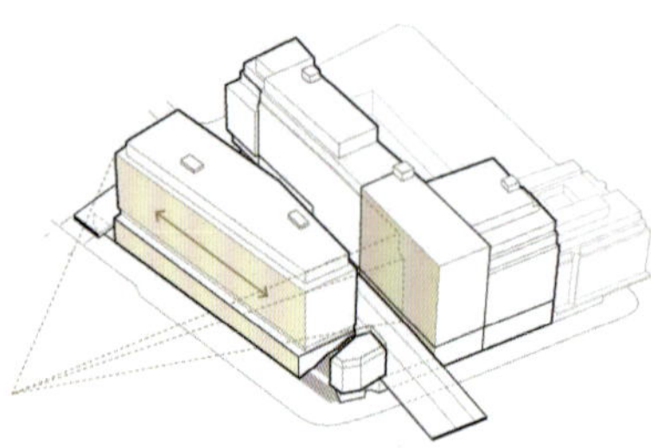

Back ground wall effect

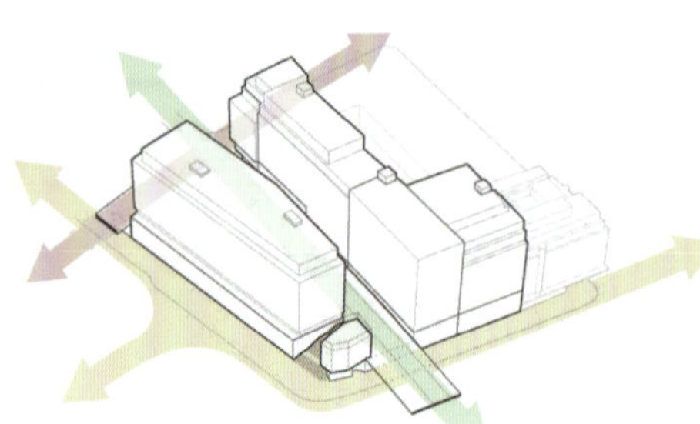

Reconnecting passages

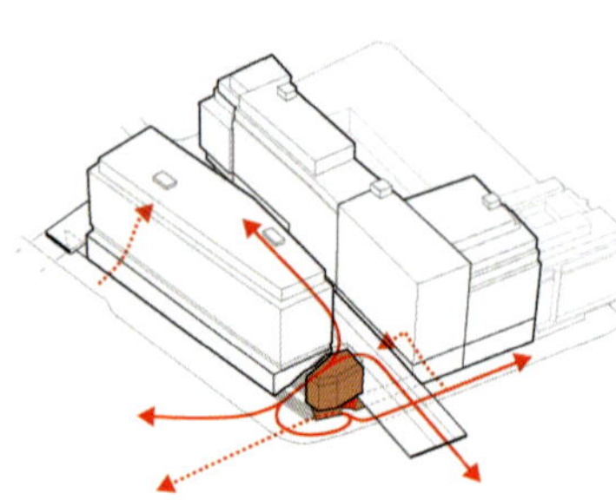

Recreating the hub of the site

Diagrams

## SERGELHUSET

Stockholm, Sweden
Photos: © Marge Arkitekter

Sergelhuset building complex is located next to Sergels Torg in the heart of Stockholm. The property is intersected by Malmskillnadsgatan, a street challenged by spatial isolation despite its central location.
In our winning proposal for Vasakronan to redesign the complex, we emphasize visual connectivity and a differentiated program, a mix of housing, retail, restaurants and offices, in an effort to turn today's anonymous Malmskillnadsgatan into an inviting street for the city's residents and visitors. A generous staircase is added, connecting the street with the bustling Sergels Torg. By keeping the structural framework of the building intact and re-using the original facade stone, the environmental impact is minimized.

Der Gebäudekomplex Sergelhuset liegt neben dem Sergels Torg im Herzen von Stockholm. Das Grundstück wird von der Malmskillnadsgatan durchschnitten, einer Straße, die trotz ihrer zentralen Lage durch die räumliche Isolation beeinträchtigt ist.
In unserem siegreichen Vorschlag zur Neugestaltung des Komplexes legen wir Wert auf visuelle Konnektivität und ein differenziertes Programm, eine Mischung aus Wohnen, Einzelhandel, Restaurants und Büros, um aus der heutigen anonymen Malmskillnadsgatan eine einladende Straße für die Bewohner und Besucher der Stadt zu machen. Eine großzügige Treppe verbindet die Straße mit dem belebten Sergels Torg. Durch die Beibehaltung des strukturellen Rahmens des Gebäudes und die Wiederverwendung der Ziegel der ursprünglichen Fassade wird die Umweltbelastung minimiert.

Le complexe immobilier Sergelhuset est situé à côté de Sergels Torg, au cœur de Stockholm. La propriété est traversée par Malmskillnadsgatan, une rue qui, malgré sa situation centrale, est confrontée à l'isolement spatial.
Dans notre proposition gagnante de réaménagement du complexe, nous mettons l'accent sur la connectivité visuelle et un programme différencié. Un mélange de logements, de commerces, de restaurants et de bureaux, dans un effort de transformer l'anonyme Malmskillnadsgatan d'aujourd'hui en une rue accueillante pour les résidents et les visiteurs de la ville. Un généreux escalier est ajouté, reliant la rue à l'effervescence du Sergels Torg. En gardant la structure du bâtiment intacte et en réutilisant les briques de la façade originale, l'impact environnemental est réduit au minimum.

El complejo de edificios Sergelhuset está situado junto a Sergels Torg en el corazón de Estocolmo. La propiedad está atravesada por Malmskillnadsgatan, una calle desafiada por el aislamiento espacial a pesar de su ubicación en el centro de la ciudad.
En nuestra propuesta ganadora para rediseñar el complejo, enfatizamos la conectividad visual y un programa diferenciado, una mezcla de viviendas, comercios, restaurantes y oficinas, en un esfuerzo por convertir el anónimo Malmskillnadsgatan de hoy en día en una calle atractiva para los residentes y visitantes de la ciudad. Se añade una generosa escalera, que conecta la calle con el bullicio de Sergels Torg. Manteniendo intacto el marco estructural del edificio y reutilizando los ladrillos de la fachada original, se minimiza el impacto ambiental.

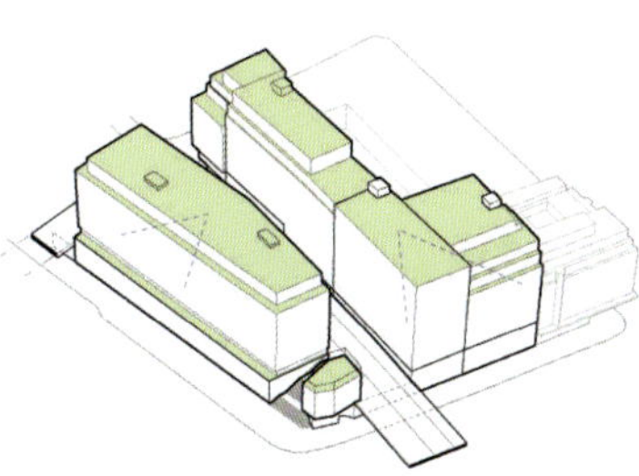

Active and green roof landscapes

## VILLA HEDBERG

Åhus, Sweden
Photos: © Johan Fowelin

In a serene setting where the beach meets the pines, Marge Architects were commissioned to design a summer house for a family of four. With neighbouring houses in close proximity to the north and south, and a public beach to the east, the brief was to create a truly private space for the client. As the family has its everyday life in the city, they needed a house that could be completely shut down during winter. By accommodating the wishes of the client on three different building briefs, a private house, a sauna and a guest house, a protected outdoor space was created, harbouring the family's need for privacy. From here, sightlines extend to the horizon and the sea, yet the characteristic roof remains the sole element visible from the beach.

In einer ruhigen Umgebung, wo der Strand auf die Kiefern trifft, wurden Marge Architects beauftragt, ein Sommerhaus für eine vierköpfige Familie zu entwerfen. Mit Nachbarhäusern in unmittelbarer Nähe im Norden und Süden und einem öffentlichen Strand im Osten bestand die Aufgabe darin, einen wirklich privaten Raum für den Bauherrn zu schaffen. Da die Familie ihren Alltag in der Stadt hat, brauchte sie ein Haus, das im Winter komplett stillgelegt werden kann. Durch die Berücksichtigung der Wünsche des Bauherrn auf drei verschiedenen Baustellen, einem Privathaus, einer Sauna und einem Gästehaus, wurde ein geschützter Außenraum geschaffen, der dem Bedürfnis der Familie nach Privatsphäre Rechnung trägt. Von hier aus reichen die Sichtachsen bis zum Horizont und zum Meer, wobei das charakteristische Dach das einzige vom Strand aus sichtbare Element bleibt.

Dans un cadre serein où la plage rencontre les pins, Marge Architects a été chargé de concevoir une maison d'été pour une famille de quatre personnes. Avec des maisons voisines à proximité immédiate au nord et au sud et une plage publique à l'est, la mission consistait à créer un espace véritablement privé pour le client. Comme la famille a sa vie quotidienne en ville, elle avait besoin d'une maison qui puisse être complètement fermée pendant l'hiver. En répondant aux souhaits du client sur trois projets de construction différents - une maison privée, un sauna et une maison d'hôtes - un espace extérieur protégé a été créé, respectant le besoin d'intimité de la famille. De là, les lignes de vue s'étendent jusqu'à l'horizon et la mer, mais le toit caractéristique reste le seul élément visible depuis la plage.

En un entorno sereno donde la playa se encuentra con los pinos, se encargó a Marge Arkitekter el diseño de una casa de verano para una familia de cuatro personas. Con las casas vecinas muy cerca del norte y del sur, y una playa pública al este, el encargo consistió en crear un espacio verdaderamente privado para el cliente. Como la familia tiene su vida cotidiana en la ciudad, necesitaban una casa que pudiera cerrarse completamente durante el invierno. En respuesta a los deseos del cliente, se construyeron una casa privada, una sauna y una casa de huéspedes en tres edificios diferentes, lo cual dio lugar a un espacio exterior protegido donde preservar la privacidad de la familia. Desde aquí, las líneas de visión se extienden hasta el horizonte y el mar, aunque el característico techo sigue siendo el único elemento visible desde la playa.

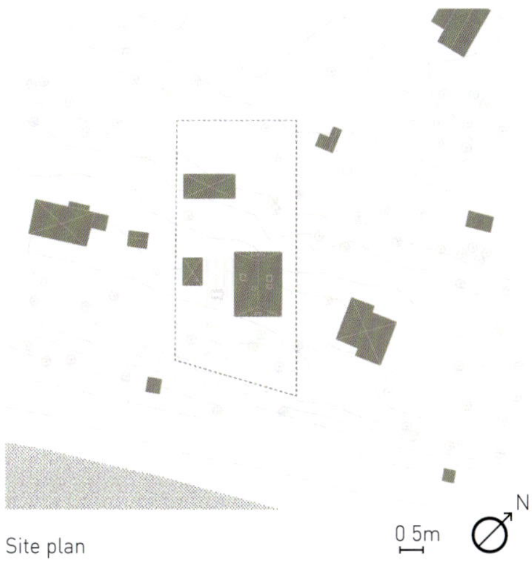

Site plan

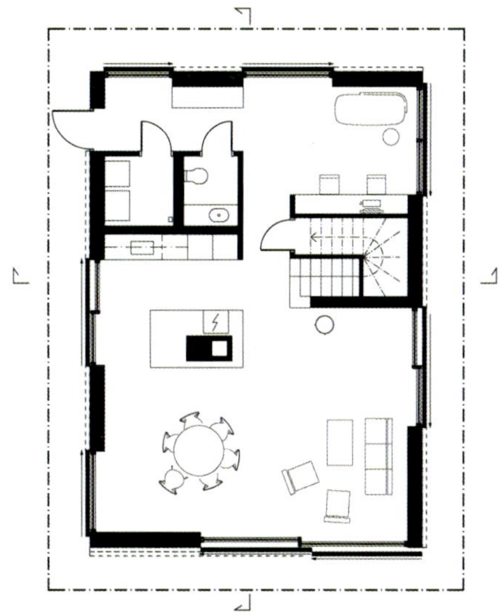
Ground floor plan

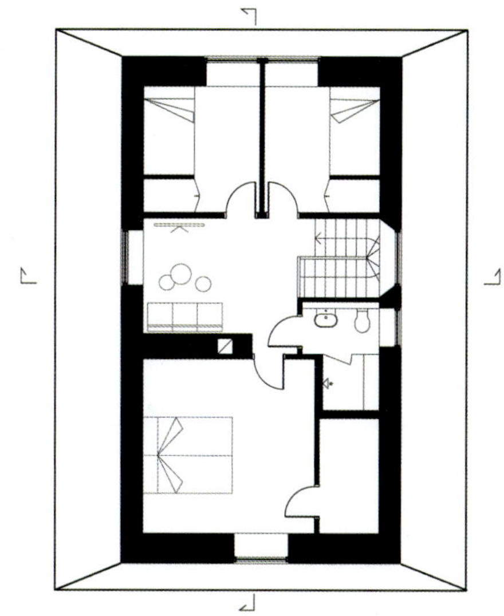
First floor plan

## NATURUM TROLLSKOGEN

Öland, Sweden
Photos: © Johan Fowelin, Piero Valpiani

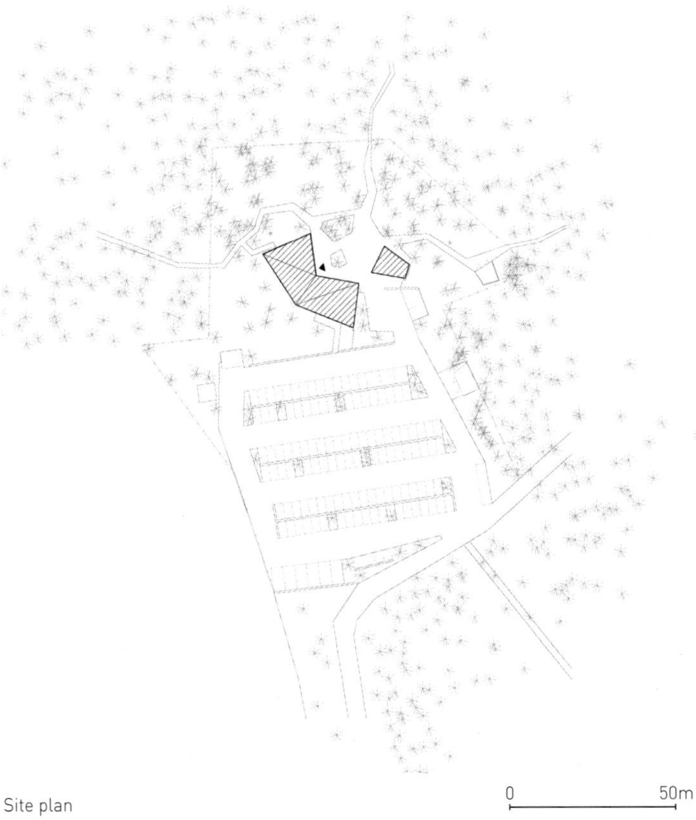


Site plan

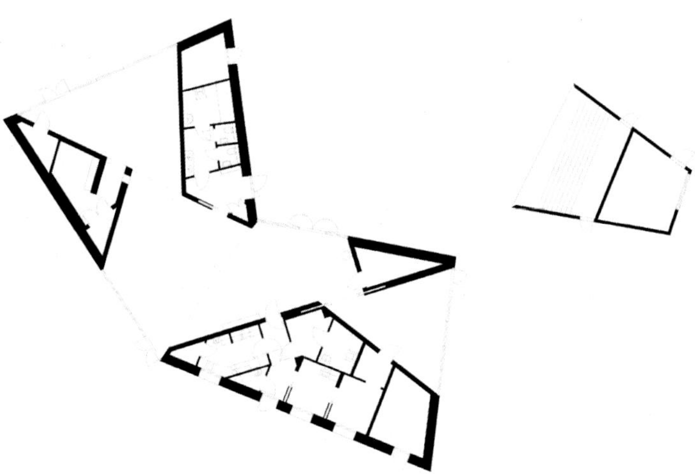

Ground floor plan

In 2014 we won an invited competition to design the new Naturum of Trollskogen as an entry point and knot for exploration of the Natural Reserve of Trollskogen. The Naturum Trollskogen consists of an information node, an exhibition building and a weather shelter, which function together or individually depending on the opening hours of the Naturum. From the information point, hiking trails lead further out into the nature reserve.
The buildings are interlaced between the trees, subordinate to nature. The design principle is based on an interaction between landscape and building, where forest clearings and exhibition spaces are knitted, spatially extending into each other. The form and materiality of the buildings relate to the creeping pines and pebble beaches of the surrounding area.

Im Jahr 2014 gewannen wir einen Wettbewerb für den Entwurf des neuen Naturum von Trollskogen als Eingangspunkt und Knotenpunkt für die Erforschung des Naturschutzgebietes Trollskogen. Das Naturum Trollskogen besteht aus einem Informationspunkt, einem Ausstellungsgebäude und einem Wetterschutzhaus, die je nach Öffnungszeiten des Naturums gemeinsam oder einzeln funktionieren. Vom Informationspunkt aus führen Wanderwege weiter hinaus in das Naturschutzgebiet.
Die Gebäude sind zwischen den Bäumen verschachtelt und der Natur untergeordnet. Das Gestaltungsprinzip basiert auf einer Interaktion zwischen Landschaft und Gebäude, wobei Waldlichtungen und Ausstellungsräume räumlich ineinander gestrickt sind. Form und Materialität der Gebäude nehmen Bezug auf die Kiefernwälder und Kiesstrände der Umgebung.

En 2014, nous avons remporté un concours sur invitation pour concevoir le nouveau Naturum de Trollskogen comme point d'entrée et nœud pour l'exploration de la réserve naturelle de Trollskogen. Le Naturum de Trollskogen se compose d'un nœud d'information, d'un bâtiment d'exposition et d'un abri contre les intempéries, qui fonctionnent ensemble ou individuellement selon les heures d'ouverture du Naturum. Depuis le point d'information, des sentiers de randonnée mènent plus loin dans la réserve naturelle.
Les bâtiments sont entrelacés entre les arbres, subordonnés à la nature. Le principe de conception est basé sur une interaction entre le paysage et le bâtiment, où les clairières forestières et les espaces d'exposition sont tricotés, se prolongeant dans l'espace l'un dans l'autre. La forme et la matérialité des bâtiments sont en rapport avec les pins rampants et les plages de galets des environs.

En 2014 ganamos un concurso para diseñar el nuevo Naturum de Trollskogen como punto de entrada y nudo para la exploración de la Reserva Natural de Trollskogen. El Naturum Trollskogen consiste en un centro de información, un edificio de exposición y un refugio meteorológico, que funcionan juntos o individualmente dependiendo del horario de apertura del Naturum. Desde el punto de información, los senderos de excursión conducen a la reserva natural.
Los edificios están entrelazados entre los árboles, subordinados a la naturaleza. El principio de diseño se basa en una interacción entre el paisaje y el edificio, donde los claros del bosque y los espacios de exposición se tejen, extendiéndose espacialmente entre sí. La forma y la materialidad de los edificios se relacionan con los pinos y las playas de guijarros de los alrededores.

Kafé
Café

## RÖHSSKA MUSEUM

Göteborg, Sweden
Photos: © Johan Fowelin

The Röhsska Museum of Design and Craft opened in 1916 as Sweden's sole museum dedicated to both design and crafts. After an invited competition, Marge Architects were chosen to re-design the Museum Shop, the reception desk and the seating furniture in anticipation of the Museum's re-opening in 2019.
In the new design for the Röhsska Museum shop and entrance area, materials and colours are used to bring the institution closer to its audience, lending the visitor a helping hand in navigating the history-laden spaces of the century-old institution. Visual hints help invoke curiosity in the design of the building and facilitates an understanding of its natural spatial sequence, while industrial felt dampens vibration, allowing for a more complex and inclusive soundscape.

Das Röhsska-Museum für Design und Kunsthandwerk wurde 1916 als Schwedens einziges Museum eröffnet, das sich sowohl dem Design als auch dem Kunsthandwerk widmet. Nach einem Wettbewerb wurden Marge Architects ausgewählt, den Museumsshop, den Empfangstresen und die Sitzmöbel im Hinblick auf die Wiedereröffnung des Museums im Jahr 2019 neu zu gestalten.
Bei der Neugestaltung des Shops und des Eingangsbereichs des Röhsska Museums wurden Materialien und Farben verwendet, um die Institution dem Publikum näher zu bringen und dem Besucher die Navigation durch die geschichtsträchtigen Räume der Jahrhunderte alten Institution zu erleichtern. Visuelle Hinweise machen neugierig auf die Gestaltung des Gebäudes und erleichtern das Verständnis der natürlichen räumlichen Abfolge, während Industriefilz Vibrationen dämpft und eine komplexere und umfassendere Klanglandschaft ermöglicht.

Le musée du design et de l'artisanat de Röhsska a ouvert ses portes en 1916. C'est le seul musée de Suède consacré à la fois au design et à l'artisanat. Après un concours sur invitation, Marge Architects a été choisi pour redessiner la boutique du musée, la réception et les sièges en prévision de la réouverture du musée en 2019.
Dans le nouveau design de la boutique et de l'entrée du musée Röhsska, les matériaux et les couleurs sont utilisés pour rapprocher l'institution de son public, donnant ainsi au visiteur un coup de pouce pour naviguer dans les espaces chargés d'histoire de cette institution centenaire. Des indices visuels aident à susciter la curiosité dans la conception du bâtiment et facilitent la compréhension de sa séquence spatiale naturelle, tandis que le feutre industriel amortit les vibrations, ce qui permet d'obtenir un paysage sonore plus complexe et plus inclusif.

El Museo de Diseño y Artesanía de Röhsska abrió en 1916 como el único museo de Suecia dedicado tanto al diseño como a la artesanía. Después de un concurso, Marge Arkitekter fueron elegidos para rediseñar la tienda del museo, el mostrador de recepción y el mobiliario de los asientos en previsión de la reapertura del museo en 2019.
En el nuevo diseño de la tienda y la zona de entrada del Museo Röhsska, se utilizan materiales y colores para acercar la institución a su público, ayudando al visitante a navegar por los espacios cargados de historia de la centenaria institución. Los indicios visuales ayudan a invocar la curiosidad en el diseño del edificio y facilitan la comprensión de su secuencia espacial natural, mientras que el fieltro industrial amortigua las vibraciones, permitiendo un paisaje sonoro más complejo e inclusivo.

Margen Wigow Arkitektkontor AB was started in 2000 and is run by Cecilia Margen Wigow architect SAR / MSA. The office specializes in new and refurbished villas and holiday homes. We are driven by job satisfaction and a genuine interest in architecture. The aim is to create environments of high architectural value based on the client's wishes, the conditions of the site and the project budget. The ambition is to follow all the stages of the project from sketch to building follow-up in order to implement the architectural ideas down to the detail level.

Margen Wigow Arkitektkontor AB wurde im Jahr 2000 gegründet und wird von Cecilia Margen Wigow, Architektin SAR / MSA, geleitet. Das Büro ist auf neue und renovierte Villen und Ferienhäuser spezialisiert. Unser Antrieb sind Arbeitszufriedenheit und ein echtes Interesse an Architektur. Ziel ist es, Umgebungen von hohem architektonischem Wert zu schaffen, basierend auf den Wünschen des Kunden, den Bedingungen des Standortes und dem Projektbudget. Es wird angestrebt, alle Phasen des Projekts von der Skizze bis zur Bauausführung zu verfolgen, um die architektonischen Ideen bis ins Detail umzusetzen.

# MARGEN WIGOW ARKITEKTKONTOR

Margen Wigow Arkitektkontor AB a été créée en 2000 et est dirigée par Cecilia Margen Wigow architecte SAR / MSA. Le bureau est spécialisé dans les villas et maisons de vacances neuves et rénovées. Nous sommes motivés par la satisfaction professionnelle et un véritable intérêt pour l'architecture. L'objectif est de créer des environnements à haute valeur architecturale en fonction des souhaits du client, des conditions du site et du budget du projet. L'ambition est de suivre toutes les étapes du projet, de l'esquisse au suivi de la construction, afin de mettre en œuvre les idées architecturales dans les moindres détails.

Margen Wigow Arkitektkontor AB se inició en 2000 y está dirigido por Cecilia Margen Wigow arquitecto SAR / MSA. La oficina se especializa en villas nuevas y renovadas y casas de vacaciones. Nos impulsa la satisfacción del trabajo y un interés genuino en la arquitectura. El objetivo es crear ambientes de alto valor arquitectónico basado en los deseos del cliente, las condiciones del lugar y el presupuesto del proyecto. La ambición es seguir todas las etapas del proyecto desde el boceto hasta el seguimiento de la construcción para llevar a cabo las ideas arquitectónicas hasta el nivel de detalle.

SEASIDE CABINS

VILLA T

HOLIDAY HOME

## SEASIDE CABINS

Archipelago of Stockholm, Sweden
Photos: © Åke E:son Lindman

The island is located at the far end of Stockholm's outer archipelago. The new buildings are built in a valley facing a sheltered bay. The wish has been to create a modern variant of the older shanty towns, which still today remain on individual islands in Stockholm. The direction of the houses and the slope of the roof follow the shape of the mountains and are covered with sedum roofs. The façades are lined with wooden panels painted with mud paint. The main building consists of a single large room where each function is divided by the different floor levels made of solid pine boards. The walls, ceilings and furnishings are made of pine plywood. On the island there is no electricity so all houses have a fireplace for heating, refrigerator and stove powered by gas, lamps of kerosene and water pumped up by hand outdoors.

Die Insel liegt am äußersten Ende des Stockholmer Außenschärengartens. Die neuen Gebäude sind in einem Tal mit Blick auf eine geschützte Bucht gebaut. Der Wunsch war es, eine moderne Variante der älteren Barackensiedlungen zu schaffen, die heute noch auf einzelnen Inseln in Stockholm stehen. Die Ausrichtung der Häuser und die Neigung des Daches folgen der Form der Berge. Sie sind mit Sedumdächern gedeckt. Die Fassaden sind mit Holztafeln verkleidet, die mit Lehmfarbe gestrichen sind. Das Hauptgebäude besteht aus einem einzigen großen Raum, in dem jede Funktion durch die verschiedenen Geschossebenen aus massiven Kiefernbrettern unterteilt ist. Die Wände, Decken und Einrichtungsgegenstände sind aus Kiefernsperrholz gefertigt. Auf der Insel gibt es keine Elektrizität, daher verfügen alle Häuser über einen Kamin zum Heizen, Kühlschrank und Herd, die mit Gas betrieben werden, Lampen mit Kerosin und Wasser, die von Hand ins Freie gepumpt werden.

L'île est située à l'extrémité de l'archipel extérieur de Stockholm. Les nouveaux bâtiments sont construits dans une vallée qui fait face à une baie abritée. Le souhait a été de créer une variante moderne des anciens bidonvilles, qui se trouvent encore aujourd'hui sur des îles individuelles de Stockholm. L'orientation des maisons et la pente du toit suivent la forme des montagnes et sont recouvertes de toits de sedum. Les façades sont revêtues de panneaux de bois peints avec de la peinture à la boue. Le bâtiment principal est constitué d'une seule grande pièce où chaque fonction est divisée par les différents niveaux de plancher en planches de pin massif. Les murs, les plafonds et le mobilier sont en contreplaqué de pin. Sur l'île, il n'y a pas d'électricité, donc toutes les maisons ont une cheminée pour le chauffage, un réfrigérateur et une cuisinière au gaz, des lampes au kérosène et de l'eau pompée à la main à l'extérieur.

La isla está situada en el extremo más alejado del archipiélago exterior de Estocolmo. Los nuevos edificios están construidos en un valle que da a una bahía protegida. Se ha querido crear una variante moderna de los antiguos barrios de chabolas, que aún hoy permanecen en ciertas islas de Estocolmo. La dirección de las casas y la inclinación del tejado siguen la forma de las montañas y están cubiertas con tejados de sedum. Las fachadas están revestidas con paneles de madera pintados con pintura de barro. El edificio principal consiste en una única habitación grande donde cada función está dividida por los diferentes niveles del suelo hechos de tableros de pino macizo. Las paredes, los techos y los muebles están hechos de contrachapado de pino. En la isla no hay electricidad, por lo que todas las casas tienen una chimenea para la calefacción, un refrigerador y una estufa que funcionan con gas, lámparas de queroseno y agua bombeada a mano en el exterior.

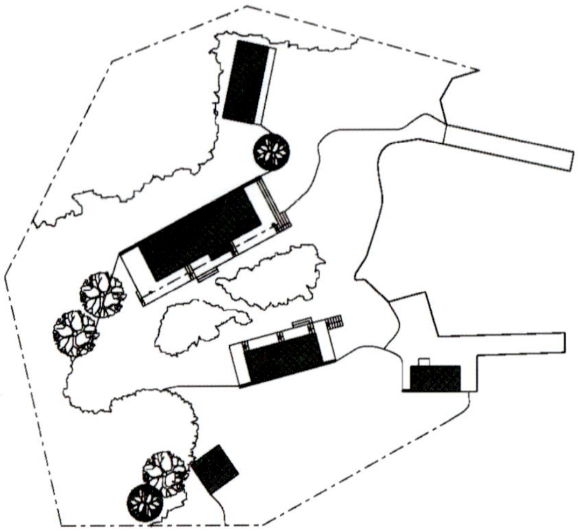

Site plan

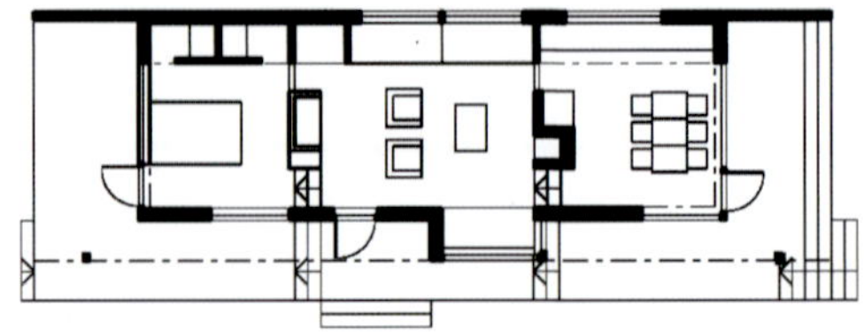

Floor plan

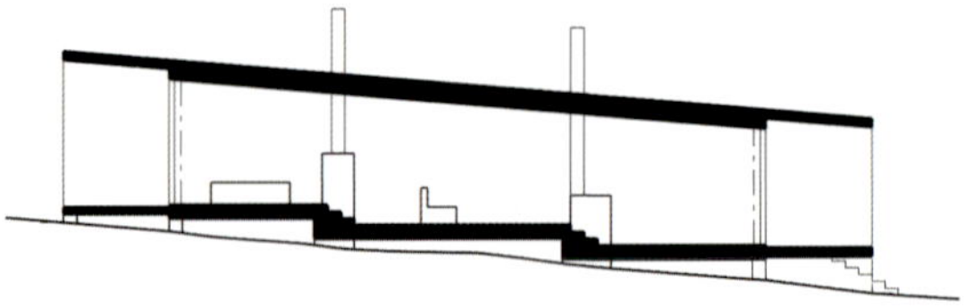

Section

## VILLA T

Archipelago of Stockholm, Sweden
Photos: © Åke E:son Lindman

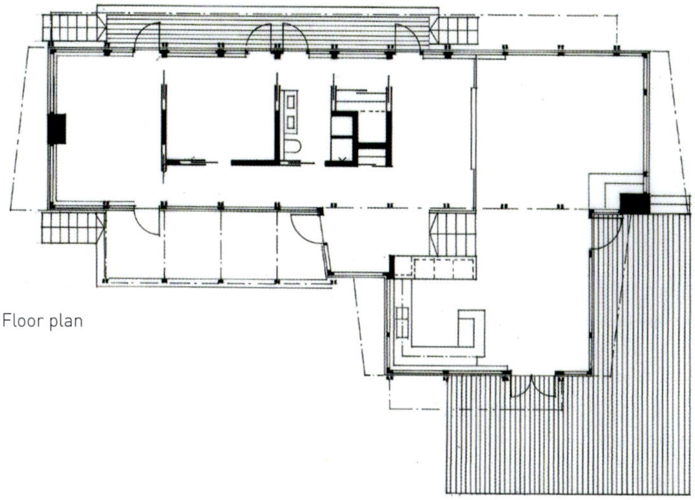

Floor plan

The headland in the middle archipelago faces two distinct landscape spaces. In the southeast you have a wide view of a larger bay and in the northwest there is a protected harbor bay. The elongated volumes of the building range between the two characters of the site; the calm harbor and the wilder bay. Two narrow, mutually displaced volumes, large glass surfaces and a visible frame with partially exposed pillars contribute to the character of the house. Add to this the material choices: granite pedestals, pale red wood panels and grassy ceilings to anchor the building in its context. The site's natural level differences are reflected inside. The interior materials are light with walls and ceilings of white painted landscape smooth panel, light gray joinery, floors of white oiled birch and planed limestone.

Die Landzunge im mittleren Archipel steht zwei unterschiedlichen Landschaftsräumen gegenüber. Im Südosten hat man einen weiten Blick auf eine größere Bucht und im Nordwesten gibt es eine geschützte Hafenbucht. Die langgestreckten Gebäudevolumina bewegen sich zwischen den beiden Charakteren des Geländes, dem ruhigen Hafen und der wilderen Bucht. Zwei schmale, gegeneinander verschobene Volumina, große Glasflächen und ein sichtbarer Rahmen mit teilweise freiliegenden Säulen tragen zum Charakter des Hauses bei. Hinzu kommt die Wahl der Materialien: Granitsockel, hellrote Holzpaneele und Grasdecken, die das Gebäude in seinem Kontext verankern. Die natürlichen Niveauunterschiede des Ortes spiegeln sich im Inneren wider. Die Materialien im Inneren sind hell mit Wänden und Decken aus weiß gestrichenen, glatten Paneelen, hellgrauen Tischlerarbeiten, Böden aus weiß geölter Birke und gehobeltem Kalkstein.

Le promontoire de l'archipel central fait face à deux espaces paysagers distincts. Au sud-est, vous avez une vue large sur une baie plus grande et au nord-ouest, une baie portuaire protégée. Les volumes allongés du bâtiment se situent entre les deux caractères du site : le port calme et la baie plus sauvage. La caractère de la maison est accentué par deux volumes étroits, décalés l'un par rapport à l'autre, de grandes surfaces vitrées et un cadre visible avec des piliers partiellement exposés. Ajoutez à cela les choix de matériaux : piédestaux en granit, panneaux de bois rouge pâle et plafonds herbeux pour ancrer le bâtiment dans son contexte. Les différences naturelles de niveau du site se reflètent à l'intérieur. Les matériaux intérieurs sont légers avec des murs et des plafonds en panneau lisse de paysage peint en blanc, des menuiseries gris clair, des sols en bouleau huilé blanc et en pierre calcaire rabotée.

El promontorio del archipiélago medio se enfrenta a dos espacios paisajísticos distintos. En el sureste tiene una amplia vista de una bahía más grande y en el noroeste hay una bahía portuaria protegida. Los volúmenes alargados de la construcción oscilan entre los dos aspectos del lugar: un puerto tranquilo y la bahía más salvaje. Dos volúmenes estrechos, mutuamente desplazados, grandes superficies de vidrio y un marco visible con pilares parcialmente expuestos contribuyen al carácter de la casa. A esto se suman las opciones materiales: pedestales de granito, paneles de madera de color rojo pálido y techos de hierba para anclar el edificio en su contexto. Las diferencias de nivel del terreno se reflejan en el interior. Los materiales son ligeros, con paredes y techos de paneles lisos de paisaje pintados de blanco, carpintería gris claro, suelos de abedul blanco aceitado y piedra caliza cepillada.

## HOLIDAY HOME

Archipelago of Stockholm, Sweden
Photos: © Åke E:son Lindman

The site where the four buildings are located consists of a beautiful meadow that slopes down to the sea. The level differences in the ground are reflected in the building's volume structures where floor levels and ceilings descend towards the sea. The façades are adorned with wooden panels painted with mud paint. Large glass sections of teak with sliding doors facing the sea make the boundary between the outside and the inside disappear. In the main building, the bedrooms are located on the highest level and a central living room, kitchen and dining area face panoramic views of the sea on the middle and lowest levels. A fireplace is located in the centre of the living area. Walls and ceilings and joinery are painted in white and the floors are covered with limestone and teak.

Das Gelände, auf dem sich die vier Gebäude befinden, besteht aus einer schönen Wiese, die zum Meer hin abfällt. Die Höhenunterschiede des Bodens spiegeln sich in den Volumenstrukturen des Gebäudes wider, wo Bodenebenen und Decken zum Meer hin abfallen. Die Fassaden sind mit Holztafeln geschmückt, die mit Schlammfarbe gestrichen sind. Große Glasflächen aus Teakholz mit Schiebetüren zum Meer hin lassen die Grenze zwischen außen und innen verschwinden. Im Hauptgebäude befinden sich die Schlafzimmer auf der höchsten Ebene und ein zentrales Wohnzimmer, Küche und Essbereich mit Panoramablick auf das Meer auf der mittleren und untersten Ebene. In der Mitte des Wohnbereichs befindet sich ein Kamin. Die Wände und Decken sowie die Tischlerarbeiten sind weiß gestrichen, und die Böden sind mit Kalkstein und Teakholz belegt.

Le site où se trouvent les quatre bâtiments est constitué d'une belle prairie qui descend en pente jusqu'à la mer. Les différences de niveau du sol se reflètent dans les structures volumétriques du bâtiment, où les niveaux des sols et des plafonds descendent vers la mer. Les façades sont ornées de panneaux en bois peints avec de la peinture à la boue. De grandes sections de verre en teck avec des portes coulissantes orientées vers la mer font disparaître la frontière entre l'extérieur et l'intérieur. Dans le bâtiment principal, les chambres sont situées au niveau le plus élevé et un salon central, une cuisine et une salle à manger font face à des vues panoramiques sur la mer aux niveaux intermédiaire et inférieur. Une cheminée est située au centre de la zone de séjour. Les murs, les plafonds et les menuiseries sont peints en blanc et les sols sont recouverts de calcaire et de teck.

El terreno donde se encuentran los cuatro edificios consiste en una hermosa pradera que desciende hasta el mar. Las diferencias de nivel se reflejan en las estructuras de volumen del edificio donde los niveles de suelo y techos descienden hacia el mar. Las fachadas están adornadas con paneles de madera pintados con pintura de barro. Grandes secciones de vidrio de teca con puertas corredizas que miran al mar hacen desaparecer el límite entre el exterior y el interior. En el edificio principal, los dormitorios están situados en el nivel más alto y una sala de estar central, la cocina y el comedor tienen vistas panorámicas al mar en los niveles medio y bajo. En el centro de la sala de estar hay una chimenea. Las paredes y los techos y la carpintería están pintados de blanco y los suelos están cubiertos de piedra caliza y teca.

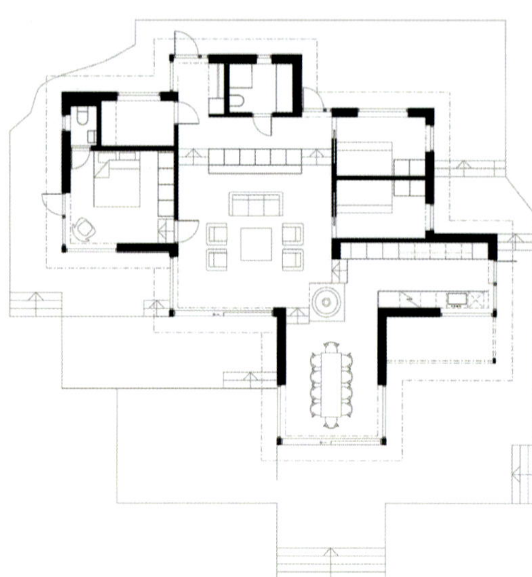

Floor plan

Martin Kallesø Arkitekter is a small one man award-winning architectural studio in Valby, Copenhagen practicing architecture for both private and corporate clients. Founded in 2010 by principal architect Martin Kallesø ( The Royal Danish Academy of Fine Arts - School of Architecture KADK ), the studio specializes in bespoke residential, corporate architecture and competitions. Seen throughout Denmark, the work represents a continued evaluation and refinement of art & craft, firmly rooted in the local building tradition of the place. The studio always works with the relationship between building and context / topography. Each project from the studio has a contextual approach.
Martin Kallesø Arkitekter is the recipient of The Dreyer Foundation Scholarship and the Danish Art Foundation Working Scholarship both in 2019.
Martin Kallesø is also appointed censor and guest critic at The Royal Danish Academy of Fine Arts - School of Architecture (KADK) and at Aarhus School of Architecture.

Martin Kallesø Arkitekter ist ein kleines, preisgekröntes Ein-Mann-Architekturbüro in Valby, Kopenhagen, das Architektur sowohl für Privat- als auch für Firmenkunden praktiziert. Das Büro wurde 2010 von Martin Kallesø (Königlich Dänische Akademie der Schönen Künste – Architekturschule KADK) gegründet und hat sich auf maßgeschneiderte Wohn- und Unternehmensarchitektur sowie Wettbewerbe spezialisiert. In ganz Dänemark beachtet, stellt das Werk eine kontinuierliche Bewertung und Verfeinerung von Kunst und Handwerk dar, die fest in der lokalen Bautradition des Ortes verwurzelt ist. Das Atelier arbeitet immer mit der Beziehung zwischen Gebäude und Kontext/Topographie. Jedes Projekt des Ateliers hat einen kontextuellen Ansatz.
Martin Kallesø Arkitekter ist Stipendiat der Dreyer-Stiftung und des Arbeitsstipendiums der Dänischen Kunststiftung, beide im Jahr 2019.
Martin Kallesø ist auch als Zensor und Gastkritiker an der Königlich Dänischen Kunstakademie – Schule für Architektur (KADK) und an der Architekturschule in Aarhus tätig.

# MARTIN KALLESØ ARKITEKTER

Martin Kallesø Arkitekter est un petit studio d'architecture de Valby, à Copenhague, qui s'adresse à des clients privés et des entreprises. Fondé en 2010 par l'architecte principal Martin Kallesø (Académie royale danoise des beaux-arts - École d'architecture KADK), le studio est spécialisé dans l'architecture résidentielle et d'entreprise sur mesure et dans les concours. Vu dans tout le Danemark, le travail représente une évaluation et un raffinement continus de l'art et de l'artisanat, fermement ancrés dans la tradition de construction locale du lieu. La relation entre le bâtiment et le contexte / la topographie est au cœur du travail du studio. Chaque projet de l'atelier a une approche contextuelle.
Martin Kallesø Arkitekter est le bénéficiaire de la bourse de la Fondation Dreyer et de la bourse de travail de la Fondation danoise pour l'art, toutes deux en 2019.
Martin Kallesø est également nommé censeur et critique invité à l'Académie royale danoise des beaux-arts - École d'architecture (KADK) et à l'École d'architecture d'Aarhus.

Martin Kallesø Arkitekter es un pequeño aunque premiado estudio de arquitectura en Valby, Copenhague, que practica la arquitectura para clientes privados y corporativos. Fundado en 2010 por el arquitecto principal Martin Kallesø ( perteneciente a La Real Academia Danesa de Bellas Artes - Escuela de Arquitectura KADK ), el estudio se especializa en arquitectura residencial, corporativa y concursos a medida. Respetado en toda Dinamarca, el trabajo representa una evaluación y un refinamiento continuo del arte y la artesanía, firmemente arraigado en la tradición de construcción local. El estudio trabaja siempre con la relación entre la construcción, el contexto y la topografía. Cada proyecto del estudio tiene un enfoque contextual.
Martin Kallesø Arkitekter es beneficiario de la beca de la Fundación Dreyer y de la beca de trabajo de la Fundación Danesa de Arte, ambas en 2019.
Martin Kallesø es también censor y crítico invitado en la Real Academia Danesa de Bellas Artes - Escuela de Arquitectura (KADK) y en la Escuela de Arquitectura de Aarhus.

ADMINISTRATION BUILDING

SINGLE FAMILY HOUSE

SKOGFINN MUSEUM (COMPETITION PROPOSAL)

## ADMINISTRATION BUILDING

Stårup, Nykøbing Sj., Denmark
Photos: © Jacob Hoffmann

The building is placed with reference to its surroundings. The ground site borders a pine plantation and forest. There was a desire to emphasize the forest´s verticality by designing an administration building that was elongated and distinctly horizontal. In addition, the building has a sloping, tilted façade and sky lighting which gives it an orientation towards the forest and the sky.
The administration building has a matt black external sinus plate cladding to adapt to the existing surrounding factory building. Inside the main corridor, the administration building is cladded with Troldtekt® on the tilted façade. The floor in the main corridor is cladded with dark grey floor tiles. Inside the various offices and facility locker rooms the floor is cladded with thin oak staves.

Das Gebäude wurde mit Bezug zu seiner Umgebung platziert. Das Grundstück grenzt an eine Pinienplantage und Wald. Es bestand der Wunsch, die Vertikalität des Waldes durch den Entwurf eines langgestreckten und deutlich horizontalen Verwaltungsgebäudes zu betonen. Darüber hinaus hat das Gebäude eine schräge, geneigte Fassade und eine Oberbeleuchtung, die dem Gebäude eine Orientierung zum Wald und zum Himmel gibt.
Das Verwaltungsgebäude hat eine mattschwarze Sinusplatten-Außenverkleidung, die sich an das bestehende benachbarte Fabrikgebäude anpasst. Innerhalb des Hauptkorridors ist das Verwaltungsgebäude an der geneigten Fassade mit Troldtekt® verkleidet. Der Fußboden im Hauptkorridor ist mit dunkelgrauen Bodenplatten verkleidet. In den verschiedenen Büros und Umkleideräumen ist der Fußboden mit dünnen Eichendauben verkleidet.

Le bâtiment est placé en référence à son environnement. Le site au sol borde une plantation de pins et une forêt. On a voulu souligner la verticalité de la forêt en concevant un bâtiment administratif allongé et nettement horizontal. De plus, le bâtiment possède une façade inclinée lui donnant une orientation vers la forêt et le ciel. Cela permet un éclairage naturel.
Le bâtiment administratif a un revêtement extérieur en tôle sinusoïdale noir mat pour s'adapter au bâtiment d'usine existant qui l'entoure. À l'intérieur du couloir principal, le bâtiment administratif est revêtu de Troldtekt® sur la façade inclinée. Le sol du couloir principal est revêtu de carreaux gris foncé. À l'intérieur des différents bureaux et vestiaires, le sol est revêtu de fines douves de chêne.

El edificio está situado en referencia a su entorno. El terreno bordea una plantación de pinos y un bosque. Se quiso enfatizar la verticalidad del bosque diseñando un edificio administrativo alargado y claramente horizontal. Además, el edificio tiene una fachada inclinada y gracias a su orientación, goza de iluminación natural.
El edificio de la administración tiene un revestimiento de placas exteriores de color negro mate para adaptarse al edificio industrial que lo rodea. En el exterior, el edificio está revestido de placas de madera aglomerada Troldtekt®. El suelo del pasillo principal está revestido con baldosas de color gris oscuro. En el interior de las diversas oficinas y vestuarios de las instalaciones el suelo se remató con finas tablillas de roble.

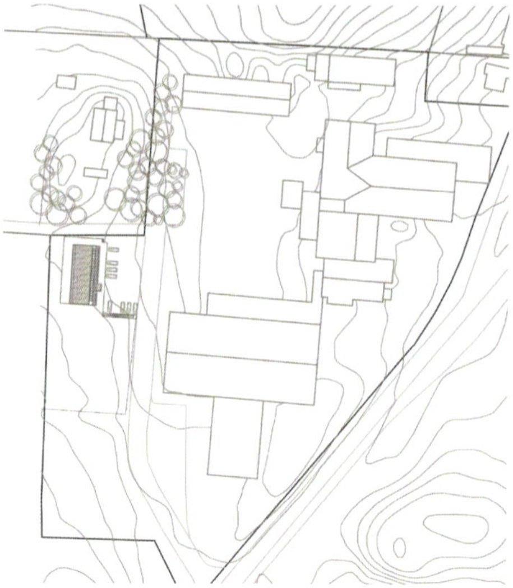

Site plan

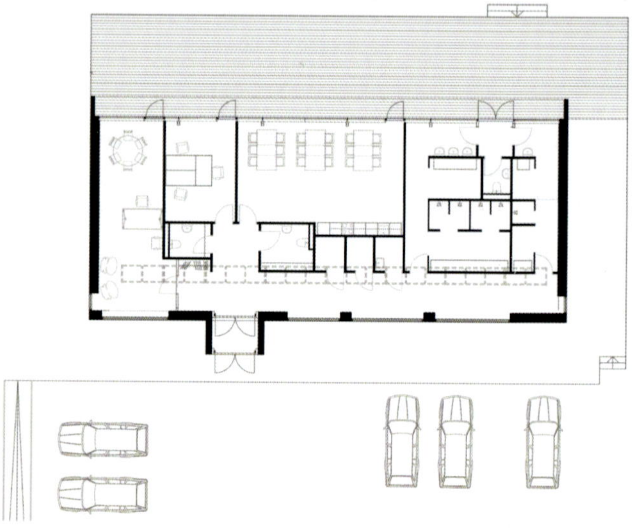

Ground floor plan

## SINGLE FAMILY HOUSE

Varpelev, Stevns, Denmark
Photos: © Jacob Hoffmann

The instruction was to design a 150 m$^2$ home for a small family. The overall main idea was to reinterpret the traditional Danish white painted three parted farmhouses from the 18th century which are common in the surrounding landscape of Varpelev, shaped by the last ice age. The building consists of three parts: a long section which holds the entrance/ hallway, a pantry, kitchen, a small playroom and a studio with huge panorama windows facing the pristine landscape. The mid sections consists only a large living room connected to the kitchen and to the third part of the house which contains another playroom, bathroom and master bedroom also with panorama windows. The house is built of light weight concrete blocks plastered and painted white to ecco the traditional farmhouses. Windows are made of teak wood. The interior is all white with oak planks on the floor.

Die Anweisung lautete, ein 150 m$^2$ großes Haus für eine kleine Familie zu entwerfen. Die Grundidee bestand darin, die traditionellen dänischen, weiß gestrichenen, dreiteiligen Bauernhäuser aus dem 18. Jahrhundert, die in der von der letzten Eiszeit geprägten Landschaft von Varpelev üblich sind, neu zu interpretieren. Das Gebäude besteht aus drei Teilen: einem langen Abschnitt, der den Eingang/Flur beherbergt, einer Speisekammer, einer Küche, einem kleinen Spielzimmer und einem Atelier mit riesigen Panoramafenstern mit Blick auf die unberührte Landschaft. Der mittlere Teil besteht nur aus einem großen Wohnzimmer, das mit der Küche und dem dritten Teil des Hauses verbunden ist, in dem sich ein weiteres Spielzimmer, ein Badezimmer und ein Hauptschlafzimmer ebenfalls mit Panoramafenstern befinden. Das Haus ist aus leichten Betonblöcken gebaut, die verputzt und weiß gestrichen wurden, um die traditionellen Bauernhäuser zu eccotieren. Die Fenster sind aus Teakholz gefertigt. Das Innere ist ganz in Weiß gehalten, mit Eichenbohlen auf dem Boden.

Les instructions étaient de concevoir une maison de 150 m$^2$ pour une petite famille. L'idée principale était de réinterpréter les trois fermes traditionnelles danoises peintes en blanc, datant du 18e siècle, qui sont communes dans le paysage environnant de Varpelev, façonné par la dernière période glaciaire. Le bâtiment se compose de trois parties : une longue section qui contient l'entrée/ le couloir, un garde-manger, une cuisine, une petite salle de jeux et un studio avec d'immenses fenêtres panoramiques donnant sur le paysage vierge. La partie médiane ne comprend qu'une grande salle de séjour reliée à la cuisine et à la troisième partie de la maison qui contient une autre salle de jeux, une salle de bains et une chambre principale également dotée de fenêtres panoramiques. La maison est construite en blocs de béton légers, crépis et peints en blanc pour ressembler aux fermes traditionnelles. Les fenêtres sont en bois de teck. L'intérieur est tout blanc avec des planches de chêne au sol.

El encargo consistió en diseñar una casa de 150 m$^2$ para una pequeña familia. La idea principal era reinterpretar las tradicionales granjas danesas de tres partes, pintadas en blanco, del siglo XVIII, muy comunes en el paisaje circundante de Varpelev, moldeado por la última edad de hielo. El edificio consta de tres partes: una sección larga que contiene la entrada-pasillo, una zona de almacenaje, la cocina, una pequeña sala de juegos y un estudio con enormes ventanas panorámicas que dan al paisaje. La sección media consiste en una única gran sala de estar conectada a la cocina y a la tercera parte de la casa, que contiene otra sala de juegos, un baño y el dormitorio principal, también con ventanas panorámicas. La casa está construida con bloques de hormigón ligero enlucidos y pintados de blanco siguiendo la tradición de las casas de campo. Las ventanas están hechas de madera de teca. El interior se acabó en color blanco, con tablones de roble en el suelo.

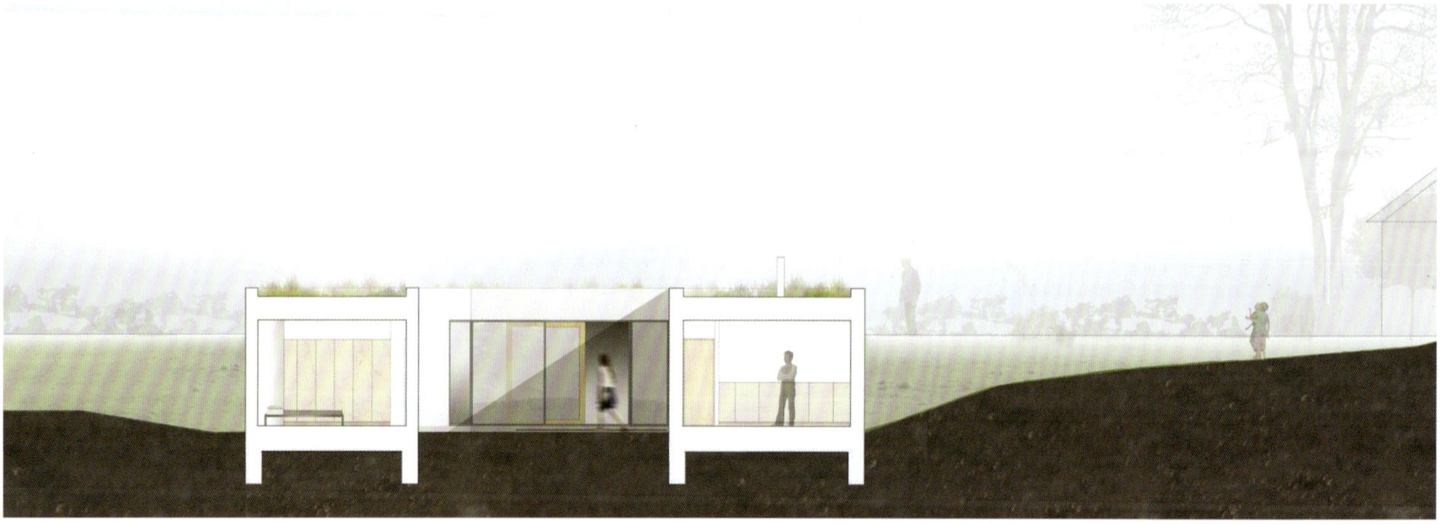

Section

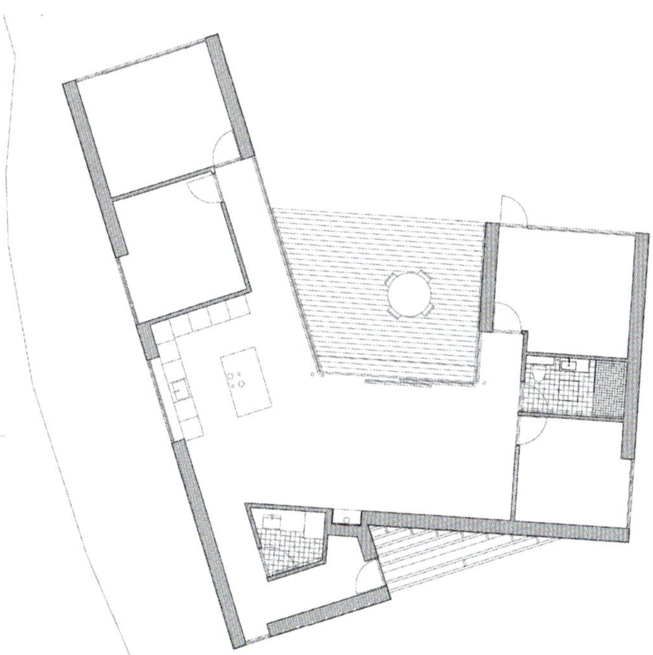

Ground floor plan

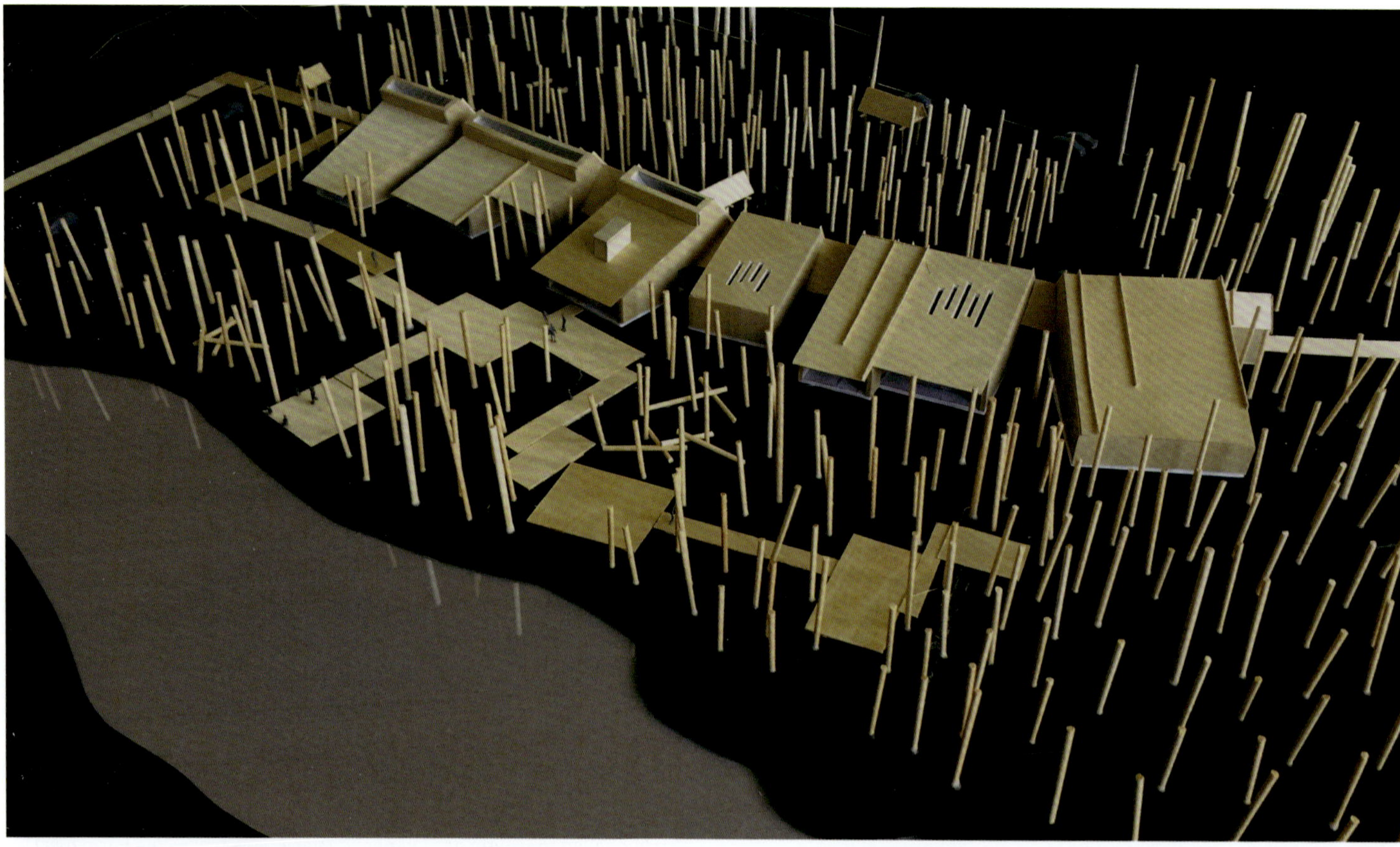

Site plan

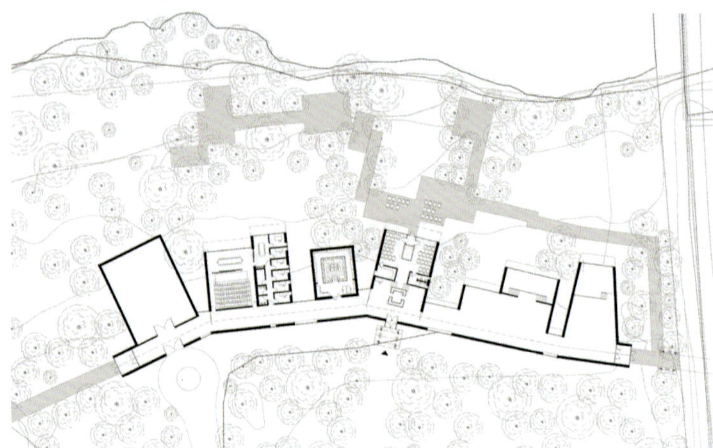

Ground floor plan

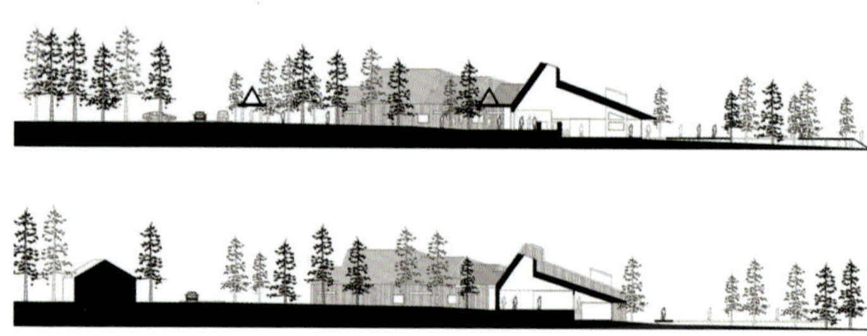

East elevation

Sections

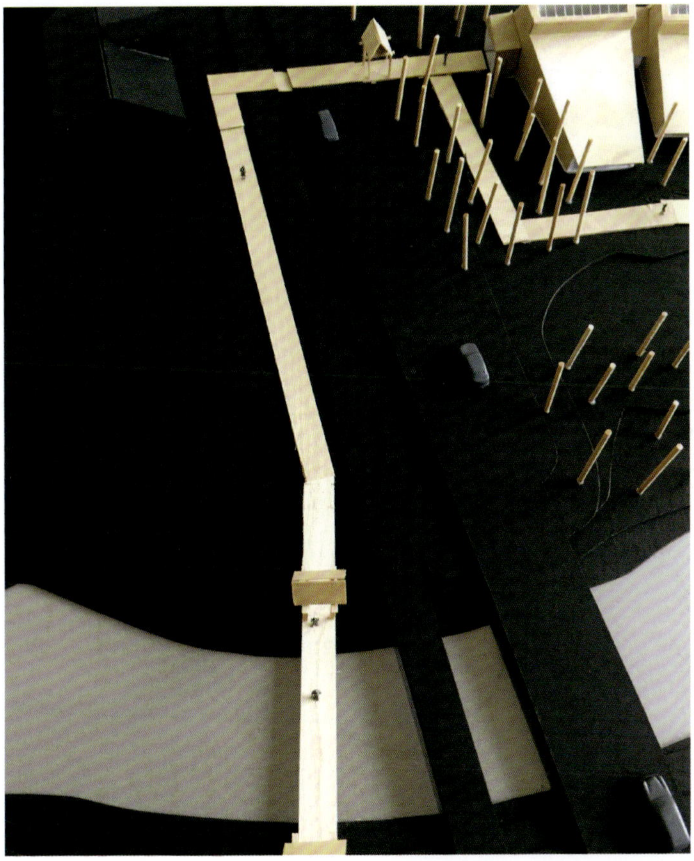

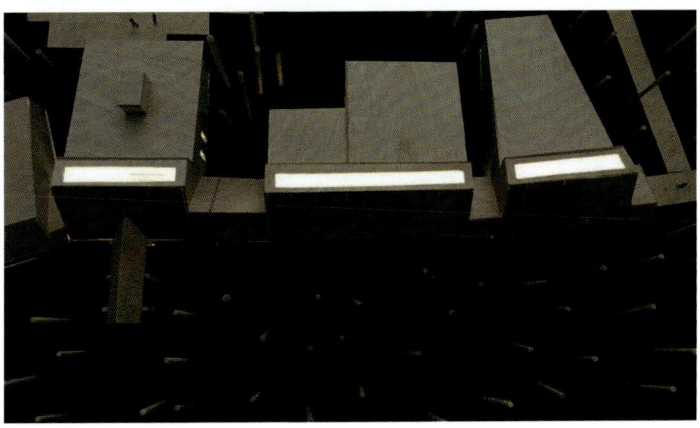

## SKOGFINN MUSEUM (COMPETITION PROPOSAL)

Svullrya, Grue Finnskog, Hedmark fylke, Norway
Photos: © Rasmus Bay Barlby

The project takes its point of departure in an analysis and poetic reading of the traditional *skogfinn* building tradition especially the slash and burn cultivation, the landscape and topography of the site. Our project consist of six houses/cabins which are gently and respectfully laid out in an east/west orientation; both along the main access road (Storbergsvegen) and next to the adjacent river Elva Rotna. These six houses/cabins are organised along a central corridor in a north/south orientation which both link the future extension of the museum (north) and the existing old Skogfinn Museum.
The mode of expression of all six houses/cabins has its origin in the traditional wooden cabin of the *skogfinns*; especially regarding the shape of the roof and the uniform choice of materials. All the façades on the buildings of the museum are cladded with local pine tree.

Das Projekt nimmt seinen Ausgangspunkt in einer Analyse und poetischen Lektüre der traditionellen Skogfinn-Bautradition, insbesondere der Brandrodung, der Landschaft und der Topographie des Ortes. Unser Projekt besteht aus sechs Häusern, die sanft und respektvoll in Ost-West-Ausrichtung angeordnet sind; sowohl entlang der Hauptzufahrtsstraße (Storbergsvegen) als auch neben dem angrenzenden Fluss Elva Rotna. Diese sechs Häuser/Hütten sind entlang eines zentralen Korridors in Nord-Süd-Ausrichtung angeordnet, die sowohl die zukünftige Erweiterung des Museums (Norden) als auch das bestehende alte Skogfinn-Museum verbinden.
Die Ausdrucksweise aller sechs Häuser/Hütten hat ihren Ursprung in der traditionellen Holzhütte der Skogfinns, insbesondere was die Form des Daches und die einheitliche Materialwahl betrifft. Alle Fassaden an den Gebäuden des Museums sind mit einheimischem Kiefernholz verkleidet.

Le point de départ du projet est une analyse et une lecture poétique de la tradition de construction du *skogfinn*, en particulier la culture sur brûlis, le paysage et la topographie du site. Notre projet consiste en six maisons et cabanes disposées de manière douce et respectueuse dans une orientation est/ouest, à la fois le long de la principale route d'accès (Storbergsvegen) et à côté de la rivière adjacente Elva Rotna. Ces six maisons/cabines sont organisées le long d'un couloir central orienté nord/sud qui relie la future extension du musée (nord) et l'ancien musée de Skogfinn existant.
Le mode d'expression des six maisons/cabines trouve son origine dans la cabine en bois traditionnelle des skogfinns, notamment en ce qui concerne la forme du toit et le choix uniforme des matériaux. Toutes les façades des bâtiments du musée sont revêtues de pins locaux.

El proyecto toma su punto de partida en un análisis y lectura poética de la tradición de construcción de *Skogfinn*, especialmente el cultivo de roza y quema, el paisaje y la topografía del lugar. Nuestro proyecto consiste en seis casas/cabañas que están dispuestas de forma suave y respetuosa en una orientación este/oeste; tanto a lo largo de la carretera principal de acceso (Storbergsvegen) como junto al río Elva Rotna adyacente. Estas cabañas están organizadas a lo largo de un corredor central en una orientación norte/sur que une la futura ampliación del museo y el antiguo Museo Skogfinn existente.
El modo de expresión de las seis casas tiene su origen en la tradicional cabaña de madera de los Skogfinns; especialmente en lo que respecta a la forma del techo y la elección uniforme de los materiales. Todas las fachadas de los edificios del museo están revestidas de pino local.

The company was founded in 2012 and is currently active in the field of architecture. We run a small and personal company with a large network of contacts in the construction industry as well as in research. The company is capable of being the spider in the network for large projects, but is also happy to undertake small projects with high ambitions.

Das Unternehmen wurde 2012 gegründet und ist derzeit im Bereich der Architektur tätig. Wir führen ein kleines und persönliches Unternehmen mit einem großen Netzwerk von Kontakten in der Bauindustrie sowie in der Forschung. Das Unternehmen ist in der Lage, die Spinne im Netzwerk für große Projekte zu sein, ist aber auch gerne bereit, kleine Projekte mit hohen Ambitionen durchzuführen.

# MARX ARCHITECTURE

La société a été fondée en 2012 et est actuellement active dans le domaine de l'architecture. Nous dirigeons une petite entreprise personnelle qui dispose d'un vaste réseau de contacts dans le secteur de la construction et de la recherche. La société est capable d'être l'araignée du réseau pour les grands projets, mais elle est également heureuse d'entreprendre de petits projets avec de grandes ambitions.

La compañía fue fundada en 2012 y sigue activa en el campo de la arquitectura. Dirigimos una empresa pequeña y personal con una gran red de contactos en la industria de la construcción, e investigación. El estudio es capaz de responder frente a grandes proyectos, pero se siente cómodo también involucrándose en pequeños proyectos que representen grandes ambiciones.

▼ APARTMENT

▼ CULTUR HOUSE CYKLOPEN

▼ GALLERY

## APARTMENT

Stockholm, Sweden
Photos: © Jesper Florbrant (Urban by Esny)

The apartment is built in connection to the Swedish "million housing program" in the 60th. During the state-initiated process 100 000 apartments were built per year to address the extreme housing shortage and poor living standard. This is an enormous effort in hindsight that the population in Sweden during this time was approximately 7,7 million people. The result was a modernist concrete architecture inspired by Le Corbusier but without his finesse. Today the areas are disreputable by the broader public. At the same time many of the houses were built with a pillar frames whitish makes them highly transformable. In this project Marx Arkitektur tore down most of the walls reinventing it as an attractive open apartment where industrial design meets high end natural materials.

Die Wohnung wurde im Zusammenhang mit dem schwedischen „Millionen-Wohnprogramm" in den 60er Jahren gebaut. Während des staatlich initiierten Prozesses wurden 100 000 Wohnungen pro Jahr gebaut, um der extremen Wohnungsknappheit und dem schlechten Lebensstandard entgegenzuwirken. Dies ist im Nachhinein eine enorme Anstrengung, wenn man bedenkt, dass die Bevölkerung in Schweden in dieser Zeit etwa 7,7 Millionen Menschen umfasste. Das Ergebnis war eine modernistische Betonarchitektur, inspiriert von Le Corbusier, aber ohne dessen Finesse. Heute sind die Gebiete in der breiten Öffentlichkeit in Verruf geraten. Gleichzeitig wurden viele der Häuser mit einem weißlichen Säulenrahmen gebaut, was sie sehr wandelbar macht. Bei diesem Projekt riss Marx Arkitektur die meisten Mauern ein und erfand sie als attraktive offene Wohnung neu, in der Industriedesign auf hochwertige natürliche Materialien trifft.

L'appartement est construit dans le cadre du programme suédois « Un million de logements » au 60e siècle. Au cours du processus lancé par l'État, 100 000 appartements ont été construits chaque année pour remédier à l'extrême pénurie de logements et au faible niveau de vie. Il s'agit d'un effort énorme si l'on considère que la population suédoise à cette époque était d'environ 7,7 millions de personnes. Le résultat a été une architecture moderniste en béton inspirée par Le Corbusier mais sans sa finesse. Aujourd'hui, les quartiers sont déshonorés par le grand public. En même temps, de nombreuses maisons ont été construites avec une charpente de piliers blanchâtre, ce qui les rend très transformables. Dans ce projet, Marx Arkitektur a démoli la plupart des murs, réinventant ainsi un appartement ouvert et attrayant où le design industriel rencontre des matériaux naturels haut de gamme.

El apartamento se construyó en conexión con el «Programa del Millón de viviendas» sueco en el año 1960. Durante el proceso iniciado por el estado, se construyeron 100 000 apartamentos por año para hacer frente a la extrema escasez de viviendas y el bajo nivel de vida de una población en Suecia que durante este tiempo era de aproximadamente 7,7 millones de personas. El resultado fue una arquitectura modernista de hormigón inspirada en Le Corbusier pero sin su delicadeza. Hoy en día las zonas son de dudosa reputación para el público en general. Al mismo tiempo, muchas de las casas fueron construidas con un marco de pilares blanquecino que las hace altamente transformables. En este proyecto Marx Arkitektur derribó la mayoría de los muros, reinventando el concepto como un atractivo apartamento abierto donde el diseño industrial se une a materiales naturales de alta calidad.

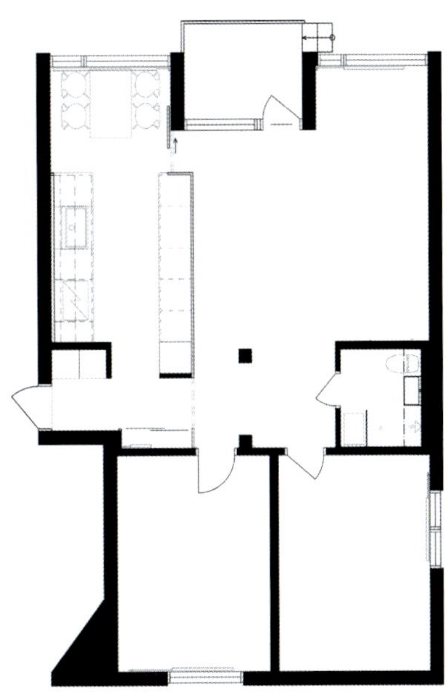

Floor plan

## CULTUR HOUSE CYKLOPEN

Stockholm, Sweden
Photos: © Johan Åström

Due to the fact of the client being a self-funded organization with a very limited budget, the project´s outsets was to have the house built by volunteers who had no former experience in construction work. The house´s outer framing was designed to act like a scaffolding during the construction period also having the quality of being easy to build for non-professional labor. The color theme of the house was designed to create a warm and welcoming feeling. Sweden, being very dark during wintertime, the colors are even more accentuated through the transparent panels, working as a friendly lantern for those passing by. The structure follows the seasons having a warm touch and accepting the outer shell to have a lower temperature closer to the outside climate, a low cost ecologism.

Aufgrund der Tatsache, dass der Kunde eine selbstfinanzierte Organisation mit einem sehr begrenzten Budget ist, sollte das Haus zu Beginn des Projekts von Freiwilligen gebaut werden, die keine Erfahrung im Baugewerbe hatten. Die äußere Umrahmung des Hauses sollte während der Bauzeit wie ein Gerüst wirken und gleichzeitig die Eigenschaft haben, dass es auch für Laien leicht zu bauen ist. Das Farbthema des Hauses wurde so gestaltet, dass es ein warmes und einladendes Gefühl vermittelt. Da Schweden im Winter sehr dunkel ist, werden die Farben durch die transparenten Paneele noch stärker betont und wirken wie eine freundliche Laterne für die Passanten. Die Struktur folgt den Jahreszeiten, indem sie sich warm anfühlt und die Außenhülle akzeptiert, um eine niedrigere Temperatur näher am Außenklima zu haben – ein kostengünstiger Ökologismus.

En raison du fait que le client est une organisation autofinancée avec un budget très limité, le projet a commencé par faire construire la maison par des volontaires qui n'avaient aucune expérience préalable dans le domaine de la construction. L'ossature extérieure de la maison a été conçue pour servir d'échafaudage pendant la période de construction, tout en ayant la qualité d'être facile à construire pour une main-d'œuvre non professionnelle. Le thème des couleurs de la maison a été conçu pour créer un sentiment de chaleur et d'accueil. La Suède étant très sombre en hiver, les couleurs sont encore plus accentuées par les panneaux transparents, qui font office de lanterne d'accueil pour les passants. La structure suit les saisons en ayant une touche chaleureuse et en acceptant que l'enveloppe extérieure ait une température plus basse et plus proche du climat extérieur, un écologisme à faible coût.

Debido a que el cliente es una organización autofinanciada con un presupuesto muy limitado, el inicio del proyecto fue hacer que la casa fuera construida por voluntarios que no tenían experiencia previa en trabajos de construcción. La propia estructura exterior de la casa fue diseñada para actuar como un andamiaje durante el período de construcción, teniendo además la cualidad de ser fácil de construir para el trabajo no profesional. El tema del color fue escogido para crear un sentimiento cálido y acogedor. En Suecia, siendo muy oscura durante el invierno, los colores se acentúan aún más a través de los paneles transparentes, funcionando como una linterna agradable para los paseantes. La estructura se adapta a las estaciones del año, teniendo un toque cálido y aceptando la cáscara exterior para tener una temperatura más baja cercana al clima exterior, un ecologismo de bajo coste.

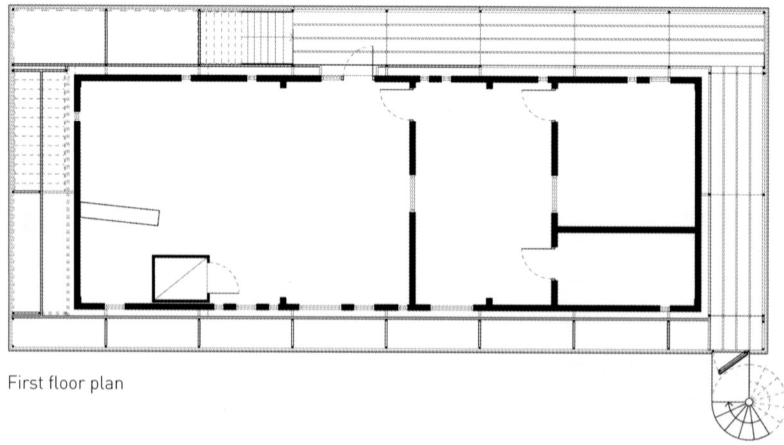

First floor plan

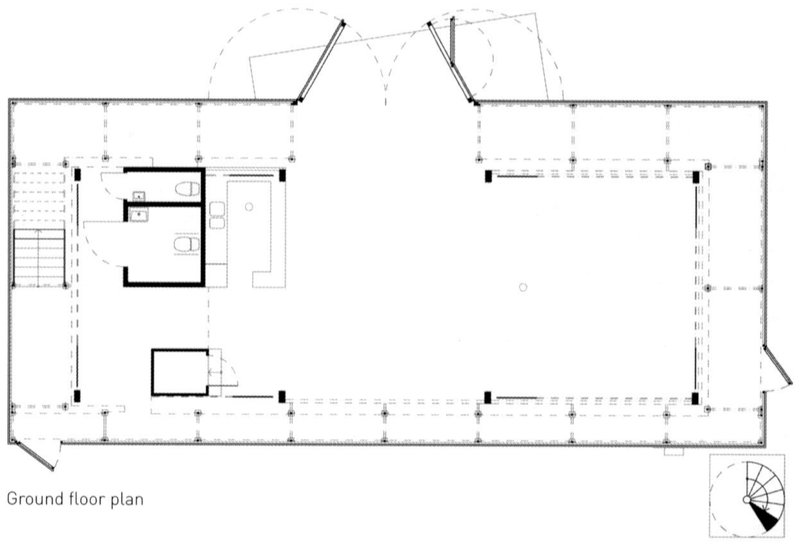

Ground floor plan

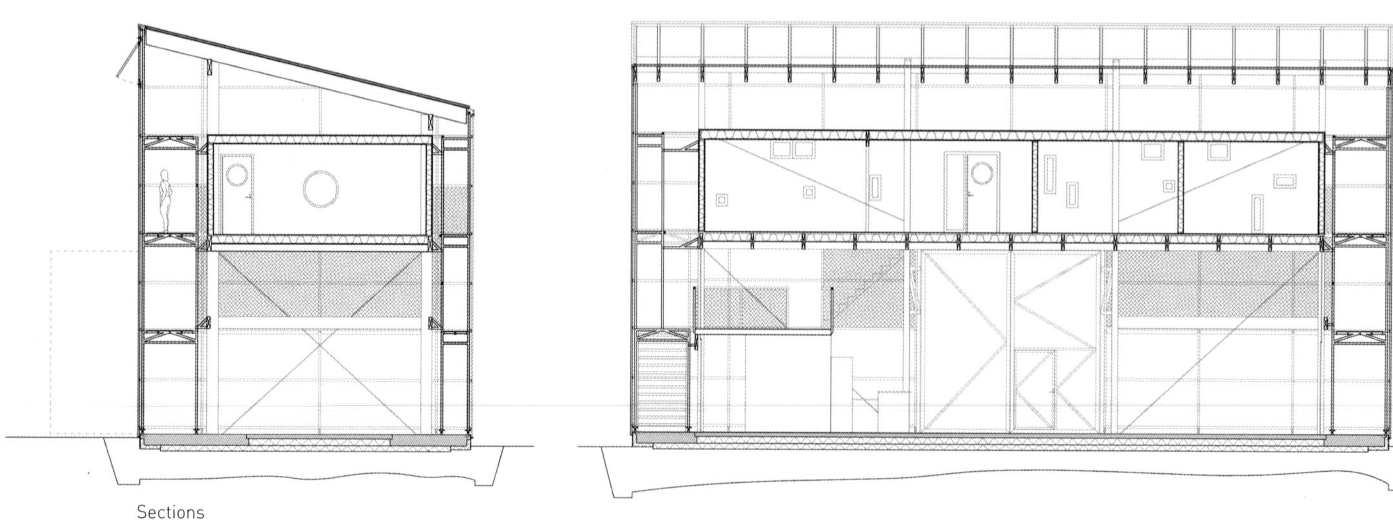

Sections

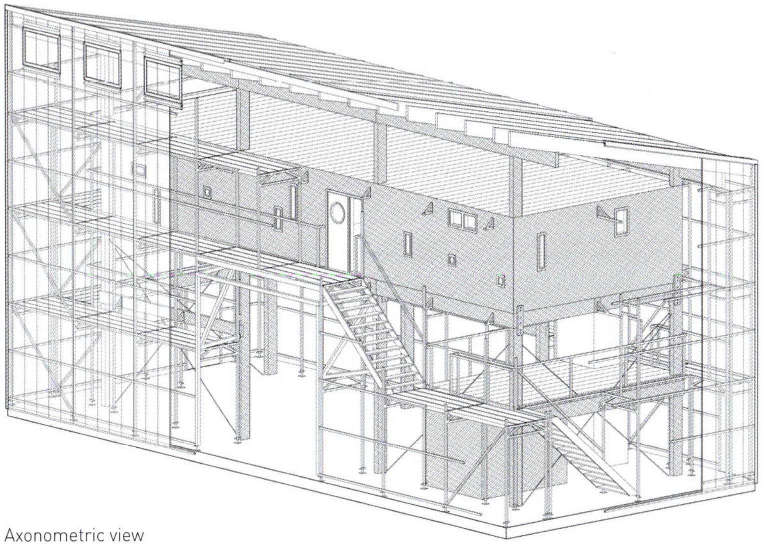

Axonometric view

## GALLERY

Stockholm, Sweden
Photos: © Johan Åström

The project, built in 2008, was included in the street art project "(Un)wanted city renewal". The artwork stated the question that if someone creates a positive change at a place dislike by the public but without permission, what is the reactions from the authority's and inhabitants of the city? Two buildings were placed into the city landscape. One of the sites was a dark concrete metro exit in a cut open down a Stockholm suburb. During a city walk in the area inhabitants claimed that they feared getting robbed. They also acknowledge the lack of social meeting points in their suburb. To address these problems, the gallery was built into one of the concrete niches making space for weekly exhibitions and giving the public space light and security. After three months the authorities demanded it to be turned down.

Das 2008 gebaute Projekt wurde in das Straßenkunstprojekt „(Un)gewollte Stadterneuerung" aufgenommen. Das Kunstwerk stellte die Frage: Wenn jemand an einem Ort, der von der Öffentlichkeit nicht gemocht wird, aber ohne Erlaubnis, eine positive Veränderung bewirkt, wie reagieren dann die Behörden und die Bewohner der Stadt? Zwei Gebäude wurden in die Stadtlandschaft gestellt. Eines der Gebäude war ein dunkler U-Bahneingang aus Beton in einem Einschnitt in einem Stockholmer Vorort. Während eines Stadtrundgangs in dem Gebiet behaupteten die Bewohner, dass sie befürchteten, ausgeraubt zu werden. Sie gaben auch an, dass es in ihrem Vorort keine sozialen Treffpunkte gab. Um diesen Problemen zu begegnen, wurde die Galerie in eine der Betonnischen gebaut, um Platz für wöchentliche Ausstellungen zu schaffen und dem öffentlichen Raum Licht und Sicherheit zu geben. Nach drei Monaten verlangten die Behörden, sie zu entfernen.

Le projet, construit en 2008, a été inclus dans le projet d'art de rue « (Un)wanted city renewal ». L'œuvre d'art posait la question suivante : si quelqu'un crée un changement positif dans un lieu que le public n'aime pas, mais sans autorisation, quelles sont les réactions des autorités et des habitants de la ville ? Deux bâtiments ont été placés dans le paysage urbain. L'un des sites était une sortie de métro en béton sombre dans une tranchée ouverte dans une banlieue de Stockholm. Au cours d'une promenade dans la ville, les habitants ont déclaré qu'ils craignaient d'être volés. Ils reconnaissent également le manque de points de rencontre sociaux dans leur banlieue. Pour remédier à ces problèmes, la galerie a été construite dans l'une des niches en béton, ce qui a permis de créer un espace pour des expositions hebdomadaires et de donner à l'espace public lumière et sécurité. Au bout de trois mois, les autorités ont exigé qu'elle soit refusée.

El proyecto, construido en 2008, se incluyó en el proyecto de arte callejero «(Un)wanted city renewal». La obra planteaba la pregunta de que si alguien crea un cambio positivo en un lugar que no le gusta al público pero que no tiene permiso, ¿cuáles son las reacciones de las autoridades y de los habitantes de la ciudad? Se colocaron dos edificios en el paisaje de la ciudad. Uno de ellos era una salida de metro de hormigón oscuro en un suburbio de Estocolmo donde los habitantes habían afirmado que temían ser robados durante un paseo. También reconocieron la falta de puntos de encuentro social en su suburbio. Para abordar estos problemas, la galería se construyó en uno de los nichos de hormigón haciendo espacio para las exposiciones semanales y dando al espacio público luz y seguridad. Después de tres meses, las autoridades exigieron que fuera derrumbada.

PAVE Architects, led by Pave Mikkonen, is a high-profile design office from Finland specialized in creating innovative and comprehensive architecture and interior design, all with their very own twist and without compromises on aesthetics.
PAVE Architects aspires to create unique buildings and sustainable environments, high in terms of quality, atmosphere and architecture, carried out with a cost-conscious and responsible service of the client. The open-minded, unprejudiced attitude, as well as the bold questioning of well-established ideas and solutions, is the core for creating and reaching new, better designs.
The relationship between buildings in their broader context, such as the local conditions and environment, gives each project an individual starting point. Therefore, with PAVE Architects, each project becomes unique as the designs stem from a clean slate.

PAVE Architects, unter der Leitung von Pave Mikkonen, ist ein hochkarätiges Designbüro aus Finnland, das sich auf die Schaffung innovativer und umfassender Architektur und Innenarchitektur spezialisiert hat, die alle ihren ganz eigenen Stil hat und keine Kompromisse bei der Ästhetik eingeht.
PAVE Architects strebt danach, einzigartige Gebäude und nachhaltige Umgebungen zu schaffen, die sich durch hohe Qualität, Atmosphäre und Architektur auszeichnen und mit einem kosten- und verantwortungsbewussten Service für den Kunden ausgeführt werden. Die aufgeschlossene, unvoreingenommene Haltung sowie das mutige Infragestellen etablierter Ideen und Lösungen ist der Kern für das Schaffen und Erreichen neuer, besserer Entwürfe.
Die Beziehung zwischen Gebäuden in ihrem breiteren Kontext, wie etwa den örtlichen Gegebenheiten und der Umgebung, gibt jedem Projekt einen individuellen Ausgangspunkt. Daher wird bei PAVE Architects jedes Projekt einzigartig, da die Entwürfe aus einer reinen Schiefertafel stammen.

# PAVE ARCHITECTS

PAVE Architects, dirigé par Pave Mikkonen, est un bureau d'études finlandais très en vue, spécialisé dans la création d'une architecture et d'un design intérieur novateurs et complets, avec leur propre touche et sans compromis sur l'esthétique.
PAVE Architects aspire à créer des bâtiments uniques et des environnements durables, de grande qualité, en termes d'atmosphère et d'architecture, réalisés avec un service au client conscient des coûts et responsable. L'ouverture d'esprit et l'absence de préjugés, ainsi que la remise en question audacieuse d'idées et de solutions bien établies, sont au cœur de la création et de la réalisation de nouveaux designs de meilleure qualité.
La relation entre les bâtiments dans leur contexte plus large, comme les conditions et l'environnement locaux, donne à chaque projet un point de départ individuel. Ainsi, avec PAVE Architects, chaque projet devient unique car les conceptions sont issues d'une ardoise vierge.

PAVE Architects, dirigido por Pave Mikkonen, es una oficina de diseño de alto perfil de Finlandia especializada en la arquitectura y el diseño de interiores innovadores y completos, todos con su propio giro y sin compromisos en la estética.
PAVE Arquitectos aspira a crear edificios únicos y entornos sostenibles, de alta calidad, proyectos llevados a cabo con un servicio responsable y consciente del presupuesto del cliente. La actitud abierta y sin prejuicios, así como el cuestionamiento audaz de ideas y soluciones bien establecidas, son la base para crear y alcanzar nuevos y mejores diseños.
La relación entre los edificios en su contexto más amplio, como las condiciones y el entorno local, otorga a cada proyecto un punto de partida individual. En PAVE Arquitectos, cada proyecto se convierte en único ya que los diseños surgen sin requisitos predeterminados.

SAUNA KÄPYLÄ

VILLA RYYSYRANTA II

DESIGN HOTEL LEVI

## SAUNA KÄPYLÄ

Oulu, Finland
Photos: © Arno de la Chapelle

The courtyard of a protected 19th century villa was enlarged with a new sauna building. The contemporary solutions of the new structure lessen the need for refurbishments on the original villa, thus protecting the valuable building heritage of the site. The annex was placed by the shoreline where a 1960s sauna was previously placed. The gable-roofed mass is embedded in the forest-like plot, with views from the sauna room opening to the sea through the fully glazed walls on the shore side.

Der Innenhof einer denkmalgeschützten Villa aus dem 19. Jahrhundert wurde mit einem neuen Saunagebäude erweitert. Die zeitgemäßen Lösungen des Neubaus verringern den Sanierungsbedarf an der ursprünglichen Villa und schützen so das wertvolle bauliche Erbe des Ortes. Der Anbau wurde an der Uferlinie platziert, wo zuvor eine Sauna aus den 1960er Jahren stand. Die giebelüberdachte Masse ist in das waldähnliche Grundstück eingebettet, wobei sich der Blick aus dem Saunaraum durch die voll verglasten Wände auf der Uferseite zum Meer hin öffnet.

La cour d'une villa protégée du XIXe siècle a été agrandie avec un nouveau bâtiment de sauna. Les solutions contemporaines de la nouvelle structure réduisent la nécessité de rénovations sur la villa d'origine, protégeant ainsi le précieux patrimoine immobilier du site. L'annexe a été placée près de la rive où se trouvait auparavant un sauna des années 1960. La masse au toit à pignon est encastrée dans le terrain en forme de forêt, avec des vues de la salle de sauna s'ouvrant sur la mer à travers les murs entièrement vitrés du côté de la rive.

El patio de una villa protegida del siglo XIX fue ampliado con un nuevo espacio para albergar una sauna a modo de anexo. Las soluciones contemporáneas de la nueva estructura disminuyen la necesidad de renovar la villa original, protegiendo así el valioso patrimonio histórico del lugar. El anexo se situó junto a la costa donde antes se encontraba una sauna de los años sesenta. El techo a dos aguas está incrustado en la parcela forestal, con vistas desde la sala de la sauna que se abre al mar a través de paredes totalmente acristaladas.

## VILLA RYYSYRANTA II

Finland
Photos: © Arno de la Chapelle

Villa Ryysyranta II is an evolution of an earlier design with the same principles of maintaining a delicate balance between the fragile beach landscape and tradition-based contemporary architecture. The sparse placement, scale and shape of the building masses and material choices with transparent design throughout root the building firmly with its surroundings. The enjoyment of the outdoors is maximized throughout the seasons.

Die Villa Ryysyranta II ist eine Weiterentwicklung eines früheren Entwurfs mit den gleichen Prinzipien der Aufrechterhaltung eines empfindlichen Gleichgewichts zwischen der fragilen Strandlandschaft und traditionsbasierter zeitgenössischer Architektur. Die spärliche Platzierung, der Maßstab und die Form der Gebäudemassen und die Materialwahl mit durchgehend transparentem Design verwurzeln das Gebäude fest in seiner Umgebung. Die Freude an der Natur wird zu jeder Jahreszeit maximiert.

La Villa Ryysyranta II est l'évolution d'une conception antérieure, avec les mêmes principes de maintien d'un équilibre délicat entre le paysage fragile de plage et l'architecture contemporaine basée sur la tradition. L'emplacement, l'échelle, la forme des masses du bâtiment et le choix des matériaux, ainsi que la transparence de la conception tout au long de la construction, ancrent fermement le bâtiment dans son environnement. Le plaisir de la vie en plein air est maximisé au fil des saisons.

Villa Ryysyranta II es una evolución de un diseño anterior con los mismos principios de mantener un delicado equilibrio entre el frágil paisaje de la playa y la arquitectura contemporánea basada en la tradición. El escaso volumen, escala y forma de los edificios y las elecciones de materiales con diseño transparente en todo el conjunto lo arraigan firmemente a su entorno. El disfrute del aire libre se maximiza a lo largo de las estaciones del año.

DESIGN HOTEL LEVI
DESIGN HOTEL LEVI
LEVI HOTEL SPA

## DESIGN HOTEL LEVI

Sirkka, Finland
Photos: © Arno de la Chapelle,
Tuukka Uimonen (photo of the hotel room)

Design Hotel Levi is a new main building for a design hotel in Levi, Finland. Rising from the landscape of Lapland, it brings a new face to the area while blending naturally into its surroundings with the combination of its contemporary language and the use of traditional materials. The hotel is carefully designed to fuse with the surrounding highlands. Inside, the elements of mood, design, and luxury will form a memorable, yet highly functional whole.

Das Design-Hotel Levi ist ein neues Hauptgebäude für ein Hotel in Levi, Finnland. Es erhebt sich aus der Landschaft Lapplands, verleiht der Gegend ein neues Gesicht und fügt sich durch die Kombination aus zeitgenössischer Sprache und der Verwendung traditioneller Materialien natürlich in die Umgebung ein. Das Hotel wurde sorgfältig entworfen, um mit dem umgebenden Hochland zu verschmelzen. Im Inneren werden die Elemente Stimmung, Design und Luxus ein einprägsames, aber dennoch hoch funktionales Ganzes bilden.

Le Design Hotel Levi est un nouveau bâtiment principal pour un hôtel design à Levi, en Finlande. S'élevant du paysage de Laponie, il apporte un nouveau visage à la région tout en se fondant naturellement dans son environnement grâce à la combinaison de son langage contemporain et à l'utilisation de matériaux traditionnels. L'hôtel est soigneusement conçu pour fusionner avec les hautes terres environnantes. À l'intérieur, les éléments d'ambiance, de design et de luxe formeront un ensemble mémorable, mais très fonctionnel.

El Hotel de Diseño Levi es un nuevo edificio principal para un hotel de diseño en Levi, Finlandia. Elevándose desde el paisaje de Laponia, aporta un nuevo rostro a la zona mientras se mezcla naturalmente con su entorno con la combinación de su lenguaje contemporáneo y el uso de materiales tradicionales. El hotel está cuidadosamente diseñado para fusionarse con las tierras altas circundantes. En el interior, los elementos de diseño y lujo formarán un conjunto memorable y altamente funcional.

Helsinki-based PES-Architects is one of the most international architecture and design firms in Finland. Founded in 1968, the office now has a multinational staff of over 70 and a Shanghai studio established in 2010. PES-Architects is known for its complex and wide-ranging building types, including airports and transport terminals, performance venues, sports facilities, arenas and mixed-used developments, as well as demanding refurbishment projects. The practice's cross-disciplinary approach is rooted in a deep understanding of the user experience.
PES-Architects partners are Pekka Salminen, Architect SAFA, Tuomas Silvennoinen Architect SAFA, Arttu Suomalainen Architect SAFA, Jarkko Salminen.

PES-Architects mit Sitz in Helsinki ist eines der internationalsten Architektur- und Designbüros in Finnland. Das 1968 gegründete Büro verfügt heute über einen multinationalen Mitarbeiterstab von über 70 Personen und ein 2010 gegründetes Studio in Shanghai. PES-Architects ist bekannt für seine komplexen und breit gefächerten Gebäudetypen, darunter Flughäfen und Verkehrsterminals, Veranstaltungsorte, Sportstätten, Arenen und gemischt genutzte Gebäude sowie anspruchsvolle Sanierungsprojekte. Der interdisziplinäre Ansatz der Praxis wurzelt in einem tiefen Verständnis für die Nutzererfahrung.
Partner von PES-Architects sind Pekka Salminen, Architekt SAFA, Tuomas Silvennoinen Architekt SAFA, Arttu Suomalainen Architekt SAFA, Jarkko Salminen.

# PES-ARCHITECTS

PES-Architects, basé à Helsinki, est l'un des cabinets d'architecture et de design les plus internationaux de Finlande. Fondé en 1968, le bureau compte aujourd'hui une équipe multinationale de plus de 70 personnes et un studio à Shanghai créé en 2010. PES-Architects est connu pour ses bâtiments complexes et variés, notamment les aéroports et les terminaux de transport, les salles de spectacle, les installations sportives, les arènes et les développements à usage mixte. Il est aussi connu pour ses projets de rénovation exigeants. L'approche interdisciplinaire de la pratique est ancrée dans une profonde compréhension de l'expérience de l'utilisateur.
Les partenaires du PSE-Architectes sont Pekka Salminen, architecte SAFA, Tuomas Silvennoinen Architect SAFA, Arttu Suomalainen Architect SAFA, Jarkko Salminen.

PES-Architects, con sede en Helsinki, es una de las firmas de arquitectura y diseño más internacionales de Finlandia. Fundada en 1968, la oficina tiene ahora una plantilla multinacional de más de 70 personas y un estudio en Shanghai desde 2010. PES-Architects es conocido por sus complejos y amplios tipos de edificios, incluyendo aeropuertos y terminales de transporte, salas de conciertos, instalaciones deportivas, pabellones y desarrollos de uso mixto, así como exigentes proyectos de renovación. El enfoque multidisciplinario del estudio se basa en una profunda comprensión de la experiencia del cliente.
Los socios de PES-Architects son Pekka Salminen, Arquitecto SAFA, Tuomas Silvennoinen Arquitecto SAFA, Arttu Suomalainen Arquitecto SAFA y Jarkko Salminen.

ICON YUNDUAN TOWER

STRAIT CULTURE AND ART CENTRE

WEST TERMINAL 2

中国-欧洲中心

## ICON YUNDUAN TOWER

Chengdu, China
Photos: © Marc Goodwin

Icon Yunduan Tower is a 192 m, high mixed-use building located in a high-tech zone on the outskirts of Chengdu. A prominent local landmark, the 47-storey complex contains commercial, hospitality and conference premises as well as offices. The adjacent, partly underground concert hall was designed by local partner CSWADI. The tower has an L-shaped plan at ground level that grows into a square towards the top, forming a sweeping façade overlooking Tianfu River and a straight edge along Tianfu Avenue. The curved elevations are defined by green terraces up to the 30th floor, while solid glass and glazed ceramic panels alternate to form a checquered pattern on the other façades. The 30 m high lobby opens towards the river.

Der Icon Yunduan Tower ist ein 192 m hohes, gemischt genutztes Gebäude in einer High-Tech-Zone am Stadtrand von Chengdu. Der 47-stöckige Komplex ist ein bedeutendes Wahrzeichen der Stadt und beherbergt Geschäfts-, Gastronomie- und Konferenzräume sowie Büros. Der angrenzende, teilweise unterirdische Konzertsaal wurde vom lokalen Partner CSWADI entworfen. Der Turm hat im Erdgeschoss einen L-förmigen Grundriss, der nach oben hin zu einem Quadrat wächst und eine geschwungene Fassade mit Blick auf den Tianfu-Fluss und eine gerade Kante entlang der Tianfu Avenue bildet. Die geschwungenen Erhebungen werden bis zum 30. Stockwerk durch grüne Terrassen definiert, während sich an den anderen Fassaden massives Glas und glasierte Keramikplatten abwechseln und ein Schachbrettmuster bilden. Die 30 Meter hohe Lobby öffnet sich zum Fluss hin.

La tour Icon Yunduan est un bâtiment polyvalent de 192 m de haut situé dans une zone de haute technologie à la périphérie de Chengdu. Ce complexe de 47 étages, qui constitue un point de repère local important, abrite des locaux commerciaux, d'accueil et de conférence, ainsi que des bureaux. La salle de concert adjacente, en partie souterraine, a été conçue par le partenaire local CSWADI. La tour a un plan en forme de L au niveau du sol qui se transforme en carré vers le sommet, formant une façade balayée qui donne sur la rivière Tianfu et une ligne droite le long de l'avenue Tianfu. Les élévations courbes sont définies par des terrasses vertes jusqu'au 30e étage, tandis que le verre massif et les panneaux de céramique vitrés alternent pour former un motif en damier sur les autres façades. Le hall de 30 m de haut s'ouvre sur la rivière.

La Torre Icon Yunduan es un edificio de uso mixto de 192 m de altura situado en una zona de alta tecnología en las afueras de Chengdu. El complejo de 47 pisos, un prominente punto de referencia local, contiene locales comerciales, de hospitalidad y de conferencias, así como oficinas. La sala de conciertos adyacente, parcialmente subterránea, fue diseñada por el socio local CSWADI. La torre tiene un plano en forma de L a nivel del suelo que crece en forma de cuadrado hacia la cima, formando una fachada amplia con vistas al río Tianfu y un borde recto a lo largo de la Avenida Tianfu. Las elevaciones curvas están definidas por terrazas verdes hasta el piso 30, mientras que los paneles de vidrio sólido y cerámica vidriada se alternan para formar un patrón de cuadros en el resto de fachadas. El vestíbulo de 30 m de altura se abre hacia el río.

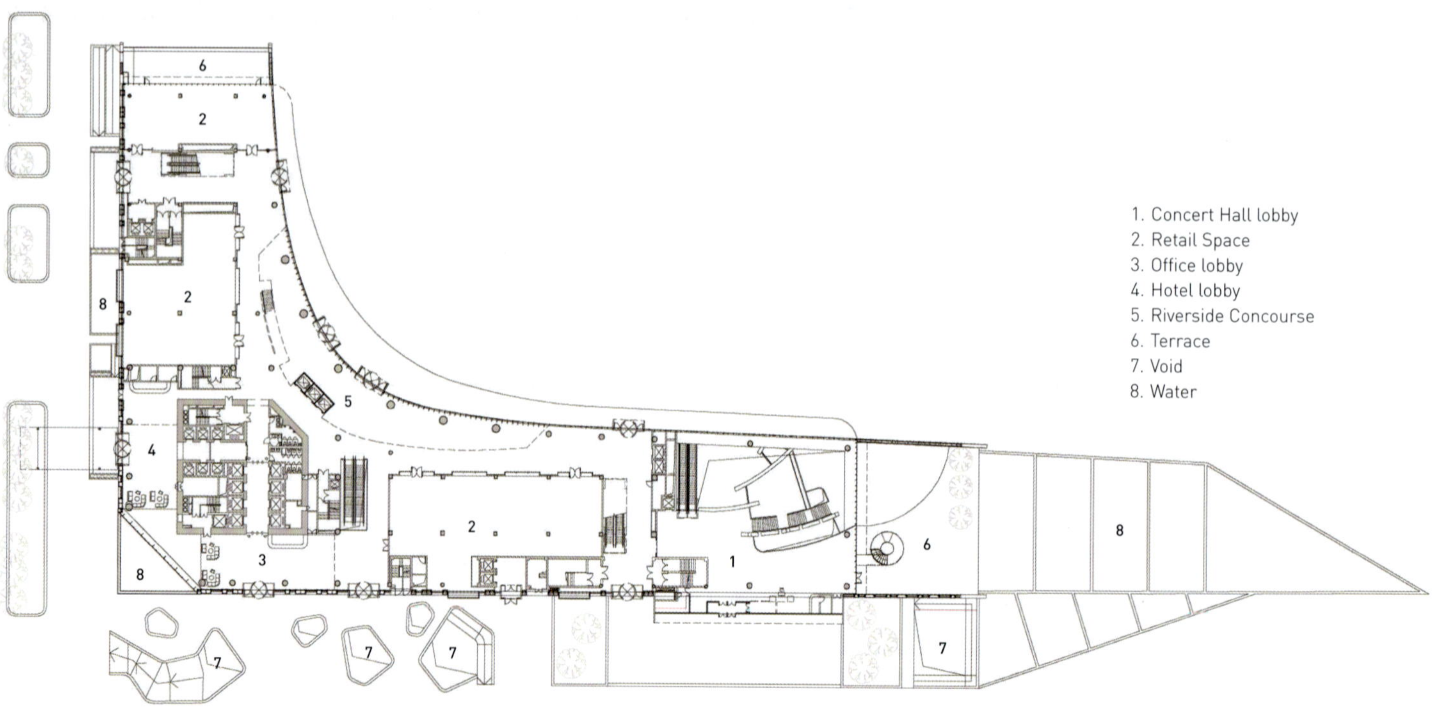
1. Concert Hall lobby
2. Retail Space
3. Office lobby
4. Hotel lobby
5. Riverside Concourse
6. Terrace
7. Void
8. Water

Floor plan

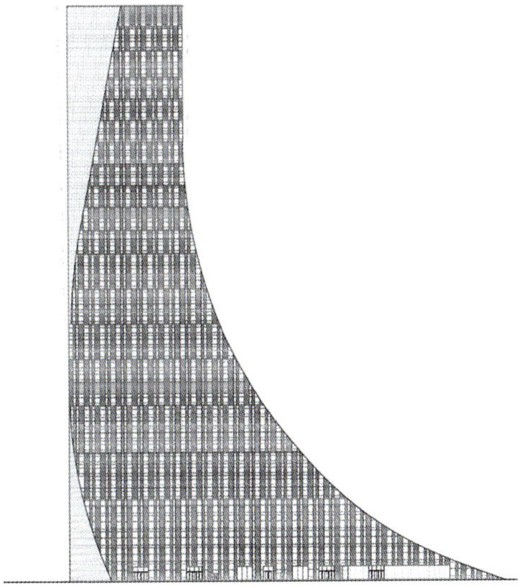

Elevation East

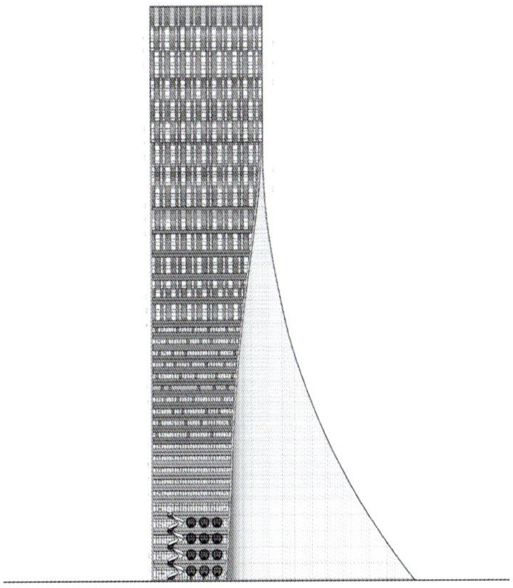

Elevation South

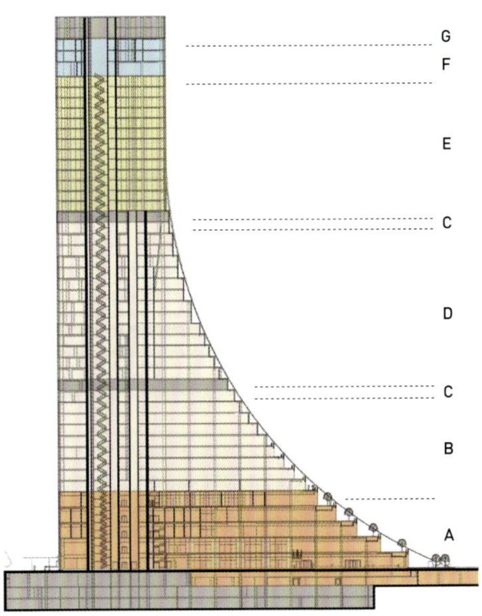


Function section diagram

A. Commercial spaces
B. Offices
C. Secure level
D. Offices
E. Apartment hotel
F. VIP Lounge, restaurant, sky bar
G. Roof, secure level, technical spaces

## STRAIT CULTURE AND ART CENTRE

Fuzhou, China
Photos: © Marc Goodwin, Virgile Simon Bertrand, Zhang Yong

Facing the Minjiang River, the Fuzhou Strait Culture and Art Centre houses an opera house, concert hall, multi-functional theatre, exhibition hall and cinema centre in five separate petal-shaped buildings. The venues are linked by a central concourse and large roof terrace, open all day to allow their flexible use. Ceramics was used throughout the complex as a functionally and aesthetically appropriate material with local historical significance. The main façades are made of ceramic louvres angled to provide shading. The artistic ceramic tile cladding of the opera and concert hall interiors was designed together with Taiwanese ceramic artist Samuel Hsuan-yu Shih according to exacting acoustic demands. Another Chinese material, bamboo, is also used for walls, flooring and detailing.

Das zum Minjiang-Fluss hin gelegene Kultur- und Kunstzentrum an der Straße von Fuzhou beherbergt in fünf separaten, blütenblattförmigen Gebäuden ein Opernhaus, einen Konzertsaal, ein multifunktionales Theater, einen Ausstellungssaal und ein Kinozentrum. Die Veranstaltungsorte sind durch eine zentrale Halle und eine große Dachterrasse miteinander verbunden, die ganztägig geöffnet sind, um eine flexible Nutzung zu ermöglichen. Im gesamten Komplex wurde Keramik als funktionell und ästhetisch angemessenes Material mit lokalhistorischer Bedeutung verwendet. Die Hauptfassaden bestehen aus Keramiklamellen, die zur Beschattung geneigt sind. Die kunstvolle Verkleidung der Opern- und Konzertsaalinnenräume mit Keramikfliesen wurde gemeinsam mit dem taiwanesischen Keramikkünstler Samuel Hsuan-yu Shih nach hohen akustischen Anforderungen gestaltet. Ein weiteres chinesisches Material, Bambus, wird ebenfalls für Wände, Bodenbeläge und Details verwendet.

Face à la rivière Minjiang, le Centre culturel et artistique du détroit de Fuzhou abrite un opéra, une salle de concert, un théâtre multifonctionnel, une salle d'exposition et un centre cinématographique dans cinq bâtiments distincts en forme de pétales. Les lieux sont reliés par un hall central et une grande terrasse sur le toit, ouverts toute la journée pour permettre une utilisation flexible. La céramique a été utilisée dans l'ensemble du complexe, considérée comme un matériau approprié d'un point de vue fonctionnel et esthétique, avec une importance historique locale. Les façades principales sont constituées de grilles de céramique inclinées pour fournir de l'ombre. Le revêtement artistique - en carreaux de céramique - des intérieurs de l'opéra et de la salle de concert a été conçu en collaboration avec l'artiste céramiste taïwanais Samuel Hsuan-yu Shih en fonction d'exigences acoustiques rigoureuses. Un autre matériau chinois, le bambou, est également utilisé pour les murs, les sols et les détails.

Frente al río Minjiang, el Centro de Cultura y Arte del Estrecho de Fuzhou alberga una ópera, una sala de conciertos, un teatro multifuncional, una sala de exposiciones y un centro de cine en cinco edificios separados en forma de pétalo. Los lugares están unidos por un vestíbulo central y una gran terraza en la azotea, abierta todo el día para permitir su uso de forma flexible. La cerámica se utilizó en todo el complejo como material funcional y estéticamente apropiado con significado histórico local. Las fachadas principales están hechas de lamas de cerámica en ángulo para proporcionar sombra. El revestimiento de cerámica artística de los interiores de la ópera y de la sala de conciertos fue diseñado junto con el artista de cerámica taiwanés Samuel Hsuan-yu Shih de acuerdo con las exigentes demandas acústicas. Otro material chino, el bambú, también se utiliza para las paredes, el suelo y los detalles.

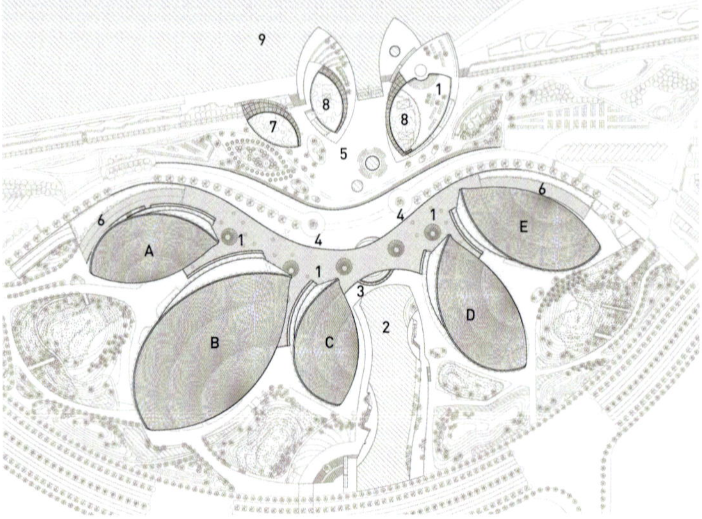


A. Multifunctional theatre
B. Grand theatre
C. Concert hall
D. Art Museum
E. Movie center

1. Public roof terrace
2. LiangCuo River
3. Spiral "EYE" stair
4. Main entrances and drop-off
5. Jasmine plaza
6. Public roof terrace ramps
7. Riverside Cafe
8. Floodgate technical spaces
9. Minjiang River

Site plan

存衣处
CLOAKROOM

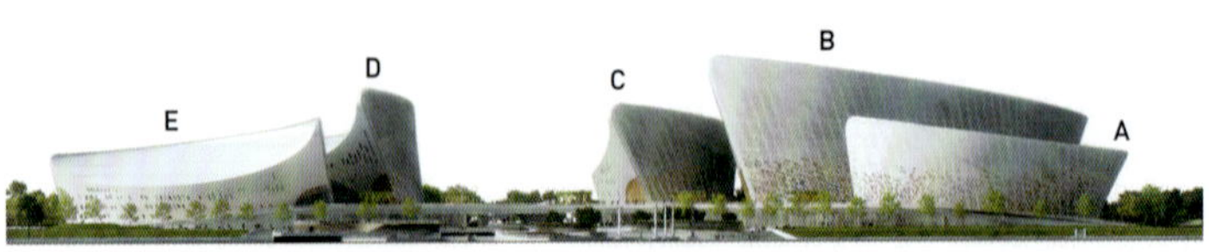


Plaza side elevation

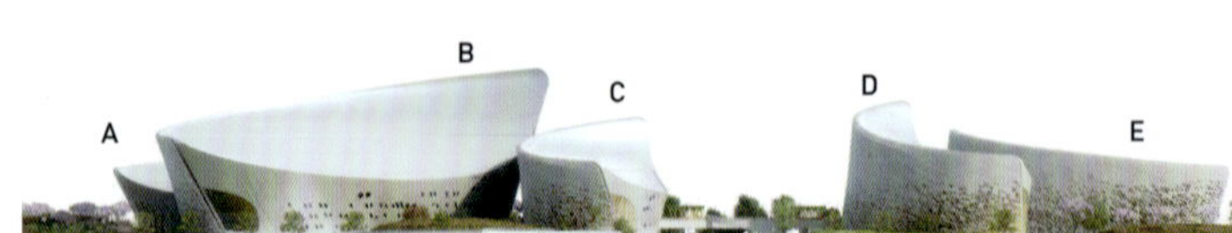


Garden side elevation

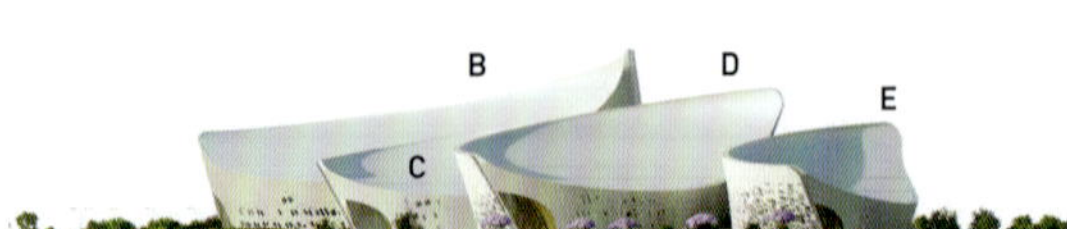


Left side elevation

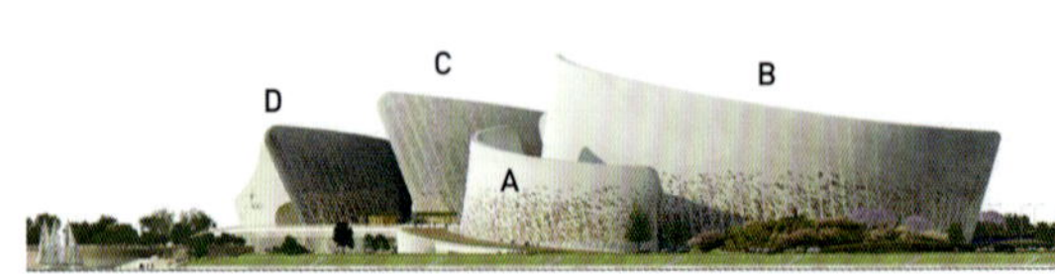


Right side elevation

A. Multipurpose hall
B. Opera h
C. Concert hall
D. Art Museum
E. Movie center

T2
ANKOMSTER
ARRIVALS
LÄNSITERMINAALI 2
VÄSTRA TERMINALEN 2
WEST TERMINAL 2
LÄHTEVÄT

## WEST TERMINAL 2

Helsinki, Finland
Photos: © Kari Palsila, Marc Goodwin

West Terminal 2 was built to meet the needs of growing ferry traffic from Helsinki West Harbour on the busy Helsinki-Tallinn route. The guiding design principle was to ensure the smooth, fast and safe transition of passengers and vehicles on and off ships and to create a landmark for the developing urban district. The terminal is compact at ground level, with a wide departure lounge raised 10 m off the ground. This allows traffic to flow under the building and minimises passengers' walking distances to and from the ships on either side. The departure lounge is a hangar-like space with a soaring timber ceiling and high glass walls opening to a view of the sea and ships. The façades and roof are of aluminium, enhancing the sculptural form of the building.

West-Terminal 2 wurde gebaut, um den Bedarf des wachsenden Fährverkehrs vom Westhafen Helsinki auf der viel befahrenen Strecke Helsinki-Tallinn zu decken. Leitgedanke des Entwurfs war es, einen reibungslosen, schnellen und sicheren Übergang von Passagieren und Fahrzeugen auf und von Schiffen zu gewährleisten und ein Wahrzeichen für den sich entwickelnden Stadtteil zu schaffen. Das Terminal ist ebenerdig kompakt und verfügt über eine breite, 10 Meter über dem Boden erhöhte Abfertigungshalle. Dies ermöglicht den Verkehrsfluss unter dem Gebäude und minimiert die Gehdistanzen der Passagiere zu und von den Schiffen auf beiden Seiten. Die Abfertigungshalle ist ein hangarähnlicher Raum mit einer aufragenden Holzdecke und hohen Glaswänden, die den Blick auf das Meer und die Schiffe freigeben. Die Fassaden und das Dach sind aus Aluminium, was die skulpturale Form des Gebäudes unterstreicht.

Le Terminal Ouest 2 a été construit pour répondre aux besoins du trafic croissant des ferries en provenance du port ouest d'Helsinki, sur la route très fréquentée Helsinki-Tallinn. Le principe directeur de la conception était d'assurer une transition douce, rapide et sûre des passagers et des véhicules à bord et en dehors des navires et de créer un point de repère pour le district urbain en développement. Le terminal est compact au niveau du sol, avec une large salle de départ surélevée de 10 m. Cela permet au trafic de passer sous le bâtiment et de réduire au minimum les distances de marche des passagers vers et depuis les navires de chaque côté. La salle d'embarquement est un espace en forme de hangar avec un plafond en bois et de hautes parois vitrées qui s'ouvrent sur la mer et les navires. Les façades et le toit sont en aluminium, ce qui renforce la forme sculpturale du bâtiment.

La Terminal 2 Oeste se construyó para satisfacer las necesidades del creciente tráfico de transbordadores del Puerto Oeste de Helsinki en la concurrida ruta Helsinki-Tallinn. El principio rector del diseño fue asegurar una transición fluida, rápida y segura de los pasajeros y vehículos dentro y fuera de los buques y crear un hito para el distrito urbano en desarrollo. La terminal es compacta a nivel del suelo, con una amplia sala de embarque elevada a 10 m. Esto permite que el tráfico fluya bajo el edificio y minimiza las distancias a pie de los pasajeros hacia y desde los buques a ambos lados. La sala de embarque es un espacio parecido a un hangar con un techo de madera elevado y altas paredes de cristal que se abren a la vista del mar y de los barcos. Las fachadas y el techo son de aluminio, lo que realza la forma escultórica del edificio.

Resell+Nicca is a Norwegian architecture firm based in Oslo. The office is working towards an inclusive and locally adapted architecture that respects and at the same time challenge its surroundings. A key element behind their work is a belief that first hand knowledge about historical, geographical, cultural and environmental conditions is essential in order to create meaningful architecture that relates to its surroundings. This often results in a modern twist on traditional Scandinavian building practice. Sustainable and environmentally friendly solutions that take nature into account is a fundamental part of the work, and an important premise for all concepts.

Resell+Nicca ist ein norwegisches Architekturbüro mit Sitz in Oslo. Das Büro arbeitet an einer integrativen und lokal angepassten Architektur, die ihre Umgebung respektiert und gleichzeitig herausfordert. Ein Schlüsselelement hinter ihrer Arbeit ist die Überzeugung, dass Wissen aus erster Hand über historische, geographische, kulturelle und Umweltbedingungen unerlässlich ist, um sinnvolle Architektur zu schaffen, die sich auf ihre Umgebung bezieht. Dies führt oft zu einer modernen Wendung in der traditionellen skandinavischen Baupraxis. Nachhaltige und umweltfreundliche Lösungen, die die Natur berücksichtigen, sind ein grundlegender Bestandteil der Arbeit und eine wichtige Voraussetzung für alle Konzepte.

# RESELL+NICCA

Resell+Nicca est un cabinet d'architecture norvégien basé à Oslo. Le travail du bureau s'articule autour d'une architecture inclusive et adaptée localement qui respecte et en même temps remet en question son environnement. Un élément clé de leur travail est la conviction qu'une connaissance de première main des conditions historiques, géographiques, culturelles et environnementales est essentielle pour créer une architecture significative en relation avec son environnement. Cela se traduit souvent par un changement de la pratique traditionnelle scandinave en matière de construction. Des solutions durables et écologiques qui tiennent compte de la nature constituent une partie fondamentale du travail et une prémisse importante pour tous les concepts.

Resell+Nicca es un estudio de arquitectura noruego con sede en Oslo. La oficina está trabajando en una arquitectura inclusiva y adaptada localmente que respete y al mismo tiempo desafíe su entorno. Un elemento clave detrás de su trabajo es la creencia de que el conocimiento de primera mano sobre las condiciones históricas, geográficas, culturales y ambientales es esencial para crear una arquitectura significativa que se relacione con su entorno. Esto a menudo da lugar a un giro moderno en la práctica tradicional de la construcción escandinava. Las soluciones sostenibles y respetuosas con el medio ambiente que tienen en cuenta la naturaleza son una parte fundamental del trabajo y una premisa importante para abordar todos los proyectos.

VILLA VOID

## CABIN RYFYLKE

Ryfylket, Norway
Photos: © Olav Resell

The cabin is situated in a gently sloping terrain on a small and lush island in the western part of Norway. Its enclosing form creates a protected and sunny outdoor space with views over the *fjord* to the south. Common spaces caters onto this side, while secondary rooms are located on the opposite side facing the forest. A dark, diamond shaped Norwegian slate stone is used on the façade, with format sizes pushed towards the maximum of what is possible to extract. Ash is chosen as the main interior material, and used as panelling on ceiling and walls, plywood on walls and solid furnishings, and as solid wood flooring on the upper level. A key element in the cabin is the concrete structure at the center. It is cast with horizontal panelling formwork, and acts as an important heat storage element.

Die Hütte liegt in einem sanft abfallenden Gelände auf einer kleinen, üppig bewachsenen Insel im westlichen Teil Norwegens. Ihre umschließende Form schafft einen geschützten und sonnigen Außenraum mit Blick über den Fjord nach Süden. Auf dieser Seite befinden sich die Gemeinschaftsräume, während die Nebenräume auf der gegenüberliegenden, dem Wald zugewandten Seite liegen. An der Fassade wird ein dunkler, rautenförmiger norwegischer Schieferstein verwendet, wobei die Formatgrößen auf das Maximum dessen, was gewonnen werden kann, ausgerichtet sind. Als Hauptmaterial für den Innenraum wurde Esche gewählt, die als Vertäfelung an Decke und Wänden, als Sperrholz an Wänden und massiven Einrichtungsgegenständen sowie als Massivholzboden im oberen Stockwerk verwendet wird. Ein Schlüsselelement in der Hütte ist die Betonstruktur in der Mitte. Sie ist mit horizontalen Schalungstafeln gegossen und dient als wichtiges Wärmespeicherelement.

La cabane est située dans un terrain en pente douce sur une petite île luxuriante dans la partie occidentale de la Norvège. Sa forme enveloppante crée un espace extérieur protégé et ensoleillé avec des vues sur le fjord au sud. Les espaces communs se trouvent de ce côté, tandis que les pièces secondaires sont situées sur le côté opposé, face à la forêt. Une pierre d'ardoise norvégienne sombre en forme de diamant est utilisée sur la façade, les formats étant poussés au maximum de ce qu'il est possible d'extraire. Le frêne est choisi comme principal matériau intérieur et utilisé comme lambris au plafond et sur les murs, comme contreplaqué sur les murs et le mobilier solide et comme plancher en bois massif au niveau supérieur. La structure en béton au centre est un élément clé de la cabine. Elle est coulée avec un coffrage de lambris horizontal et agit comme un élément important de stockage de la chaleur.

La cabaña está situada en un terreno de suave pendiente en una pequeña y exuberante isla en la parte occidental de Noruega. Su forma envolvente crea un espacio exterior protegido y soleado con vistas al fiordo del sur. Los espacios comunes se encuentran en este lado, mientras que las habitaciones secundarias se encuentran en el lado opuesto, frente al bosque. En la fachada se utiliza una piedra oscura de pizarra noruega en forma de diamante. Se elige el fresno como principal material en el interior, y se utiliza como revestimiento en el techo y las paredes. La madera contrachapada se ha utilizado también en las paredes y el mobiliario. El suelo del nivel superior es madera maciza. Un elemento esencial de la cabaña es la estructura central de hormigón, fundida con encofrado de paneles horizontales, y que actúa como importante elemento de almacenamiento de calor.

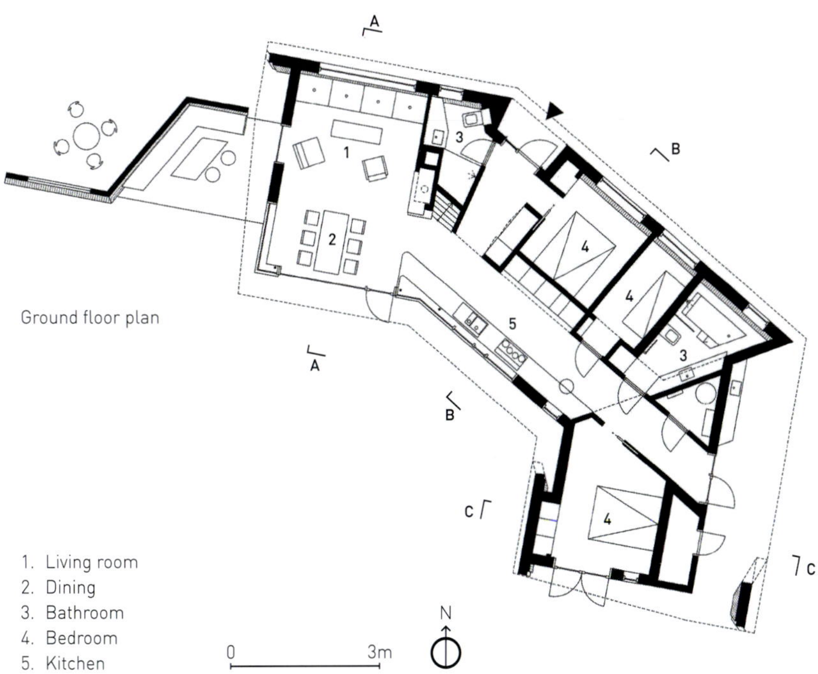


Ground floor plan

1. Living room
2. Dining
3. Bathroom
4. Bedroom
5. Kitchen

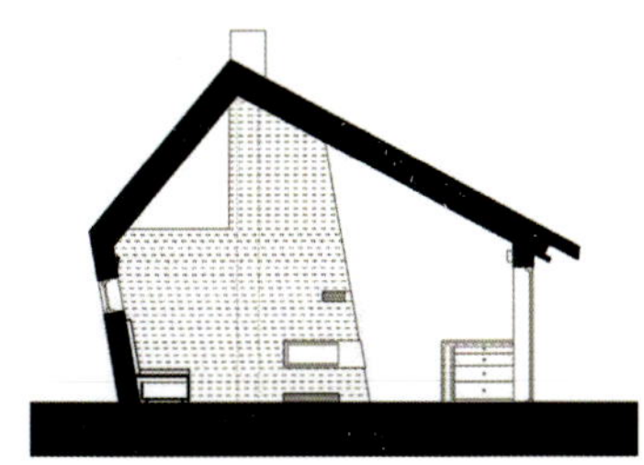

Section A-A

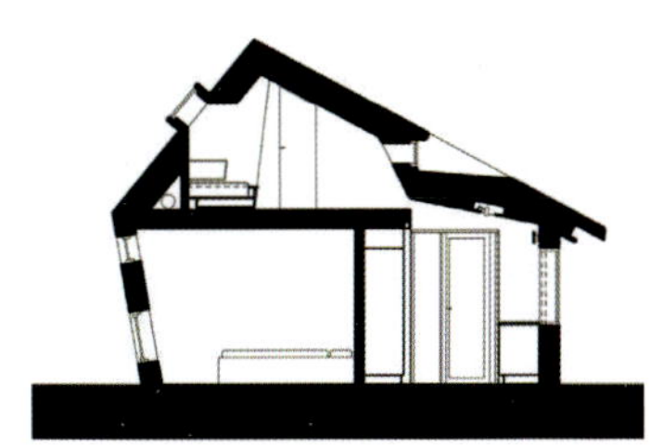

Section B-B

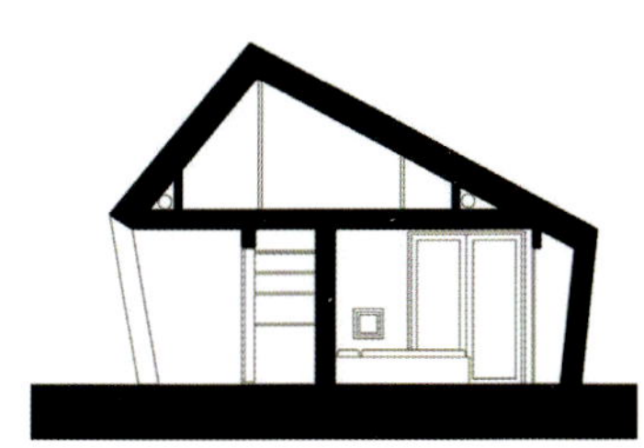

Section C-C

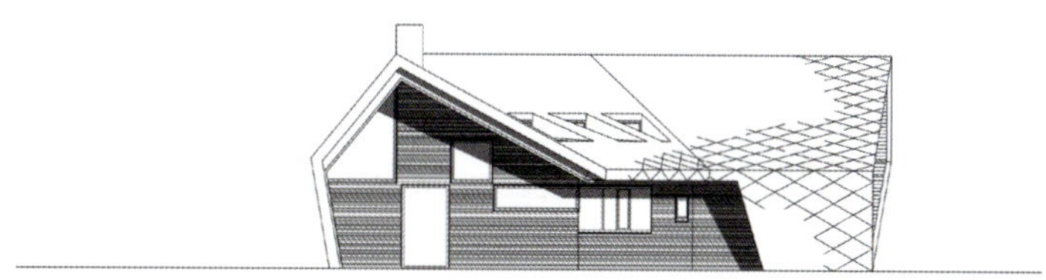

West elevation

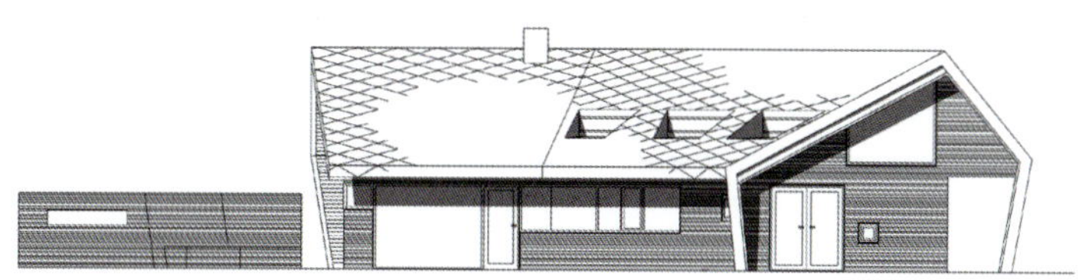

South elevation

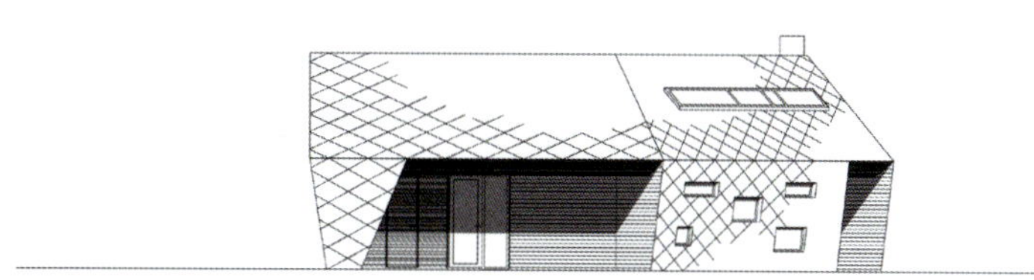

East elevation

0 3m

## VILLA VOID

Viken, Norway
Photos: © Olav Resell

Sitting on sloping terrain, the house is surrounded by tall pine trees. It has an elongated main volume inspired by other houses in the area, from which parts has been subtracted to meet functional needs. The materiality underlines this concept, with the basic shape given a precise surface enhancing its sculptural qualities, and the recessed parts held in a warmer material with more visual depth. The interior is characterized by a longitudinal main space containing living room, kitchen and dining room. These spaces are visually connected, but sit on different levels, with each one corresponding to the outside terrain. A narrow void spans a large portion of the buildings length, providing visual contact between levels, and bringing daylight down onto the back wall of the main space.

Das Haus steht auf abschüssigem Gelände und ist von hohen Pinienbäumen umgeben. Es hat ein langgestrecktes Hauptvolumen, das von anderen Häusern in der Gegend inspiriert ist und von dem Teile abgetrennt wurden, um funktionellen Bedürfnissen gerecht zu werden. Die Materialität unterstreicht dieses Konzept, wobei die Grundform eine präzise Oberfläche erhält, die ihre skulpturalen Qualitäten verstärkt, und die zurückgesetzten Teile in einem wärmeren Material mit mehr visueller Tiefe gehalten sind. Das Innere ist durch einen länglichen Hauptraum gekennzeichnet, der Wohnzimmer, Küche und Esszimmer enthält. Diese Räume sind visuell miteinander verbunden, befinden sich aber auf verschiedenen Ebenen, die jeweils dem Außengelände entsprechen. Ein schmaler Hohlraum überspannt einen großen Teil der Gebäudelänge, bietet Sichtkontakt zwischen den Ebenen und bringt Tageslicht auf die Rückwand des Hauptraumes.

Située sur un terrain en pente, la maison est entourée de grands pins. Elle possède un volume principal allongé inspiré des autres maisons de la région, dont certaines parties ont été soustraites pour répondre à des besoins fonctionnels. La matérialité souligne ce concept, la forme de base étant dotée d'une surface précise qui renforce ses qualités sculpturales et les parties en retrait étant maintenues dans un matériau plus chaud avec plus de profondeur visuelle. L'intérieur est caractérisé par un espace principal longitudinal contenant le salon, la cuisine et la salle à manger. Ces espaces sont visuellement reliés, mais se situent à des niveaux différents, chacun correspondant au terrain extérieur. Un vide étroit s'étend sur une grande partie de la longueur des bâtiments, assurant un contact visuel entre les niveaux et faisant descendre la lumière du jour sur le mur arrière de l'espace principal.

Asentada en un terreno inclinado, la casa está rodeada de altos pinos. Tiene un volumen principal alargado inspirado en otras casas de la zona, del que se han sustraído partes para satisfacer las necesidades funcionales. La materialidad subraya este concepto, con la forma básica a la que se da una superficie precisa que realza sus cualidades escultóricas, y las partes empotradas sostenidas en un material más cálido con más profundidad visual. El interior se caracteriza por un espacio principal longitudinal que contiene la sala de estar, la cocina y el comedor. Estos espacios están visualmente conectados, pero se sitúan en diferentes niveles, relacionado cada uno de ellos al terreno exterior. Un estrecho vacío abarca una gran parte de la longitud de los edificios, proporcionando contacto visual entre los niveles y llevando la luz natural a la pared trasera del espacio principal.

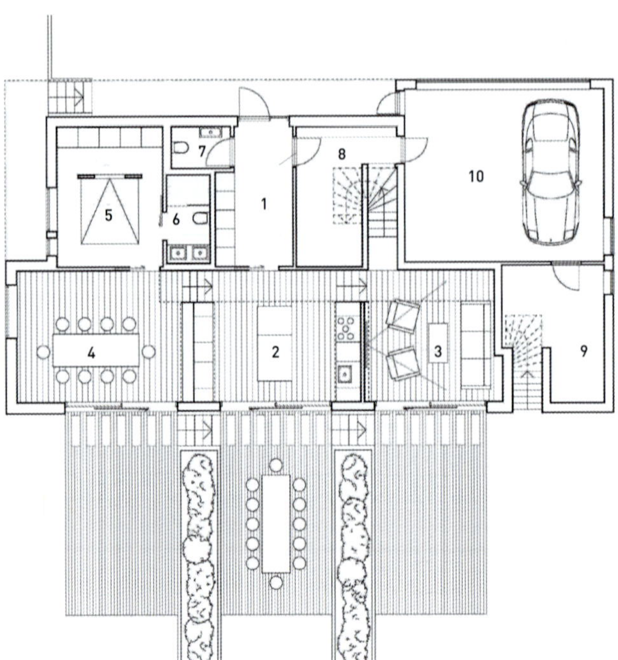

Ground floor plan

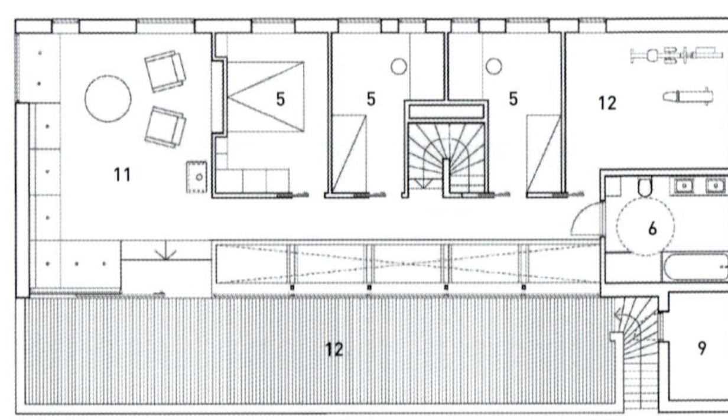

First floor plan

1. Hallway
2. Kitchen
3. Living room
4. Dining room
5. Bedroom
6. Bathroom
7. Toilet
8. Techinical room
9. Storage
10. Garage
11. Family room
12. Terrace

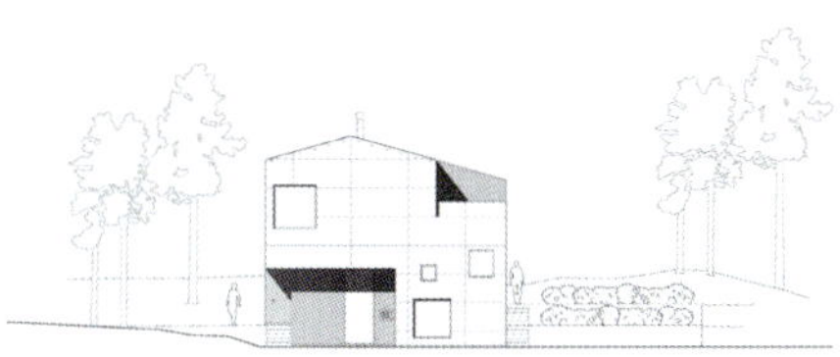

North elevation

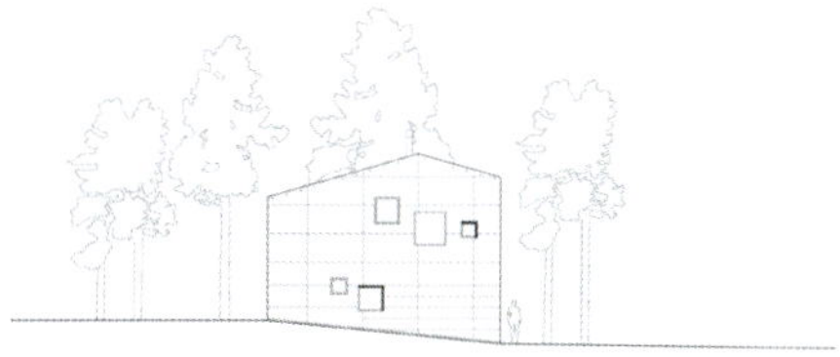

South elevation

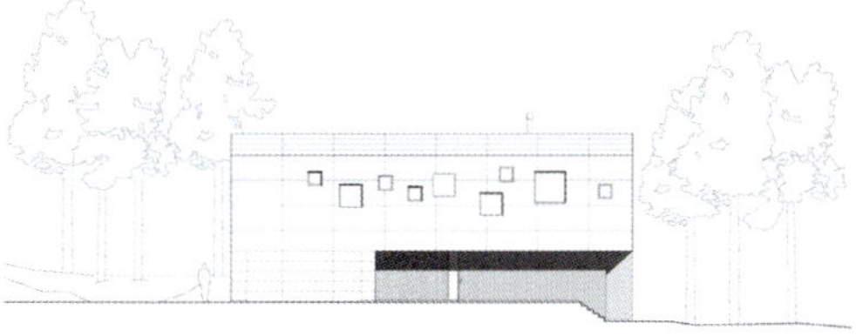

East elevation

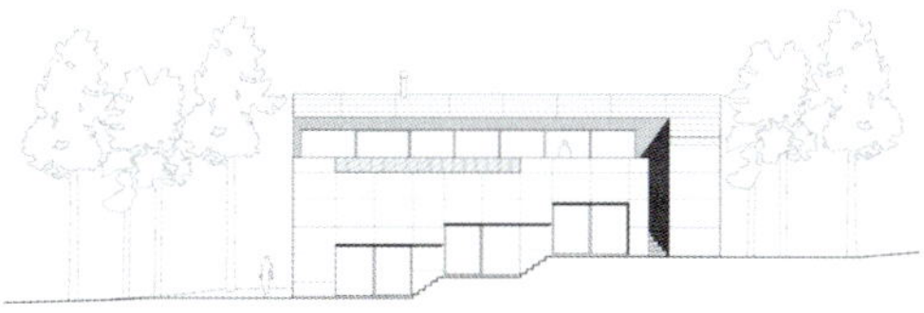

West elevation

Stinessen is committed to developing projects that are conscious of our surroundings and the people inhabiting the spaces we create. Interest, respect and curiosity are keywords to our processes. The studio provides a full range of services from architecture to interior and furniture design. We deliver tailor-made projects and products through a close interaction and dedicated service to our clients.

Stinessen setzt sich dafür ein, Projekte zu entwickeln, die sich unserer Umgebung und der Menschen, die die von uns geschaffenen Räume bewohnen, bewusst sind. Interesse, Respekt und Neugier sind Schlüsselbegriffe für unsere Prozesse. Das Atelier bietet eine umfassende Palette von Dienstleistungen von der Architektur bis zum Innen- und Möbeldesign. Wir liefern maßgeschneiderte Projekte und Produkte durch eine enge Interaktion und engagierten Service für unsere Kunden.

# STINESSEN ARKITEKTUR

Stinessen s'engage à développer des projets qui sont conscients de notre environnement et des personnes qui habitent les espaces que nous créons. L'intérêt, le respect et la curiosité sont les mots clés de nos processus. Le studio offre une gamme complète de services allant de l'architecture au design d'intérieur et de mobilier. Nous livrons des projets et des produits sur mesure grâce à une interaction étroite et un service dédié à nos clients.

Stinessen se compromete a desarrollar proyectos que sean conscientes con el entorno y de las personas que habitan los espacios que creamos. El interés, el respeto y la curiosidad son palabras clave en nuestros procesos. El estudio ofrece una gama completa de servicios desde la arquitectura hasta el diseño de interiores y mobiliario. Entregamos proyectos y productos a medida a través de una estrecha interacción y un servicio dedicado a nuestros clientes.

MANSHAUSEN

EFJORD

MALANGEN

NARVIK TOP STATION

# MANSHAUSEN

Steigen Archipelago, Norway
Photos: © Kjell Ove Storvik, Steve King, Siggen Stinessen

Manshausen Island is situated in the Steigen Archipelago off the coast of northern Norway and is home to the world´s largest population of sea eagles. The Island´s position between majestic mountains and the Barents Sea is in itself the inspiration for the design.
The resort is organized with guestrooms as individual cabins placed at the top of the rocky formations of the Island, where the positioning in the landscape ensures an immersive, yet private, view to the majestic nature and the elements outside. The shelter design endeavours to make a minimum environmental impact with minimum footprint and the use of cross laminated timber construction. The old farmhouse was renovated and converted to restaurant and library. A sauna was made in the natural pond using left over materials.

Die Insel Manshausen liegt im Steigen-Archipel vor der Küste Nordnorwegens und beheimatet die größte Seeadlerpopulation der Welt. Die Lage der Insel zwischen majestätischen Bergen und der Barentssee ist an sich schon die Inspiration für das Design.
Das Resort ist mit Gästezimmern als Einzelkabinen organisiert, die auf der Spitze der Felsformationen der Insel platziert sind, wo die Positionierung in der Landschaft einen eindringlichen, aber dennoch privaten Blick auf die majestätische Natur und die Elemente draußen gewährleistet. Bei der Gestaltung der Unterkünfte wird versucht, die Umwelt so wenig wie möglich zu belasten, mit minimalem Platzbedarf und dem Einsatz von Brettsperrholzkonstruktionen. Das alte Bauernhaus wurde renoviert und zu einem Restaurant und einer Bibliothek umgebaut. Im Naturteich wurde eine Sauna aus Materialresten errichtet.

L'île de Manshausen est située dans l'archipel de Steigen, au large des côtes du nord de la Norvège et abrite la plus grande population d'aigles de mer du monde. La position de l'île, entre des montagnes majestueuses et la mer de Barents, est une véritable source d'inspiration pour le projet.
La station est organisée en chambres d'hôtes sous forme de cabines individuelles placées au sommet des formations rocheuses de l'île, où le positionnement dans le paysage assure une vue immersive, mais privée, sur la nature majestueuse et les éléments extérieurs. La conception de l'abri s'efforce d'avoir un impact minimal sur l'environnement avec une empreinte minimale et l'utilisation de constructions en bois lamellé croisé. L'ancienne ferme a été rénovée et transformée en restaurant et en bibliothèque. Un sauna a été réalisé dans l'étang naturel en utilisant des restes de matériaux.

La isla de Manshausen está situada en el archipiélago Steigen, frente a la costa del norte de Noruega, y alberga la mayor población mundial de gaviotas. La posición de la isla entre las majestuosas montañas y el mar de Barents fue en sí misma la inspiración para el diseño.
El complejo está organizado con habitaciones de huéspedes como cabañas individuales situadas en la cima de las formaciones rocosas de la isla, donde la ubicación en el paisaje asegura una vista amplia, aunque privada, de la majestuosa naturaleza y el exterior. En el diseño de las cabañas se procura que el impacto ambiental sea mínimo utilizando una construcción de madera laminada en cruz. La antigua granja fue renovada y convertida en restaurante y biblioteca. Se hizo una sauna en el estanque natural usando los materiales sobrantes.

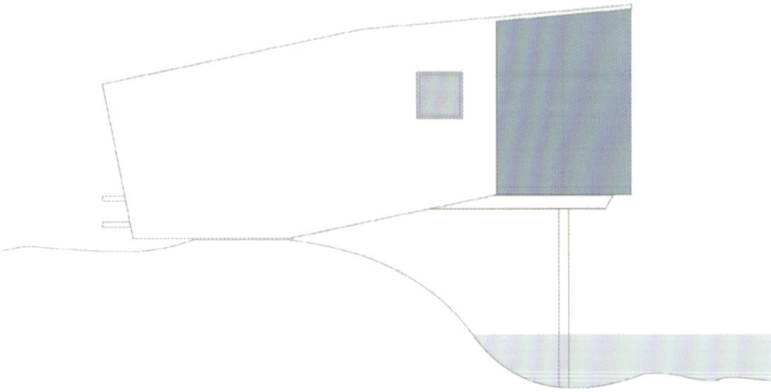

Facade elevation

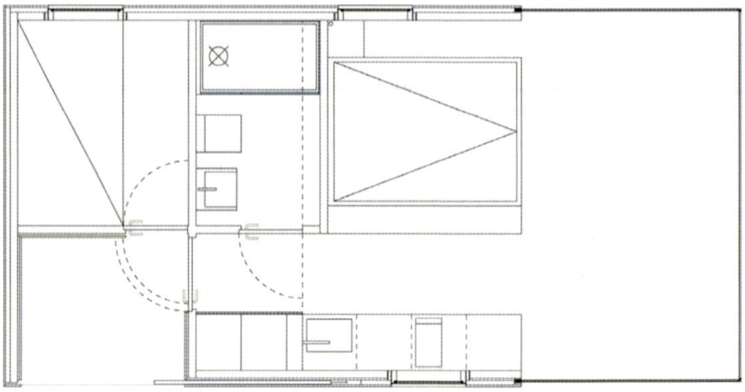

Floor plan

## EFJORD

Ofoten fiord, Norway
Photos: © Snorre Stinessen, Steve King

Efjord is a branch off the Ofoten fiord in northern Norway. The client wanted a retreat that focused on the panoramic views of the site, but which also transported them to a feeling of isolation and total privacy, away from hectic working days in the city. The conceptual layout opens and closes the building in different directions, where the eastern part of the cabin closes towards some neighbouring buildings and opens towards a ridge and the terrain on the other side. The opposite directions are sought at the front end of the cabin, opening up to the magnificent views towards the dramatic mountains and the fiord to the west.
The two volumes are slightly offset to provide for sheltered outdoor areas and views towards the fiord also from the rear volume.

Der Efjord ist ein Seitenarm des Ofotenfjords in Nordnorwegen. Der Bauherr wünschte sich einen Rückzugsort, der sich auf die Panoramablicke des Ortes konzentriert, aber auch ein Gefühl der Isolation und der totalen Privatsphäre vermittelt, fernab von hektischen Arbeitstagen in der Stadt. Das konzeptionelle Layout öffnet und schließt das Gebäude in verschiedene Richtungen, wobei sich der östliche Teil der Hütte zu einigen Nachbargebäuden hin schließt und sich zu einem Bergrücken und dem Gelände auf der anderen Seite hin öffnet. Am vorderen Ende der Hütte werden die entgegengesetzten Richtungen gesucht, die sich zu den herrlichen Aussichten auf die dramatischen Berge und den Fjord im Westen hin öffnen.
Die beiden Volumina sind leicht versetzt, um geschützte Außenbereiche und Ausblicke auf den Fjord auch vom hinteren Volumen aus zu ermöglichen.

L'Efjord est une branche du fjord d'Ofoten, dans le nord de la Norvège. Le client souhaitait une retraite axée sur les vues panoramiques du site, mais qui procure également un sentiment d'isolement et d'intimité totale, loin des journées de travail trépidantes de la ville. Le plan conceptuel ouvre et ferme le bâtiment dans différentes directions. La partie orientale de la cabane se ferme vers certains bâtiments voisins et s'ouvre vers une crête et le terrain de l'autre côté. Les directions opposées sont recherchées à l'extrémité avant de la cabane, s'ouvrant sur les vues magnifiques vers les montagnes spectaculaires et le fjord à l'ouest.
Les deux volumes sont légèrement décalés pour permettre d'abriter les espaces extérieurs et d'offrir des vues vers le fjord également depuis le volume arrière.

Efjord es una rama del fiordo de Ofoten en el norte de Noruega. El cliente deseaba un retiro que se centrara en las vistas panorámicas del lugar, pero que también los transportara a una sensación de aislamiento y total privacidad, lejos de los agitados días de trabajo en la ciudad. La disposición conceptual abre y cierra el edificio en diferentes direcciones, donde la parte oriental de la cabaña se cierra hacia algunos edificios vecinos y se abre hacia una cresta y el terreno vecino. En el extremo delantero de la cabaña se buscan las direcciones opuestas, abriéndose a las magníficas vistas hacia las dramáticas montañas y el fiordo al oeste.
Los dos volúmenes están ligeramente compensados para proporcionar zonas exteriores protegidas y vistas hacia el fiordo incluso desde el volumen trasero.

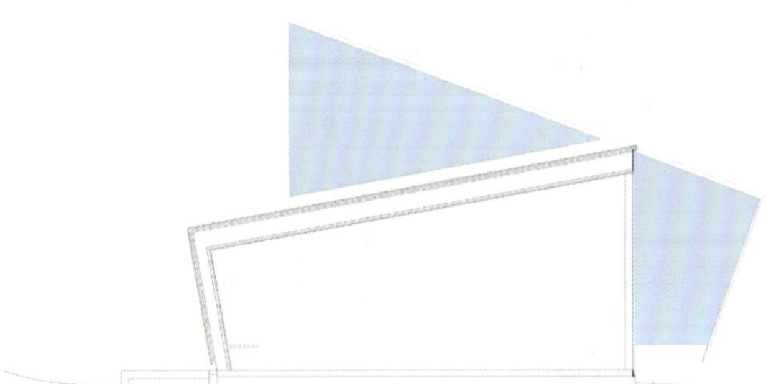

Section

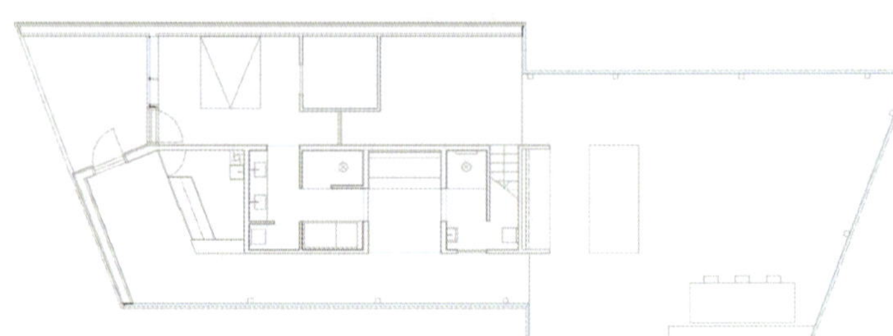

Floor plan

## MALANGEN

Mortenhals, Tromsø, Norway
Photos: © Stefano Lodola, Terje Arntsen, Steve King

The clients, a family with small children, wanted room for the larger family and friends. The conceptual layout was conceived as several individual volumes connected via in-between spaces and a central winter garden placed on a natural shelf in the land. The organisation provides both privacy and room for several activities at the same time. The central winter garden, with fireplace and outdoor kitchen, function as the entrance to the building. From here the retreat opens up to the natural clearing in the forest, entering into either the main building or the annex. Each group of rooms are conceived as separate volumes to achieve an additional layer of privacy, but also to emphasize the transition between spaces and activities while telling a story of everyday journeys.

Die Kunden, eine Familie mit kleinen Kindern, wollten Platz für die größere Familie und Freunde. Das konzeptionelle Layout wurde als mehrere Einzelvolumina konzipiert, die durch Zwischenräume und einen zentralen Wintergarten auf einer natürlichen Anhöhe im Land verbunden sind. Die Organisation bietet sowohl Privatsphäre als auch Raum für mehrere Aktivitäten zur gleichen Zeit. Der zentrale Wintergarten mit Kamin und Außenküche fungiert als Eingang zum Gebäude. Von hier aus öffnet sich der Rückzugsraum zur natürlichen Lichtung im Wald und führt entweder in das Hauptgebäude oder in den Anbau. Jede Raumgruppe ist als separates Volumen konzipiert, um eine zusätzliche Ebene der Privatsphäre zu erreichen, aber auch, um den Übergang zwischen Räumen und Aktivitäten zu betonen und gleichzeitig eine Geschichte der alltäglichen Wege zu erzählen.

Les clients - une famille avec de jeunes enfants - voulaient de la place pour la grande famille et les amis. L'agencement conceptuel a été conçu en plusieurs volumes individuels reliés par des espaces intermédiaires et un jardin d'hiver central, placé sur une étagère naturelle dans le terrain. L'organisation offre à la fois de l'intimité et de la place pour plusieurs activités en même temps. Le jardin d'hiver central, avec sa cheminée et sa cuisine extérieure, sert d'entrée au bâtiment. De là, la retraite s'ouvre sur la clairière naturelle de la forêt, en entrant soit dans le bâtiment principal, soit dans l'annexe. Chaque groupe de pièces est conçu comme un volume séparé pour obtenir une couche supplémentaire d'intimité, mais aussi pour souligner la transition entre les espaces et les activités tout en racontant une histoire de voyages quotidiens.

Los clientes, una familia con niños pequeños, necesitaban más espacio. La disposición conceptual fue concebida como varios volúmenes individuales conectados a través de espacios intermedios y un jardín de invierno central colocado en un estante natural en el terreno. La organización proporciona tanto privacidad como espacio para varias actividades al mismo tiempo. El jardín de invierno, con chimenea y cocina exterior, funciona como entrada al edificio. Desde aquí el refugio se abre al claro natural del bosque, entrando en el edificio principal o en el anexo. Cada grupo de habitaciones se concibe como volúmenes separados para lograr privacidad adicional, pero también para enfatizar la transición entre los espacios y actividades.

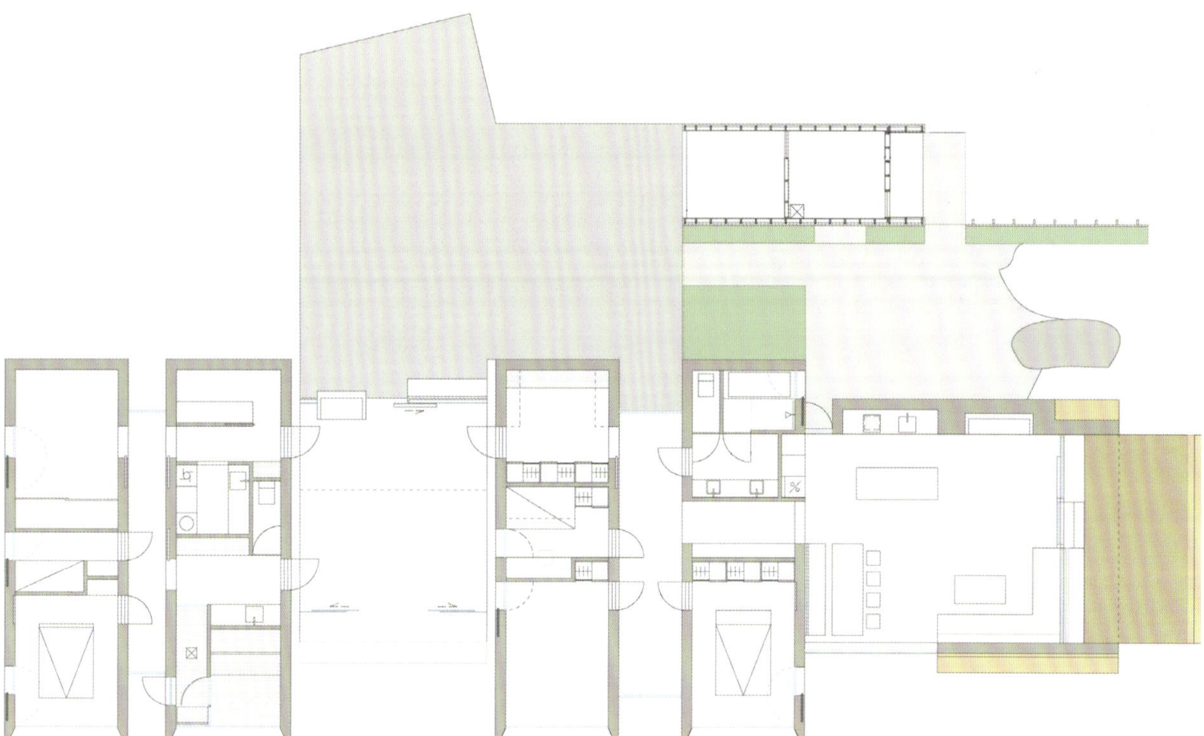

Plan

## NARVIK TOP STATION

Narvik, Norway
Photos: © Rune Dahl

The Narvik station is the mountain top station for the new gondola on the top point of the slopes in Narvikfjellet, a ski resort directly above the Narvik city centre characterised by one of the steepest height to length ratios ( from 1000 m above sea level down to the sea ), offering some amazing scenery with the view out the Ofoten fiord to the World Heritage area of Lofoten. The design seeks to express a connection between the city's industrial history and the surrounding dramatic nature. Narvik is a shipping port for the rail and ship transportation of iron ore, represented in the black metal cladding and shaping of the shelter station, positioned on the top slopes of the majestic mountain.

Die Station Narvik ist die Bergstation der neuen Gondelbahn auf dem höchsten Punkt der Pisten im Narvikfjellet, einem Skigebiet direkt oberhalb des Stadtzentrums von Narvik, das sich durch eines der steilsten Höhen-Längen-Verhältnisse auszeichnet (von 1000 m über dem Meeresspiegel bis hinunter zum Meer) und mit dem Blick über den Ofotenfjord auf das Weltkulturerbegebiet der Lofoten eine atemberaubende Landschaft bietet. Der Entwurf versucht, eine Verbindung zwischen der Industriegeschichte der Stadt und der sie umgebenden dramatischen Natur auszudrücken. Narvik ist ein Verschiffungshafen für den Eisenbahn- und Schiffstransport von Eisenerz, was sich in der schwarzen Metallverkleidung und der Formgebung der Schutzstation widerspiegelt, die sich an den oberen Hängen des majestätischen Berges befindet.

La station de Narvik est la station d'altitude de la nouvelle télécabine au sommet des pistes de Narvikfjellet, une station de ski située directement au-dessus du centre ville de Narvik. Elle est caractérisée par l'un des rapports hauteur/longueur les plus élevés (de 1000 m d'altitude à la mer), offrant des paysages étonnants avec vue sur le fjord d'Ofoten et la zone des Lofoten, inscrite au patrimoine mondial. La conception cherche à exprimer un lien entre l'histoire industrielle de la ville et la nature dramatique environnante. Narvik est un port maritime pour le transport ferroviaire et maritime de minerai de fer, caractérisé par un revêtement métallique noir et la forme de la station d'accueil, située sur les pentes supérieures de la majestueuse montagne.

La estación de Narvik es la estación de montaña en el punto más alto de las pistas de Narvikfjellet, una estación de esquí situada directamente sobre el centro de la ciudad de Narvik, caracterizada por una de las mayores desniveles de altura y longitud (desde los 1000 m sobre el nivel del mar hasta el mar), y que ofrece un paisaje asombroso con vistas al fiordo de Ofoten y a la zona de Lofoten, declarada Patrimonio de la Humanidad. El diseño busca expresar una conexión entre la historia industrial de la ciudad y la naturaleza impactante de los alrededores. Narvik, un puerto de embarque para el transporte por ferrocarril y por barco de mineral de hierro, está representado en el revestimiento de metal negro y la forma de la estación del refugio, situada en las laderas superiores de la majestuosa montaña.

Thorbjörn Andersson has practiced landscape architecture since 1981, having studied landscape architecture, architecture, and art history in Sweden and the United States. He is probably most known for his work in the urban planning and design of public spaces. A selection of these projects, which have received awards and international attention, were published in the book Platser/Places. Teaching experience includes visiting professorships at the GSD at the Harvard University, Cambridge; the EPFL in Lausanne, Switzerland; and the University of Illinois in Urbana-Champaign.
For his contribution to the field of landscape architecture, in 2009 Thorbjörn Andersson was awarded the Prince Eugene Medal from His Majesty, the King of Sweden.

Thorbjörn Andersson ist seit 1981 als Landschaftsarchitekt tätig und hat Landschaftsarchitektur, Architektur und Kunstgeschichte in Schweden und den Vereinigten Staaten studiert. Am bekanntesten ist er wohl für seine Arbeit in der Stadtplanung und Gestaltung öffentlicher Räume. Eine Auswahl dieser preisgekrönten und international beachteten Projekte wurde in dem Buch Platser/Places veröffentlicht. Seine Lehrerfahrung umfasst Gastprofessuren am GSD an der Harvard University, Cambridge, an der EPFL in Lausanne, Schweiz, und an der University of Illinois in Urbana-Champaign.
Für seinen Beitrag auf dem Gebiet der Landschaftsarchitektur wurde Thorbjörn Andersson 2009 von Seiner Majestät, dem König von Schweden, mit der Prinz-Eugen-Medaille ausgezeichnet.

# THORBJÖRN ANDERSSON WITH SWECO ARCHITECTS

Thorbjörn Andersson pratique l'architecture du paysage depuis 1981. Il a étudié l'architecture du paysage, l'architecture et l'histoire de l'art en Suède et aux États-Unis. Il est probablement plus connu pour son travail dans le domaine de l'urbanisme et de la conception d'espaces publics. Une sélection de ses projets, qui ont reçu des prix et une attention internationale, a été publiée dans le livre Platser/Places. Il a enseigné à l'Université de Harvard à Cambridge, à l'EPFL à Lausanne, en Suisse et à l'Université de l'Illinois à Urbana-Champaign.
Thorbjörn Andersson a reçu en 2009 la médaille du Prince Eugène de Sa Majesté, le Roi de Suède, pour sa contribution au domaine de l'architecture du paysage.

Thorbjörn Andersson ha practicado la arquitectura paisajista desde 1981, habiendo estudiado paisajismo, arquitectura e historia del arte en Suecia y en los Estados Unidos. Es probablemente más conocido por su trabajo en la planificación urbana y el diseño de espacios públicos. Una selección de estos proyectos, que han recibido premios y atención internacional, fueron publicados en el libro Platser/Places. Su experiencia docente incluye la docencia como profesor visitante en el GSD de la Universidad de Harvard, Cambridge, la EPFL en Lausana, Suiza y la Universidad de Illinois en Urbana-Champaign.
Por su contribución al campo de la arquitectura paisajista, en 2009 Thorbjörn Andersson fue galardonado con la Medalla del Príncipe Eugenio de

RINKEBY PANORAMA TERRACE

TOWN HALL SQUARE

## RINKEBY PANORAMA TERRACE

Stockholm, Sweden
Photos: © Åke E:son Lindman

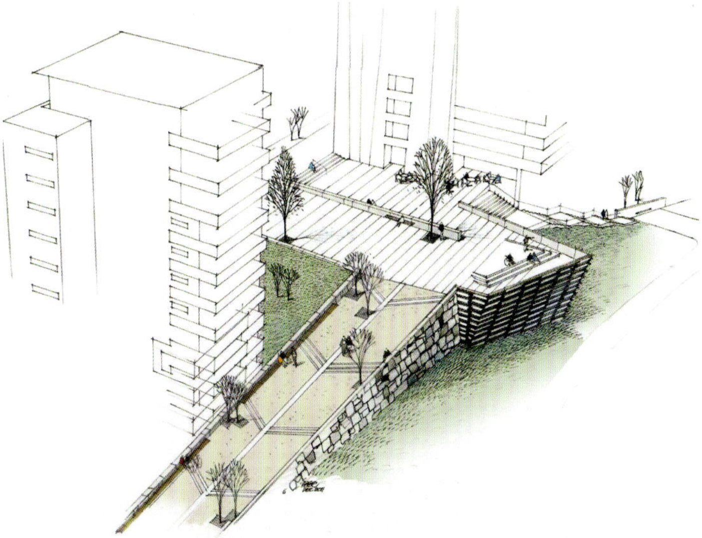

Rinkeby Panorama Terrace is a viewing platform overlooking Järva Field, a large recreational area in northern Stockholm. The panorama terrace occupies a dramatic position on the site and is linked to the field by a sloping promenade. The viewing platform on the crest of the terrace is designed to resemble a large wooden lamp. The 8 m high angled walls are constructed of planks with spaces between them that emit the light generated within. The sloping promenade is planted with the olive of the North (Eleagnus angustifolia) and articulated by eight stone sculptures by Marco Cueva, carefully positioned in the landscape. The project aimed to create a place of high experiential quality and to add pride for a socio-economic exposed area. This is one of those instances when landscape architecture makes a political and social difference.

Die Rinkeby-Panoramaterrasse ist eine Aussichtsplattform mit Blick auf das Järva Field, ein großes Erholungsgebiet im Norden Stockholms. Die Panoramaterrasse nimmt eine dramatische Position auf dem Gelände ein und ist durch eine schräge Promenade mit dem Feld verbunden. Die Aussichtsplattform auf dem Kamm der Terrasse ist so gestaltet, dass sie einer großen Holzlampe ähnelt. Die 8 Meter hohen, schrägen Wände sind aus Bohlen mit Zwischenräumen konstruiert, die das im Inneren erzeugte Licht abstrahlen. Die schräge Promenade ist mit der Olive des Nordens (Eleagnus angustifolia) bepflanzt und durch acht Steinskulpturen von Marco Cueva gegliedert, die sorgfältig in der Landschaft positioniert sind. Das Projekt zielte darauf ab, einen Ort von hoher Erlebnisqualität zu schaffen und den Stolz auf ein sozioökonomisch exponiertes Gebiet zum Ausdruck zu bringen. Dies ist einer jener Fälle, in denen Landschaftsarchitektur einen politischen und sozialen Unterschied macht.

Rinkeby Panorama Terrace est une plateforme d'observation qui surplombe Järva Field, une grande zone de loisirs dans le nord de Stockholm. La terrasse panoramique occupe une position spectaculaire sur le site et est reliée au terrain par une promenade en pente. La plateforme d'observation située sur la crête de la terrasse est conçue pour ressembler à une grande lampe en bois. Les murs en angle de 8 m de haut sont construits en planches avec des espaces entre elles qui émettent la lumière générée à l'intérieur. Des oliviers du Nord (Eleagnus angustifolia) sont plantés le long de la promenade en pente qui est articulée par huit sculptures en pierre de Marco Cueva, soigneusement positionnées dans le paysage. Le projet visait à créer un lieu qui procure une expérience de grande qualité et à ajouter de la fierté pour une zone socio-économique exposée. C'est l'un de ces cas où l'architecture du paysage fait une différence politique et sociale.

La Terraza Panorama de Rinkeby es una plataforma de observación con vistas al Campo Järva, una gran área recreativa en el norte de Estocolmo. La terraza panorámica ocupa una posición espectacular en el terreno y está unida a la montaña por un paseo inclinado. La plataforma de observación en la cresta de la terraza está diseñada para parecerse a una gran lámpara de madera. Los muros angulares de 8 m de altura están construidos con tablones con espacios entre ellos que filtran la luz generada en su interior. El paseo inclinado se ha plantado de Olivos del Norte (Eleagnus angustifolia) y articulado por ocho esculturas de piedra de Marco Cueva, cuidadosamente colocadas en el paisaje. El proyecto tenía como objetivo crear un lugar de alta calidad experiencial y añadir orgullo para un área socioeconómica expuesta. Esta es una de esos casos en los que la arquitectura paisajística marca una diferencia política y social.

COMFORT HOTEL WINN

## TOWN HALL SQUARE

Umeå, Sweden
Photos: © Mikael Lundgren, Åke E:son Lindman, August Wiklund

Rådhustorget (Town Hall Square) in Umeå provides a stately setting for the Town Hall from 1888. The city's new major public space pairs the carefully considered use of trees with a simply paved central area. An allée of maples (Acer rubrum) run along the square's east side, finishing to the west with an apple grove (Malus "Everest") which blooms white in May. The canopies of these trees hover over a set of shallow canals that resembles a system of irrigation channels. Six stone amphorae, an artwork by sculptor Pål Svensson, are the source of the water. The paving in this part of the square is laid out as a carpet, with a pattern inspired from a local weaving technique using two colours of granite. The central part of the square is purposely kept open to host events of different kinds that vary with the seasons.

Der Rådhustorget (Rathausplatz) in Umeå bietet eine stattliche Kulisse für das Rathaus von 1888. Der neue große öffentliche Platz der Stadt verbindet die durchdachte Verwendung von Bäumen mit einem einfach gepflasterten zentralen Bereich. Eine Ahornallee (Acer rubrum) zieht sich entlang der Ostseite des Platzes und endet im Westen mit einem Apfelhain (Malus „Everest"), der im Mai weiß blüht. Die Baumkronen dieser Bäume schweben über einer Reihe von flachen Kanälen, die einem System von Bewässerungskanälen ähneln. Sechs Steinamphoren, ein Kunstwerk des Bildhauers Pål Svensson, sind die Quelle des Wassers. Das Pflaster in diesem Teil des Platzes ist als Teppich ausgelegt, mit einem Muster, das von einer lokalen Webtechnik inspiriert ist, bei der zwei Granitfarben verwendet werden. Der zentrale Teil des Platzes ist absichtlich offen gehalten, um Veranstaltungen verschiedener Art zu beherbergen, die mit den Jahreszeiten variieren.

Le Rådhustorget (place de l'hôtel de ville) à Umeå offre un cadre majestueux à l'hôtel de ville depuis 1888. Le nouvel espace public majeur de la ville associe l'utilisation réfléchie des arbres à une zone centrale simplement pavée. Une allée d'érables (Acer rubrum) longe le côté est de la place, se terminant à l'ouest par une pommeraie (Malus « Everest ») qui fleurit en blanc au mois de mai. Les auvents de ces arbres planent au-dessus d'un ensemble de canaux peu profonds qui ressemblent à un système de canaux d'irrigation. Six amphores en pierre, une œuvre du sculpteur Pål Svensson, sont la source de l'eau. Le dallage de cette partie de la place est disposé comme un tapis, avec un motif inspiré d'une technique de tissage locale utilisant deux couleurs de granit. La partie centrale de la place est volontairement ouverte pour accueillir divers événements qui varient selon les saisons.

Rådhustorget (Plaza del Ayuntamiento) en Umeå proporciona un escenario majestuoso para el Ayuntamiento desde 1888. El nuevo gran espacio público de la ciudad combina el uso cuidadosamente considerado de los árboles con una zona central pavimentada de forma sencilla. Un conjunto de arces (Acer rubrum) recorre el lado este de la plaza y termina al oeste con un manzano (Malus «Everest») que florece en mayo. Las copas de estos árboles se ciernen sobre un conjunto de canales poco profundos que se asemejan a un sistema de canales de irrigación. Seis ánforas de piedra, obra del escultor Pål Svensson, son la fuente desde la que mana el agua. El pavimento de esta parte de la plaza está dispuesto en forma de alfombra, con un patrón inspirado en una técnica de tejido local que utiliza dos colores de granito. La parte central de la plaza se mantiene abierta a propósito para albergar eventos de diferentes tipos que varían según las estaciones.

URBAN POWER was founded by the architects Sara Bjelke, Arne Cermak Nielsen and Rune Veile in 2013, with the objective of creating holistic solutions within architecture, public space and urban planning.
Regardless of scale or type, urban cohesion is always the driving force to create value for the surroundings, society, the users and clients. The cohesive approach combines and balances parameters essential for livable and resilient urban environments. Diversity, multifunctionality and connectivity are all key elements of the URBAN POWER process, where solutions are tested, evaluated and transformed as an open and visible project development.
URBAN POWER is navigating between impact and effect in the search for durable, affordable and sustainable solutions that bring new power to urban areas.

URBAN POWER wurde 2013 von den Architekten Sara Bjelke, Arne Cermak Nielsen und Rune Veile mit dem Ziel gegründet, ganzheitliche Lösungen in Architektur, öffentlichem Raum und Stadtplanung zu schaffen.
Unabhängig von Maßstab oder Typologie ist der städtische Zusammenhalt immer die treibende Kraft hinter der Wertschöpfung für Umwelt, Gesellschaft, Nutzer und Kunden. Der kohäsive Ansatz kombiniert und balanciert die wesentlichen Parameter für eine lebenswerte und widerstandsfähige städtische Umwelt. Vielfalt, Multifunktionalität und Konnektivität sind Schlüsselelemente des URBAN POWER-Konstruktionsprozesses, bei dem Lösungen als offene und sichtbare Projektentwicklung getestet, bewertet und umgesetzt werden.
URBAN POWER navigiert zwischen Wirkung und Wirkung bei der Suche nach dauerhaften, erschwinglichen und nachhaltigen Lösungen, die neue Kraft in städtische Gebiete bringen.

# URBAN POWER

URBAN POWER a été fondé par les architectes Sara Bjelke, Arne Cermak Nielsen et Rune Veile en 2013, dans le but de créer des solutions holistiques dans les domaines de l'architecture, de l'espace public et de l'urbanisme.
Quelle que soit l'échelle ou la typologie, la cohésion urbaine est toujours le moteur de la création de valeur pour l'environnement, la société, les utilisateurs et les clients. L'approche cohésive combine et équilibre les paramètres essentiels pour un environnement urbain vivable et résilient. La diversité, la multifonctionnalité et la connectivité sont des éléments clés du processus de conception de l'URBAN POWER, où les solutions sont testées, évaluées et transformées en un développement de projet ouvert et visible.
URBAN POWER navigue entre impact et effet dans la recherche de solutions durables, abordables et viables qui apportent une nouvelle puissance aux zones urbaines.

URBAN POWER fue fundada por los arquitectos Sara Bjelke, Arne Cermak Nielsen y Rune Veile en 2013, con el objetivo de crear soluciones holísticas dentro de la arquitectura, el espacio público y la planificación urbana.
Independientemente de la escala o tipología, la cohesión urbana es siempre su fuerza motriz para crear valor para el entorno, la sociedad, los usuarios y los clientes. El enfoque cohesivo combina y equilibra los parámetros esenciales para un entorno urbano habitable y resistente. La diversidad, la multifuncionalidad y la conectividad son elementos clave del proceso de diseño de URBAN POWER, en el que las soluciones se prueban, evalúan y transforman como un desarrollo de proyecto abierto y visible.
URBAN POWER navega entre el impacto y el efecto en la búsqueda de soluciones duraderas, asequibles y sostenibles que aporten un nuevo poder a las zonas urbanas.

HOLMENE

INTERNATIONAL PEOPLE'S COLLEGE

HAMAR HILLS

## HOLMENE

Hvidovre, Denmark
Photos: © Urban Power

The project "Holmene" prescribes an innovative way of planning industrial areas. The urban power emerge with the interaction between knowledge, intensive industry, super nature and an integrated flood barrier - constructed as an archipelago of $CO_2$-neutral industrial islands. Located just south of Copenhagen, the Holmene project is the largest land reclamation project in Scandinavia which solves several challenges of the region with new opportunities: sites for knowledge, intensive industry close to highly skilled labour, universities and an international airport. Renewable energy is used primarily from biogas provided by an energy producing waste water cleaning plant, which enables $CO_2$ neutral production. Part of Holmene is dedicated to a recreational landscape, that attracts wildlife and a diverse vegetation, while protecting the existing and future areas against flooding.

Das Projekt „Holmene" schreibt eine innovative Art der Planung von Industriegebieten vor. Die urbane Kraft entsteht durch das Zusammenspiel von Wissen, intensiver Industrie, Supernatur und einer integrierten Hochwasserbarriere – aufgebaut als ein Archipel $CO_2$-neutraler Industrieinseln. Das Holmene-Projekt liegt südlich von Kopenhagen und ist das größte Landgewinnungsprojekt in Skandinavien. Es löst mehrere Herausforderungen der Region mit neuen Chancen: Standorte für Wissen, intensive Industrie in der Nähe von hochqualifizierten Arbeitskräften, Universitäten und einem internationalen Flughafen. Erneuerbare Energie wird hauptsächlich aus Biogas genutzt, das von einer energieproduzierenden Abwasserreinigungsanlage geliefert wird, die eine $CO_2$-neutrale Produktion ermöglicht. Ein Teil von Holmene ist einer Erholungslandschaft gewidmet, die Wildtiere und eine vielfältige Vegetation anzieht und gleichzeitig die bestehenden und zukünftigen Gebiete vor Überschwemmungen schützt.

Le projet « Holmene » propose une manière innovante de planifier les zones industrielles. La puissance urbaine émerge avec l'interaction entre la connaissance, l'industrie intensive, la nature et une barrière intégrée contre les inondations - construite comme un archipel d'îles industrielles neutres en $CO_2$. Situé juste au sud de Copenhague, est le plus grand projet de mise en valeur des terres en Scandinavie. Il résout plusieurs défis de la région avec de nouvelles opportunités : des sites pour la connaissance, une industrie intensive à proximité d'une main-d'œuvre hautement qualifiée, des universités et un aéroport international. L'énergie renouvelable est utilisée principalement à partir du biogaz fourni par une usine de nettoyage des eaux usées productrice d'énergie, qui permet une production neutre en $CO_2$. Une partie de Holmene est consacrée à un paysage récréatif, qui attire la faune et une végétation diversifiée, tout en protégeant les zones existantes et futures contre les inondations.

El proyecto «Holmene» prescribe una forma innovadora de planificar las zonas industriales. El poder urbano emerge con la interacción entre el conocimiento, la industria intensiva, la super naturaleza y una barrera de inundación integrada, construida como un archipiélago de islas industriales neutra de $CO_2$. Es el mayor proyecto de recuperación de tierras de Escandinavia que resuelve varios retos de la región con nuevas oportunidades: lugares para el conocimiento, industria intensiva de mano de obra altamente cualificada, universidades y un aeropuerto internacional. La energía renovable se utiliza principalmente a partir del biogás proporcionado por una planta de limpieza de aguas residuales que produce energía, lo que permite una producción neutra de $CO_2$. Una parte de Holmene está dedicada a un paisaje recreativo, que atrae a la vida salvaje y a una vegetación diversa, a la vez que protege las zonas existentes y futuras de posibles inundaciones.

## INTERNATIONAL PEOPLE'S COLLEGE

Elsinore, Denmark
Photos: © Urban Power

The extension of the International People's College becomes the new social heart of the building. The extension, by Steen Eiler Rasmussen, complements the complex with a contemporary and highly sustainable landmark.
Placed in the centre is a Hall of the United Nations, where students from all over the world will interact with local students as delegates in virtual Model UN-conferences. This key feature will have a prominent location were the urban power emerge by the interaction of inside and outside, adapting to the distinctive sloped topography of the site.
The hall and adjacent space are highly multifunctional and framed by a compact wooden building for minimized resource consumption and a viable economy, with the highest sustainable ambitions when the extension is completed in 2021.

Der Erweiterungsbau des International People's College wird zum neuen sozialen Herzstück des Gebäudes. Der Erweiterungsbau von Steen Eiler Rasmussen ergänzt den Komplex um ein zeitgemäßes und höchst nachhaltiges Wahrzeichen.
Im Zentrum befindet sich ein Saal der Vereinten Nationen, in dem Studenten aus aller Welt als Delegierte in virtuellen Modell-UN-Konferenzen mit lokalen Studenten interagieren können. Dieses Hauptmerkmal wird einen prominenten Ort schaffen, an dem die urbane Kraft durch die Interaktion von innen und außen entsteht und sich an die charakteristische geneigte Topographie des Geländes anpasst.
Die Halle und der angrenzende Raum sind hochgradig multifunktional und werden von einem kompakten Holzgebäude eingerahmt, das für einen minimalen Ressourcenverbrauch und eine tragfähige Wirtschaftlichkeit sorgt und nach Abschluss der Erweiterung im Jahr 2021 die höchsten Nachhaltigkeits-Ambitionen hat.

L'extension du Collège populaire international devient le nouveau cœur social du bâtiment. Réalisée par Steen Eiler Rasmussen, elle complète le complexe avec un point de repère contemporain et hautement durable.
Au centre, se trouve une salle des Nations Unies où des étudiants du monde entier interagiront avec des étudiants locaux en tant que délégués, lors de conférences virtuelles de simulation des Nations Unies. Cet élément clé aura une place de choix là où la puissance urbaine émerge par l'interaction de l'intérieur et de l'extérieur, en s'adaptant à la topographie inclinée caractéristique du site.
Le hall et l'espace adjacent sont hautement multifonctionnels et encadrés par un bâtiment en bois compact pour une consommation de ressources réduite au minimum et une économie viable. Ce projet a de grandes ambitions en matière de durabilité lorsque l'extension sera terminée en 2021.

La ampliación del International People's College se convierte en el nuevo corazón social del edificio. La ampliación de Steen Eiler Rasmussen complementa el complejo con un hito contemporáneo y altamente sostenible.
En el centro se encuentra el Salón de las Naciones Unidas, donde estudiantes de todo el mundo interactuarán con estudiantes locales como delegados en conferencias virtuales en una ubicación prominente donde el poder urbano surgirá por la interacción del interior y el exterior, adaptándose a la distintiva topografía inclinada del terreno.
El salón y el espacio adyacente son altamente multifuncionales y están enmarcados por un edificio compacto de madera para minimizar el consumo de recursos y una economía viable, con las más altas ambiciones sostenibles cuando se complete la ampliación en 2021.

## HAMAR HILLS

Hamar, Norway
Photos: © Urban Power

The city of Hamar is replacing villas with traditional residential blocks. "Hamar Hills" introduces a new typology that brings urban power to the area by mediating the density of the apartment blocks with the residential qualities of the villa.
The housing scheme consists of several housing types, each appealing to different generations and income groups. The landscape ranges from small private spaces to inviting green stretches that ties Hamar Hills together with the surrounding neighborhood.
Common and shared facilities ensure a lively community, where both the indoor and outdoor qualities serve as an attractive alternative to the traditional single-family home. Hamar Hills will be carried out as a timber construction with a low carbon footprint, green roofs and a biodiverse landscape.

Die Stadt Hamar ersetzt Villen durch traditionelle Wohnblöcke. „Hamar Hills" führt eine neue Typologie ein, die urbane Macht in das Gebiet bringt, indem sie die Dichte der Wohnblöcke mit den Wohnqualitäten einer Villa verbindet.
Das Wohnungsbauprogramm besteht aus mehreren Wohnungstypen, die jeweils unterschiedliche Generationen und Einkommensgruppen ansprechen. Das Spektrum reicht von kleinen Privaträumen bis hin zu einladenden Grünflächen, die die Hamar Hills mit der umliegenden Nachbarschaft verbinden.
Gemeinsame und gemeinsam genutzte Einrichtungen sorgen für eine lebendige Gemeinschaft, in der sowohl die Innen- als auch die Außenqualitäten eine attraktive Alternative zum traditionellen Einfamilienhaus darstellen. Hamar Hills wird als Holzkonstruktion mit einem niedrigen $CO_2$-Fußabdruck, grünen Dächern und einer biologisch vielfältigen Landschaft ausgeführt.

La ville de Hamar remplace les villas par des blocs résidentiels traditionnels. « Hamar Hills » introduit une nouvelle typologie qui apporte une puissance urbaine à la région en faisant la médiation entre la densité des immeubles d'habitation et les qualités résidentielles de la villa.
Le programme de logement comprend plusieurs types de logements, chacun s'adressant à des générations et des groupes de revenus différents. Le paysage va de petits espaces privés à des étendues vertes accueillantes qui relient Hamar Hills au quartier environnant.
Les installations communes et partagées assurent une communauté vivante, où les qualités intérieures et extérieures constituent une alternative attrayante à la maison individuelle traditionnelle. Hamar Hills sera réalisé en bois avec une faible empreinte carbone, des toits verts et un paysage biodiversifié.

La ciudad de Hamar está reemplazando las villas por conjuntos residenciales tradicionales. «Hamar Hills» introduce una nueva tipología que aporta poder urbano a la zona mediando la densidad de los bloques de apartamentos con las cualidades residenciales de la villa.
El plan de viviendas consta de varios tipos de viviendas, cada uno de ellos atractivo para diferentes generaciones y distintos tipos de posibilidades económicas. El paisaje abarca desde pequeños espacios privados hasta atractivos tramos verdes que unen Hamar Hills con el vecindario circundante.
Las instalaciones compartidas aseguran una comunidad animada, en la que tanto las cualidades interiores como exteriores sirven como alternativa atractiva a la tradicional casa unifamiliar. Hamar Hills se llevará a cabo como una construcción de madera con una baja huella de carbono, techos verdes y un paisaje biodiverso.

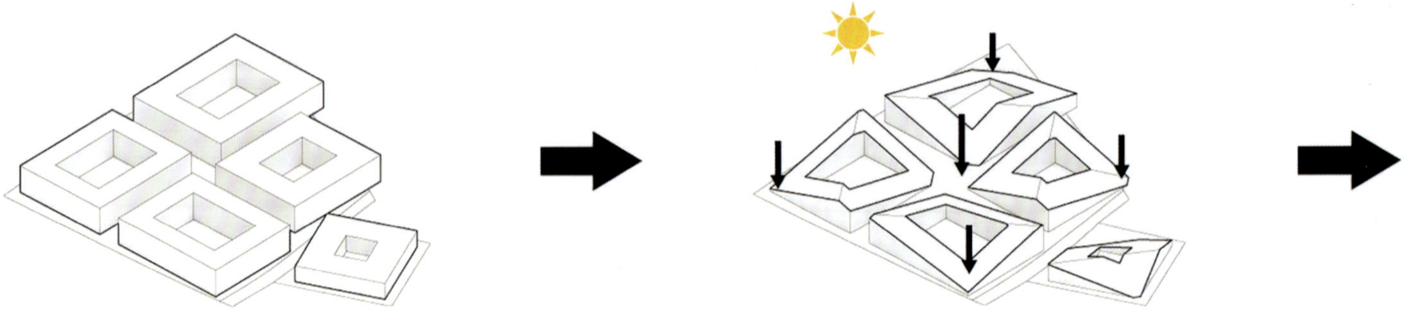

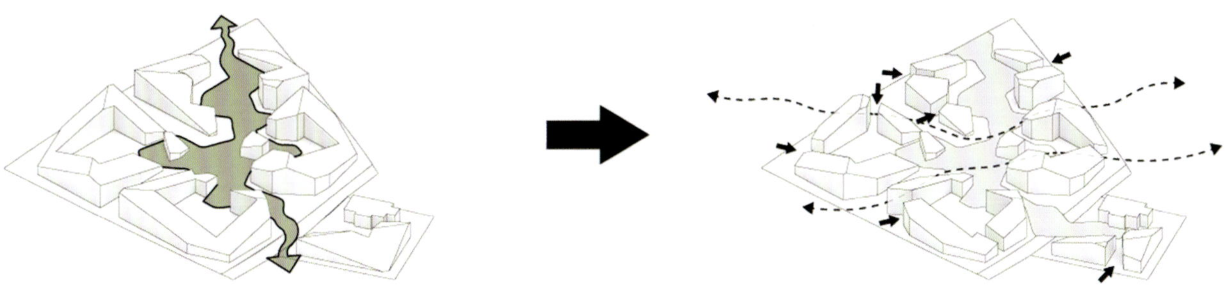

Wåhlin Arkitekter was founded in 1994 by Per Wåhlin as an investment in innovative and contemporary architecture. We see a breadth of assignments as an advantage for our customers. We are 10 employees who work with every kind of project, from senior housing to shopping malls. The company also works with restoration, rebuilding and renovation of public premises. All types of assignments make us committed and motivated. The company stands for experience and creativity and works with design in all its stages and with all types of buildings. We believe that a project is highly dependent on a smooth working method and the ability to communicate properly. The office is located in Stockholm.

Wåhlin Arkitekter wurde 1994 von Per Wåhlin als Investition in innovative und zeitgenössische Architektur gegründet. Wir sehen eine breite Palette von Aufträgen als Vorteil für unsere Kunden. Wir sind 10 Mitarbeiter, die mit jeder Art von Projekt arbeiten, von Seniorenwohnungen bis hin zu Einkaufszentren. Das Unternehmen arbeitet auch mit der Restaurierung, dem Umbau und der Renovierung von öffentlichen Gebäuden. Alle Arten von Aufträgen machen uns engagiert und motiviert. Das Unternehmen steht für Erfahrung und Kreativität und arbeitet mit Design in all seinen Phasen und mit allen Arten von Gebäuden. Wir glauben, dass ein Projekt in hohem Maße von einer reibungslosen Arbeitsweise und der Fähigkeit, richtig zu kommunizieren, abhängt. Das Büro befindet sich in Stockholm.

# WÅHLIN ARKITEKTER

Wåhlin Arkitekter a été fondé en 1994 par Per Wåhlin comme un investissement dans l'architecture innovante et contemporaine. Nous considérons qu'une large gamme de missions est un avantage pour nos clients. Nous sommes dix employés qui travaillent sur tous types de projets, des logements pour personnes âgées aux centres commerciaux. L'entreprise travaille également à la restauration, à la reconstruction et à la rénovation de locaux publics. Nous sommes engagés et motivés pour tous les types de missions. L'entreprise est synonyme d'expérience et de créativité et travaille avec le design dans toutes ses étapes et avec tous les types de bâtiments. Nous pensons qu'un projet dépend fortement d'une méthode de travail harmonieuse et de la capacité à communiquer correctement. Le bureau est situé à Stockholm.

Wåhlin Arkitekter fue fundada en 1994 por Per Wåhlin como una inversión en arquitectura innovadora y contemporánea. Vemos la amplitud de los encargos como una ventaja para nuestros clientes. Somos 10 empleados que trabajamos con todo tipo de proyectos, desde viviendas para ancianos hasta centros comerciales. La empresa también trabaja en la restauración, reconstrucción y renovación de locales públicos. Todo tipo de tareas nos hace sentir comprometidos y motivados. La empresa representa la experiencia y la creatividad y trabaja con el diseño en todas sus etapas y con todo tipo de edificios. Creemos que un proyecto depende en gran medida de un método de trabajo fluido y de la capacidad de comunicarse adecuadamente. La oficina está situada en Estocolmo.

UPPSALA CENTRAL STATION

VILLA BJÖRKNÄS

VILLA KUMMELN

POCKET SHOP
Pressbyrån
SJ
TELE2
UL

## UPPSALA CENTRAL STATION

Uppsala, Sweden
Photos: © Ola Österling

Uppsala's new central station is the hub of the plan for Uppsala Travel Center, which was inaugurated in December 2011. The assignment was to design a new terminal building that would meet today's needs for the approximately 67,000 travelers who pass the station each day. The terminal building contains customer service and ticket handling, as well as restaurants, cafés and shops.

Der neue Hauptbahnhof von Uppsala ist der Dreh- und Angelpunkt des Plans für das Uppsala Travel Center, das im Dezember 2011 eingeweiht wurde. Die Aufgabe bestand darin, ein neues Terminalgebäude zu entwerfen, das den heutigen Bedürfnissen der rund 67.000 Reisenden entspricht, die täglich am Bahnhof vorbeikommen. Im Terminalgebäude befinden sich der Kundenservice und die Ticketabwicklung sowie Restaurants, Cafés und Geschäfte.

La nouvelle gare centrale d'Uppsala est au cœur du projet d'Uppsala Travel Center, qui a été inauguré en décembre 2011. La mission consistait à concevoir un nouveau terminal qui répondrait aux besoins actuels des quelque 67 000 voyageurs qui passent chaque jour devant la gare. L'aérogare comprend le service clientèle et la gestion des billets, ainsi que des restaurants, des cafés et des boutiques.

La nueva estación central de Uppsala es el centro del plan para el Centro de Viajes de Uppsala, que se inauguró en diciembre de 2011. La tarea consistió en diseñar una nueva terminal que satisficiera las necesidades actuales de los aproximadamente 67 000 viajeros que pasan por la estación cada día. El edificio contiene el servicio de atención al cliente y la gestión de los billetes, así como restaurantes, cafés y tiendas.

SUSHI
YAMA
SUSHI
YAMA

# VILLA BJÖRKNÄS

Stockholm, Sweden
Photos: © Ola Österling

Villa Björknäs is a 200 m² villa located in Stockholm, completed in 2008. On the site there is a huge mountain ridge whose stone gave the inspiration to let the building's façades be characterized by the inherent nature of the materials; iron that rusts unevenly, wood that grays and shows twigs and chips and the shiny transparency of the glass. In this case, we have selected corten steel, larch wood and flat glass. Between the standing dense façade sections, floor-high glass sections open. The verticality of the façade contrasts sharply with the long stretch of the building along the six-meter-high mountain ridge. To the west, the interior opens into a large combined kitchen and living room that ends on a huge terrace over a dramatic cliff.

Die Villa Björknäs ist eine 200 m² große Villa in Stockholm, die 2008 fertiggestellt wurde. Auf dem Grundstück befindet sich ein riesiger Bergrücken, dessen Stein die Inspiration dazu gab, die Fassaden des Gebäudes durch die inhärente Natur der Materialien charakterisieren zu lassen: Eisen, das ungleichmäßig rostet, Holz, das grau wird und Zweige und Späne zeigt, und die glänzende Transparenz des Glases. In diesem Fall haben wir Cortenstahl, Lärchenholz und Flachglas gewählt. Zwischen den stehenden dichten Fassadenabschnitten öffnen sich bodenhohe Glasabschnitte. Die Vertikalität der Fassade steht in scharfem Kontrast zu der langen Ausdehnung des Gebäudes entlang des sechs Meter hohen Bergrückens. Im Westen öffnet sich der Innenraum in eine große Wohnküche, die auf einer riesigen Terrasse über einer dramatischen Klippe endet.

La Villa Björknäs est une villa de 200 m² située à Stockholm, achevée en 2008. Sur le site se trouve une énorme crête montagneuse dont la pierre a donné l'inspiration pour que les façades du bâtiment. Elles sont caractérisées par la nature inhérente des matériaux : le fer qui rouille de manière inégale, le bois qui grise et montre des brindilles et des éclats et la transparence brillante du verre. Dans ce cas, nous avons choisi l'acier corten, le bois de mélèze et le verre plat. Entre les parties denses de la façade, s'ouvrent des sections de verre de la hauteur du sol. La verticalité de la façade contraste fortement avec la longue étendue du bâtiment le long de la crête montagneuse de six mètres de haut. À l'ouest, l'intérieur s'ouvre sur la combinaison d'une grande cuisine et d'un salon qui se termine sur une immense terrasse surplombant une falaise spectaculaire.

La Villa Björknäs, de 200 m² y situada en Estocolmo, fue terminada en 2008. En el lugar hay una enorme cresta de montaña cuya piedra sirvió de inspiración para que las fachadas del edificio se caracterizaran por la naturaleza inherente de los materiales; el hierro que se oxida de forma desigual, la madera que se agrieta y muestra ramitas y astillas y la brillante transparencia del cristal. En este caso, hemos seleccionado acero corten, madera de alerce y vidrio plano. Entre las densas secciones de la fachada, se abren secciones de vidrio a la altura del suelo. La verticalidad de la fachada contrasta fuertemente con el largo tramo del edificio a lo largo de la cresta de la montaña de 6 m. de altura. Al oeste, el interior se abre en una gran cocina y sala de estar que termina en una enorme terraza sobre un dramático acantilado.

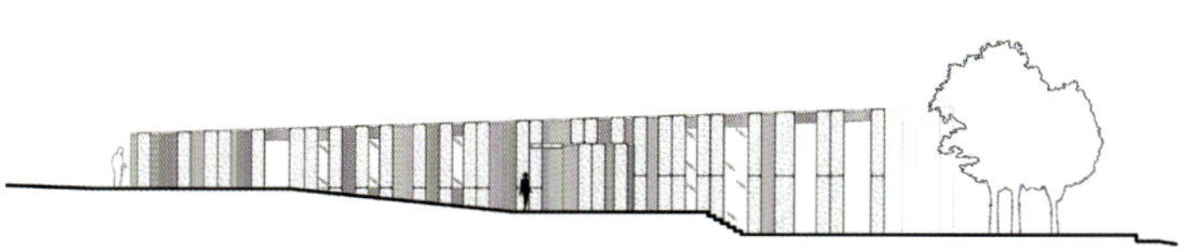

Elevations

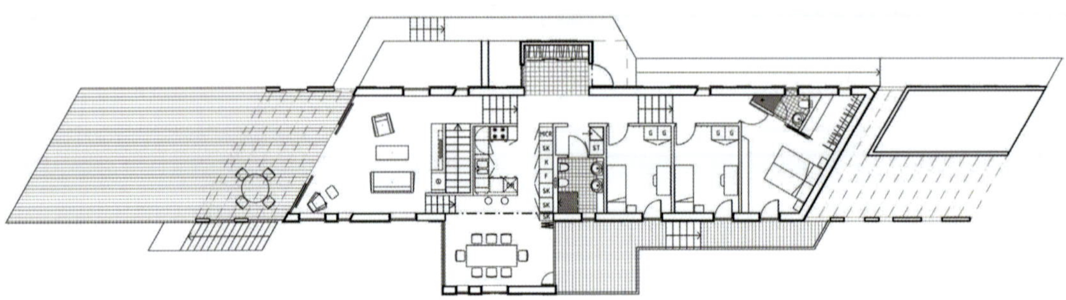

First floor plan

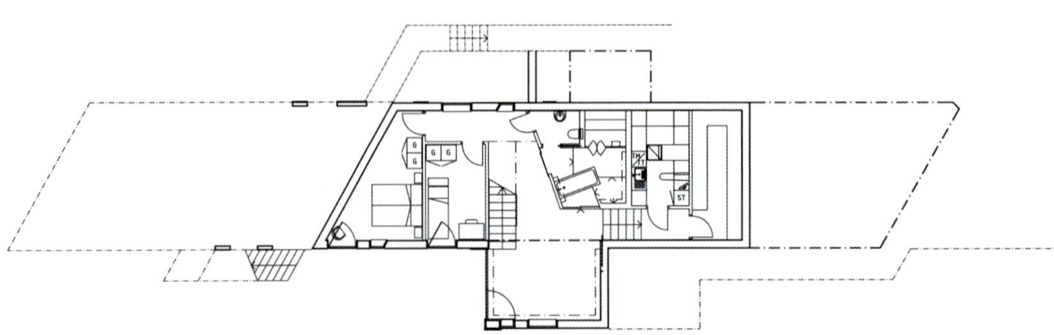

Ground floor plan

STELLA

## VILLA KUMMELN

Stockholm, Sweden
Photos: © Ola Österling

The project was built on a high site where the customer wanted to access the fantastic view of the bay and the ground floor would only serve as an entrance. We designed a house that up to 90% consisted of an staircase. More living space was demanded as the family expected to increase. We then added a volume below the protruding stairs which proved to work excellent both functionally and aesthetically. The seemingly simple and minimalist house bodies are in fact a piece of advanced engineering art built with a concrete core and steel frame that can withstand the large spans at the heavily projecting parts. The large profileless glass surfaces convey a sense of boundlessness, like a huge aquarium. When the darkness falls, the house glows like a giant lantern.

Das Projekt wurde an einer hochgelegenen Stelle gebaut, wo der Kunde den fantastischen Blick auf die Bucht genießen wollte und das Erdgeschoss nur als Eingang dienen sollte. Wir entwarfen ein Haus, das bis zu 90% aus einer Treppe bestand. Es wurde mehr Wohnfläche gefordert, da die Familie erwartete, dass der Wohnraum wachsen würde. Wir fügten dann ein Volumen unter der vorstehenden Treppe hinzu, das sich sowohl funktionell als auch ästhetisch hervorragend einfügte. Die scheinbar einfachen und minimalistischen Hauskörper sind in Wirklichkeit ein Stück fortschrittlicher Ingenieurskunst, gebaut mit einem Betonkern und einem Stahlrahmen, der den großen Spannweiten an den stark vorspringenden Teilen standhalten kann. Die großen profillosen Glasflächen vermitteln ein Gefühl der Grenzenlosigkeit, wie bei einem riesigen Aquarium. Bei Einbruch der Dunkelheit leuchtet das Haus wie eine riesige Laterne.

Le projet a été construit sur un site élevé où le client voulait accéder à la vue fantastique de la baie et où le rez-de-chaussée ne servirait que d'entrée. Nous avons conçu une maison dont jusqu'à 90 % des éléments étaient constitués d'un escalier. Il fallait plus d'espace de vie, car la famille devait s'agrandir. Nous avons alors ajouté un volume sous les escaliers en saillie qui s'est avéré excellent tant sur le plan fonctionnel qu'esthétique. Le corps de la maison, d'apparence simple et minimaliste, est en fait une œuvre d'art d'ingénierie avancée construite avec un noyau en béton et une armature en acier qui peut supporter les grandes portées des parties en saillie. Les grandes surfaces vitrées sans profil donnent une impression d'immensité, comme un immense aquarium. Quand la nuit tombe, la maison brille comme une lanterne géante.

El proyecto se construyó en un lugar alto donde el cliente quería acceder a la fantástica vista de la bahía, de forma que la planta baja solo serviría como entrada. Diseñamos una casa alrededor principalmente de una escalera. Se exigía más espacio para vivir, ya que la familia esperaba crecer en número. Añadimos un volumen debajo de las escaleras que resultó ser excelente tanto funcional como estéticamente. Los cuerpos de la casa, aparentemente simples y minimalistas, son de hecho una pieza de arte de ingeniería avanzada construida con un núcleo de hormigón y un marco de acero que puede filtrar la luz en las partes más salientes. Las grandes superficies de vidrio sin perfiles transmiten una sensación de infinito, en forma de un gran acuario. Cuando cae la oscuridad, la casa brilla como una linterna gigante.

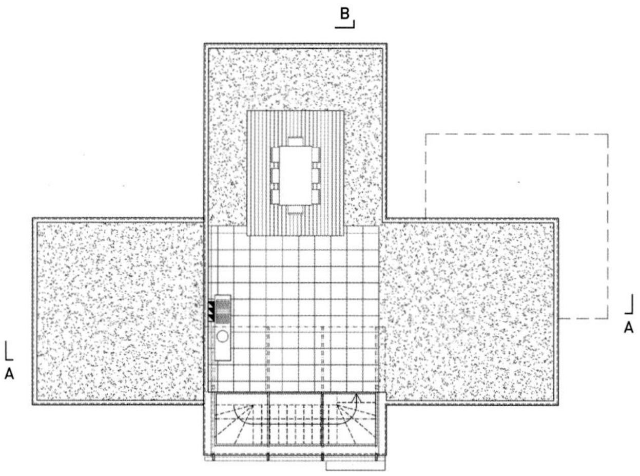


Roof floor plan

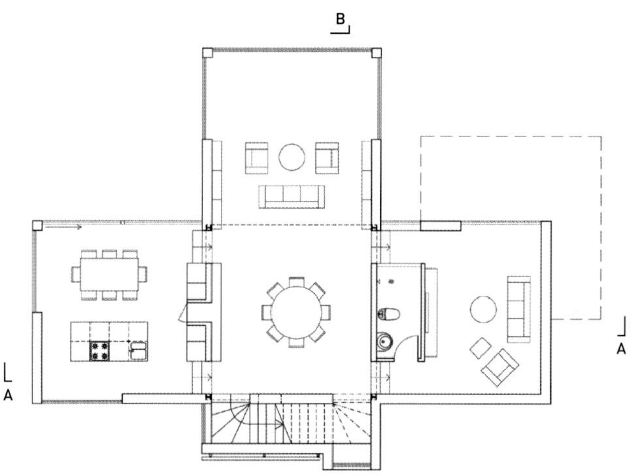


First floor plan

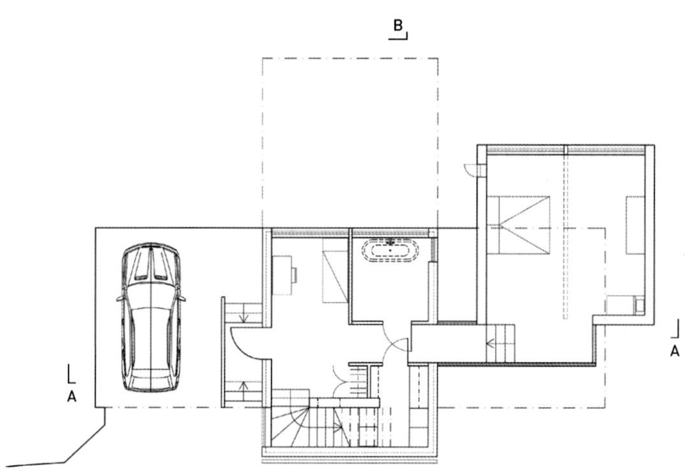


Ground floor plan

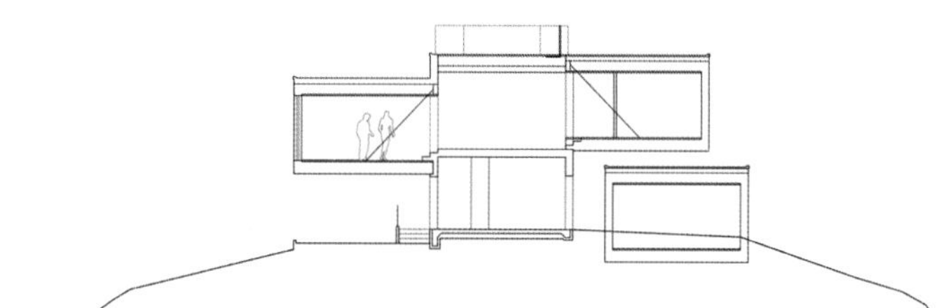

Section A-A

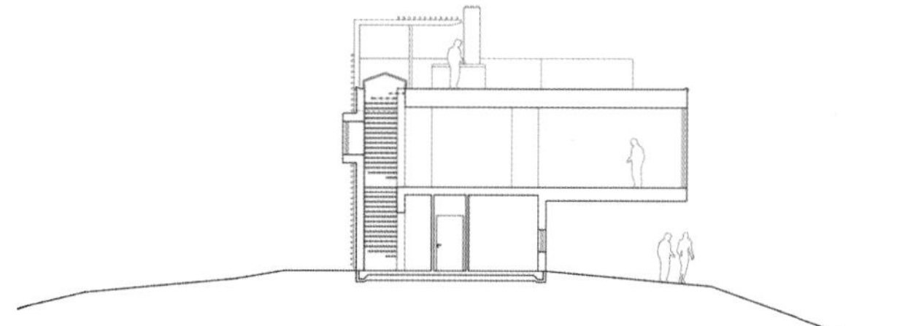

Section B-B

**PES-ARCHITECTS**
STRAIT CULTURE AND ART CENTRE

© Marc Goodwin

**AIX ARCHITECTER**
www.aix.se

**KATA FARM**
Lead Architect: Magnus Silfverhielm.
Architect Team: Klas Eriksson, Anders Widegren, Henrik Strid, Lotta Lindgren
Area: 260 m²
Year: 2017

**DRESSYRHALLEN**
Lead Architect: Eva Göransson, AIX.
Architect Team: Eva Göransson, Lars Johansson, Katja Hillström, Martin Berg, Stina Svantesson, AIX.
Static Design: Magnus Emilsson, Limträteknik and Lars Johansson, AIX Architects
Area: 940 m²
Year: 2011

**ARKÍS ARCHITECTS**
www.ark.is

**HOLMEN AQUATICS CENTER**
Architects: ARKÍS architects
Client: Asker Municipalitye
Year: 2013-2017

**ÁSTJÖRN PARISH HALL**
Architects: ARKÍS architects
Client: Ástjarnarsókn
Year: 2014-2017

**VILLA PANORAMA**
Architects: ARKÍS architects
Client: Private
Year: 2008-2010

**FJAÐRÁRGLJÚFUR VIEWING PLATFORM**
Architects: ARKÍS architects
Client: Skaftárhreppur
Year: 2017

**DELIN ARKITEKTKONTOR**
www.delinarkitektkontor.se

**LUNDNÄS HOUSE**
Architect: Buster Delin
Awarded the Swedish Window Award 2016

**FORTUNEN ARKITEKTUR**
www.fortunen.no

**BRYGGENS MUSEUM´S PERMANENT EXHIBITION (2017-2019)**
Architects: Fortunen Arkitektur
Client: Bymuseet i Bergen
Builder: DONAR AS
Graphic Designer: Tine Erika Fuglseth
Collaborators: Bymuseet i Bergen, Bright AS, Silje Sandodden Kise, Erstad & Lekven Bergen AS
Area: 700 m²
Year: 2018-2019

**HESTAD CHAPEL REST AREA**
Architects: Fortunen Arkitektur
Client: National Tourist Routes
Area: 400 m²
Year: 2018-Ongoing

**LOGEN THEATER**
Architects: Fortunen Arkitektur
Client: Hordaland Teater
Builder: OBAS AS
Collaborators: 3RW architects
Area: 1.600 m²
Year: 2016-2018

**GUDMUNDUR JONSSON ARKITEKTKONTOR**
www.gudmundurjonsson.com

**CASA G**
Architect: Gudmundur Jonsson
Engineering: VSÓ
Builder: Jáverk and Viðhald og Nýsmíði
Year: 2012
Area: 504 m²

**CASA MYHRER HAUGE**
Architect: Gudmundur Jonsson
Engineering: Emil Thor Gudmundsson
Builder: Askhus AS
Year: 2019
Area: 301 m² BRA
Client: Målfrid Myhrer Hauge & Øystein Hauge
Awards: Nominated to City of Oslo Architecture Awards

**JAN HENRIK JANSEN ARKITEKTER**
www.janhenrikjansen.dk

**BIRKEDAL**

**LANDHUS I MIDTJYLLAND**

**VILLA KORUP**

**KNUT HJELTNES**
www.hjeltnes.as

**WEEKEND HOUSE STRAUME**
Architect: Knut Hjeltnes sivilarkitekter MNAL AS.
Project architects: Knut Hjeltnes (pl), Tora Arctander, Nils Joneid, Sieglinde Muribø, Hans-Kristian Hagen, Maria Nesvaag (model).
Structural engineer: Siv.ing. Finn-Erik Nilsen AS.
Builder: Handverksbygg AS
Steel: Hasund Mekaniske Verksted AS
Windows and glass: Nordvestvinduet AS
Furnishings and stairs: CKI AS/AM Entreprenør AS
Area: 149.5 m²
Year: 2016

**LUND HAGEM ARKITEKTER**
www.lundhagem.no

**CABIN KVITFJELL**
Architect: Lund Hagem Arkitekter
Area: Gross areas: main cabin, approx. 120 m² + annex, approx. 30 m² + carport
Year: 2016

**LILLE ARØYA**
Architect: Lund Hagem Arkitekter
Area: 75 m²
Year: 2014

## MARGE ARKITEKTER
www.marge.se

**SERGELHUSET**
Status: Ongoing
Area: 85,500 m²
Type: Overall design concept, rebuild and new-build of offices, residentials, and commercial facilities, city development
Scope: Winning competition proposal, building permission, developed design, construction drawings
Client: Vasakronan
Contractors: Zengun, Veidekke
Artist: Gunilla Klingberg
Landscape: Karavan Landskap

**VILLA HEDBERG**
Completed: 2018
Area: 208 m²
Type: New-build of private house, guest house, and sauna
Client: Private

**NATURUM TROLLSKOGEN**
Completed: 2018
Area: 420 m²
Type: New-build of visitor centre in nature reserve
Scope: Winning competition proposal, developed design, construction drawings including lead consultants
Client: Länsstyrensen, Kalmar County
Contractor: NCC
Landscape: Karavan Landskap
Awards: Nominated for Stenpriset 2019

**RÖHSSKA MUSEUM**
Completed: 2019
Area: 250 m²
Type: Interior and design for the entrance and shop as well as new benches
Scope: Winning competition proposal, developed design, construction drawings
Client: The Röhsska Museum

## MARGEN WIGOW ARKITEKTKONTOR
www.margenwigow.se

**SEASIDE CABINS**
Arkitekt: Margen Wigow arkitektkontor AB, Cecilia Margen Wigow and Per Wigow
Constructor: Svedbergs bygg & byggprojektering, Kjellåke Svedberg
Year: 2012
Area: 150 m²
Client: Private

**VILLA T**
Arkitekt: Margen Wigow arkitektkontor AB, Cecilia Margen Wigow and Per Wigow
Year: 2001
Area: 130 m²
Client: Private

**HOLIDAY HOME**
Arkitekt: Margen Wigow arkitektkontor AB, Cecilia Margen Wigow
Constructor: Konkret rådgivande ingenjörer, Olle Norrman
Year: 2019
Area: Main Building: 143 m²; Guest house: 53 m²; Sauna: 15 m²; Storage: 18 m²
Client: Private

## MARTIN KALLESØ ARKITEKTER
www.kallesoearkitekt.dk

**ADMINISTRATION BUILDING**
Architect: Martin Kallesø
Builder: Sjællands Pelsdyrfoder
Area: 240 m²
Contractor: 3T Byggeentreprise A/S
Year: 2017

**SINGLE FAMILY HOUSE**
Architect: Martin Kallesø
Client: Private
Area: 150 m²
Contractor: KDC Byg
Year: 2014

**SKOGFINN MUSEUM (COMPETITION PROPOSAL)**
Architect: Martin Kallesø
Area: 1,670 m²
Collaborator: Rasmus Bay Barlby, industrial designer MDD

## MARX ARCHITECTURE
www.marxarkitektur.se

**APARTMENT**
Architect: Marx Architecture
Scope: Reprograming life in the modernist concrete block

**CULTUR HOUSE CYKLOPEN**
Architect: Marx Architecture

**GALLERY**
Architect: Marx Architecture
Scope: (un)Wanted city renewal,

## PAVE ARCHITECTS
www.pavearkkitehdit.fi

**SAUNA KÄPYLÄ**
Architect: PAVE Architects
Year: 2017
Area: 117 m²
Function: Sauna building

**VILLA RYYSYRANTA II**
Architect: PAVE Architects
Year: 2017
Area: 160 m²
Function: Leisure home

**DESIGN HOTEL LEVI**
Architect: PAVE Architects
Year: 2019
Area: 3,390 m²
Function: New main building of a hotel, 77 hotel rooms

## PES-ARCHITECTS
www.pesark.com

**ICON YUNDUAN TOWER**
Architects: PES-Architects
Architectural design / PES-Architects: Tuomas Silvennoinen (chief designer), Pekka Salminen, Tristan Hughes, Emanuel Lopes, Toivo Moustgaard
Local architects: China South West Architecture and Design Institute (CSWADI): Qian Fang, Qiu Xiaoyong, Wang Yongwei, Feng Tailin, Zhu Yanqing
Year: 2017
Client/contractor: Chengdu Hi-Tech Investment Group Co. Ltd.
Main contractor: China State Construction Engineering Corp. Ltd.
Technical design: China Southwest Architectural Design and Research Institute, CSWADI
Lighting design: a+g Licht, Germany
Function: Mixed-use
Total floor area: 103,650 m² (tower), total project ca 160,000 m²
Finish materials: Glass/ceramic facades
Structure: Concrete/steel

**STRAIT CULTURE AND ART CENTRE**
Architects: PES-Architects
Lead designers, architecture and interior: Pekka Salminen (chief designer), Martin Lukasczyk (project architect), Lai Linli (project manager), Samuel Hsuan-yu Shih (opera and concert hall ceramic interior)
Local Architect: CCEDGC Co.,Ltd., Xu Zongwu
Year: 2018
Client: Fuzhou New Town Development Investment Group Co.,Ltd.
Special consultants: Eckhard Kahle (Kahle Acoustics), Henrik Möller (Akukon Oy), acoustics; Matti Haaramo (Vahanen Oy), steel structures; Harri Ripatti (Climaconsult Oy), HVAC; Wilfried Kramb (ag+Licht GbR), lighting; Gretel Hemgård (Hemgård Landscape Design), landscape; Nick Li (Schmidlin Façade Shanghai Co.,Ltd), curtain wall; Lu Yi (Gold Mantis Construction Decoration Co.,Ltd), interiors
Function: Cultural venue: opera house (1,600 seats), concert hall (1,000 seats), multi-functional theatre (700 seats), art exhibition hall, cinema centre
Area: 153,000 m²
Materials: Steel, concrete, bamboo and ceramics

**WEST TERMINAL 2**
Architects: PES-Architects
Design team: Tuomas Silvennoinen (chief designer), Pekka Mäkelä (project manager), Emanuel Lopes, Hanna Eskelinen
Year: 2017

Client: Port of Helsinki
Construction company: YIT Rakennus Oy
Structural engineering: Sweco Rakennetekniikka Oy
Consulting: Viator Oy, Indepro Oy
Building technology: Ramboll Finland Oy
Electrical: Granlund Oy
Function: Ferry terminal
Area: 12,900 m²
Structure: Reinforced steel frame, pre-fabricated concrete elements

**RESELL+NICCA**
www.resellnicca.no

**CABIN RYFYLKE**
Architect: Olav Resell
Co-architect: Pirll Oslo
Year: 2014

**VILLA VOID**
Architects: Olav Resell, Nicca Gade Christensen
Year: 2017
Function: Single Family House

**STINESSEN ARKITEKTUR**
www.snorrestinessen.com

**MANSHAUSEN**
Architect: Snorre Stinessen
Furniture design: Snorre Stinessen & Lindahl Design

**EFJORD**
Architect: Snorre Stinessen

**MALANGEN**
Architect: Snorre Stinessen

**NARVIK TOP STATION**
Architect: Snorre Stinessen
Team member: Emanuela Bonardi
Structural Engineering: Indira AS
Gondola: Bartholet

**THORBJÖRN ANDERSSON WITH SWECO ARCHITECTS**
www.thorbjorn-andersson.com
www.sweco.se

**RINKEBY PANORAMA TERRACE**
Design team: Thorbjörn Andersson, PeGe Hillinge, Anna Norén, Joel Lundqvist, Fredrik Toller, Catrin Jonsson, Staffan Sundström, Ronny Brox, Alexander Cederroth (lighting), Marco Cueva (sculpture)
Client: City of Stockholm
Area: 4,000 m²
Year: 2017

**TOWN HALL SQUARE**
Design team: Thorbjörn Andersson, PeGe Hillinge, Tobias Phersson, Fredrik Schönfeldt, Niklas Ödmann (lighting), Pål Svensson (sculpture)
Client: City of Umeå
Area: 9,000 m²
Year: 2018

**URBAN POWER**
www.urbanpower.dk

**HOLMENE**
Architect Team: Arne Cermak Nielsen, Rune Veile, Sara Buhl Bjelke, Hannah Knudsen, Ewelina Purta, Kinga Murawska, Ida Lykke Christensen, Agnija Rubene, Tien-Yi Su
Function: Green technology hub, sustainable industries, Energy producing Waste Water and Bio waste Treatment Plant, flood Barrier, nature park and recreational Areas
Site area: 3,080,000 m²
Floor area: 1,500,000 m²
Year: 2016-2045
Client: Hvidovre Municipality
Collaborators: COWI, DHI, MOE | tetraplan, Rambøll, Aglaja
Status: Expected construction start by 2023

**INTERNATIONAL PEOPLE'S COLLEGE**
Architect Team: Rune Veile, Sara Buhl Bjelke, Arne Cermak Nielsen, Kathrine Blichsted Brauer, Niels Kjærgaard, Christian Jensen, Jan Ole Hansen, Kinga Murawska, Ewelina Purta, Michael Dragschitz, Tien-Yi Su, Javier Gutierrez Sainz
Function: Lecture Hall, Class Rooms, Social Spaces
Site area: 12,000 m²
Floor area: 1,100 m² extension, 250 m² renovation
Year: 2018-2021
Client: International People's College
Collaborators: Henry Jensen rådgivende ingeniører, Gade & Mortensen Akustik, Weile arkitekter
Status: Invited Competition, winning entry. Completion 2021

**HAMAR HILLS**
Architect Team: Rune Veile, Sara Buhl Bjelke, Arne Cermak Nielsen, Kinga Murawska, Alexander Bredgaard, Sabela Barreiro, Tien-Yi Su, Michael Dragschitz
Function: Housing, Urban Space
Site area: 20,000 m²
Floor area: 24,400 m²
Year: 2018-2022
Client: Hamar municipality
Status: 1st prize in open international competition. Expected construction start by 2021

**WÅHLIN ARKITEKTER**
www.wahlinarkitekter.se

**UPPSALA CENTRAL STATION**
Lead Architect: Per Wåhlin
Year: 2008-2011
Area: 2,400 m²

**VILLA BJÖRKNÄS**
Lead Architect: Per Wåhlin
Year: 2007-2008
Area: 200 m²

**VILLA KUMMELN**
Lead Architect: Per Wåhlin
Year: 2005-2006
Area: 200 m²